Goethe in East Germany, 1949–1989

Studies in German Literature, Linguistics, and Culture

Edited by James Hardin
(*South Carolina*)

Daniel J. Farrelly

Goethe in East Germany, 1949–1989

Toward A History of Goethe Reception in the GDR

CAMDEN HOUSE

First published 1998
Camden House
Drawer 2025
Columbia, SC 29202–2025 USA

Camden House is an imprint of Boydell & Brewer Inc.
PO Box 41026, Rochester, NY 14604–4126 USA
and of Boydell & Brewer Limited
PO Box 9, Woodbridge, Suffolk IP12 3DF, UK

ISBN: 1–57113–065–9

Library of Congress Cataloging-in-Publication Data
Farrelly, Daniel J., 1934–
    Goethe in East Germany, 1949-1989 : toward a history of Goethe
reception in the GDR / Daniel J. Farrelly.
        p.   cm. – (Studies in German literature, linguistics, and
culture)
    Includes bibliographical references and index.
    ISBN 1–57113–065–9 (alk. paper)
    1. Goethe, Johann Wolfgang von, 1749– 1832– Appreciation– Germany
(East) 2. Criticism—Germany (East)—History. I. Title.
II. Series: Studies in German literature, linguistics, and culture
(Unnumbered)
PT2166.F37 1998
831'.6—dc21   97-32934
                                                            CIP

This publication is printed on acid-free paper.
Printed in the United States of America

For
Una
Noreen, Ciara, Mark, and Frank
my sister Margaret

Contents

Acknowledgments   viii

Preface   ix

Part One: Orientation

1: Introduction   3

2: Official Cultural Policy (*Kulturpolitik*)   5

3: Writing the History   12

4: Religion versus Society: 31
    Transcendence versus Immanence

Part Two: Interpretations

5: Introduction   43

6: Early Poems: Subjectivity/Objectivity   47

7: *The Sorrows of Young Werther*   54

8: *Egmont, Iphigenie,* and *Tasso*   64

9: *Wilhelm Meister's Apprenticeship*   72

10: *Faust*   88

11: *Elective Affinities (Die Wahlverwandtschaften)*   130

12: Resonance in the West   147

Works Consulted   157

Index   163

Acknowledgments

M y sincere thanks are due to the following individuals and institutions without whose assistance and advice this work would not have been possible: the UCD Arts Faculty which, under various schemes, funded research travel to Germany and provided a generous grant in aid of publication; the International Office of the Education Department, where Ms Phil Barrett was helpful — by her great courtesy and with information — in arranging visits to Berlin — visits which were jointly funded by the DAAD (German Academic Exchange Service); to Oxford University Press for permission to make use of the David Luke translation of Goethe's *Faust Part One*; the librarians of the *Germanistisches Seminar* of the Humboldt University for their unstinting help and advice; my colleagues in the Department of German at University College, Dublin; the many students of German who, over a period of ten years, were exposed to my lectures and seminars on the material of this book.

D. J. F.
January 1998

Preface

This book is written by an outsider, and yet it would not have been written at all without the indirect initiatives stemming from the GDR itself. Apart from the occasional one-day excursions into East Berlin in the mid-1970s, when unplanned visits to the Humboldt University were still discouraged by the presence of armed soldiers guarding the entrance, I had had no contact with the GDR. Then, in early 1984 came an invitation to join a small party of Irish-based Germanists visiting the GDR as guests of the GDR / Ireland Friendship Society. We were conscious of it being very much a "guided" tour, but this was only part of the reality which opened up to us. Officials from the Ministry for Education in Berlin explained aspects of GDR education policy, and then provided a tour of various educational institutions from kindergarten level up to University.

For me, the most striking feature of this tour — apart from the warmth of the welcome we received at all levels — was that the education system assigned such an extraordinarily important role to the study of Goethe and Schiller.

The following year, I was able to live in East Berlin for nearly six months — with my family — as a guest of the Humboldt University. Professor Wolfgang Stellmacher was allotted to me as my "Betreuer" — and advisor. Within three days of our arrival in East Berlin, the invitations began to come in: to conferences, staff meetings, thesis defenses, participation in seminars. Wolfgang Stellmacher was enormously generous and endlessly patient in answering my questions, directing me to articles and books I needed to read, introducing me to scholars I wanted to meet (like Hans-Dietrich Dahnke in Weimar and Werner Mittenzwei in Berlin). Peter Müller and Peter Wruck were generous and open, prepared to facilitate me wherever they could. Manuela Runge, a reader with the Aufbau-Verlag, and her husband Bernhard, a young mathematician at the Humboldt University, became our close friends. Manuela's encouragement — sometimes in the form of goading — and her generosity with books were important factors in the continuance of this project. The debt I owe to the Stellmacher family, to Peter Müller and to the Runge family cannot be repaid. I shall always admire them for their integrity and capacity for friendship.

My East German colleagues made of the outsider something of an "insider." Yet it is impossible for me to view the East German tradition with East German eyes. My knowledge of the East German scholars' achievements must fall short of what they know about themselves from within the tradition. My critical judgments — without which there would be little point in writing this book — may well seem to them inappropriate or based on an inadequate appreciation of their work. But my main concern in this project,[1] from the beginning, has been to draw attention to their work. Since 1989 it has become increasingly important to confront the danger that scholars in the West will pass over their East German colleagues' achievements in silence.

---

[1] Some of the material of this book has been published in periodicals, as early as 1991, but in much different form.

Part One: Orientation

1: Introduction

With the fall of the Berlin Wall in 1989, a forty-year tradition of literary history writing came to an abrupt end. The German Democratic Republic had sought, from its inception in 1949, gradually to establish its own culture. It had tried a complete break with the immediate past of National Socialism. But, governed as it was by the Soviet occupying force, it needed to make a clear break from the prevailing capitalist ethos and to establish new foundations for the writing of its own creative literature and for the writing of a new literary history.

The problems of both of these types of writing have a particularly German quality. While events between 1939–1945 obviously had a profound effect not only on Germany but on the whole world, the new German literature became preoccupied in a particular way with analyzing both its current situation and the factors which led to the war of which the situation was a product.

Similarly, the branch of *Germanistik* dealing with the period since the Enlightenment cast a skeptical eye on the kinds of literary history writing which had led up to and then accompanied the rise of National Socialism. Thus, by 1945, Karl Viëtor[1] was already challenging the approach based on *Geistesgeschichte* (history of the mind, spirit) as one which lived too idealistically with the history of ideas and had, as it turned out, dangerously ignored concrete social and political reality. In effect, it had even presented the literature of the Classical period and of the nineteenth century in such a way that National Socialism could, if only cynically, claim justification in its Germanic roots. Even in the post-war period, with the text-immanent approach of writers of the Emil Staiger school, it was possible to live in the other world of literature, remote from problems which, created in the past, still demanded a solution in the present.

In the GDR the need to deal with the past was no less great than in West Germany. But in the GDR this need was coupled with the Soviet-directed need to deal with the "capitalist" roots of the problem. This meant, here too, a shift away from "Geistesgeschichte." A new German socialist culture was to be born. The most obvious pillars of this tradition were going to be Marx and Engels. But a still broader base could be achieved through a link-up with the classical achievement of Goethe's and Schiller's Weimar. This would not only provide a richer cultural diet within the GDR, but it would, at the same

[1] *"Deutsche Literaturgeschichte als Geistesgeschichte." PMLA* (60) 1945: 899–916.

time, serve to validate the program for creating a new socialist culture in East Germany. While Germans in West Germany manifested profound skepticism with regard to their great writers — not least for the way these had been served up to them under the National Socialist regime — the East Germans set out to prize their classical writers free of this National Socialist connection. They could find in Goethe, Schiller, and Herder men with humanist ideas that could fairly be considered at least "pre-socialist." Here were values (and not "eternal" values) that could be used as a basis for education in socialism. It was a question of highlighting ideas — especially socialist ideas — which they considered central to Weimar Classicism but which in the past had never been in proper focus.

2: Official Cultural Policy (*Kulturpolitik*)

Within a few months of the German capitulation (May 8, 1945) orders were given in the Soviet occupied zone to build up the centers of classical culture again. This was a clear indication that Walter Ulbricht (to become, from 1960 till 1971, the most powerful political figure in the GDR) and his circle had come from exile in Moscow with a fixed cultural policy in mind: namely, to build the new order on the foundation of Germany's cultural heritage. In general, what was understood by this heritage was all the positive values which could be drawn from previous periods. These were to be carefully scrutinized and used according to their potential for contributing to the development of a progressive society.

It is perhaps surprising that, instead of drawing on the more revolutionary strands in literature, the choice was the established middle-class inheritance centered on classical Weimar. It is, again, perhaps surprising that this non-revolutionary idea stems from Lenin. By 1920, Lenin had become convinced that a proletarian culture divorced from the middle-class tradition was not feasible:

> Proletarian culture does not drop out of the skies. It is not the invention of people who describe themselves as specialists in proletarian culture. That is all complete nonsense. Proletarian culture has to be the regular, continued development of the sum of knowledge achieved by mankind under the yoke of capitalist society, characterized as it is by private property and bureaucracy.[1]

Six days later Lenin added to this speech:

> Marxism did not reject the most valuable achievements of the middle-class era, but, on the contrary, took over and worked on everything that, in more than two thousand years of human thought and human culture, was of any value. Only further work on this basis and in this direction . . . can be acknowledged as the development of a real proletarian culture. (Viëtor-Engländer: 3)

---

[1] October 2, 1920. Quoted by Viëtor-Engländer, *Faust in der DDR*, 3. Apart from quotations from *Faust Part One* and *Faust Part Two*, where I have used David Luke's translation, and apart from the use of the English version of Lukács's *Goethe und seine Zeit*, all the translations from German are my own.

Much the same view of cultural inheritance was held by Stalin when he came to power on the death of Lenin in 1924. Two years later, speaking at the first Congress of the Union of Soviet Writers, Andrei Shdanow reflected the Stalinist position when he said:

> The proletariat is the sole heir of the best that the treasury of world literature contains. The bourgeoisie dissipated its literary inheritance; we have the duty to gather it carefully, to study it and, after assimilating it critically, to develop it further. (3)

These were the criteria which the German exiles in Moscow encountered when they escaped from the National Socialists after 1933. But what ideas about cultural inheritance had these exiles brought with them to Moscow in the first place?

Around 1922, the radical left associated with the journal *Die Aktion* saw Goethe as a symbol of the SPD which it considered indistinguishable from the bourgeoisie. In KPD circles, even Johannes Becher (later to be Minister for Culture in the GDR from 1954–58) had in 1928 thought of Goethe as "the quintessence of German Philistinism." (3) But when in 1931 he was proposing for contemporary, revolutionary writers a program for learning and re-learning, he claimed that this learning process had to include the development of a dialectical relationship to the past and to the body of cultural inheritance. This called for a series of careful studies.

In the face of the National Socialist take-over, the claim to the inheritance was to be shared by the working classes and the middle-class humanists, because it was in the interest of all to wrest the cultural inheritance from the grasp of the National Socialists. Thus at the Brussels Conference of the KPD in October 1935, the Popular Front movement saw as its aim not only to rescue the inheritance but to use it as a weapon against Fascism. This strategy came to have a lasting influence on cultural policy in the GDR.

Georg Lukács was to provide the series of "careful studies" required. In opposition to the "Anti-Gestaltung" interests of Ottwalt and Brecht, Lukács favored concentration on the realistic tradition represented by Fielding, Goethe, Diderot and Balzac. Not all the German Marxists agreed with Lukács that the inheritance was identified with the past. Nor were they agreed on Lukács's ideas of what elements of the past tradition were relevant. The opposing views clashed in the Expressionism debate around 1938, in which the Marxist philosopher Ernst Bloch (in an article co-written with the musician Hanns Eisler) criticized Lukács for writing off the products of modernity as the "decaying products of a capitalist society in decline." Bloch stressed the importance of the present, claiming that the past is only important in its relation to the present. What is decisive is the reciprocal relationship: critical scrutiny of the present which thereby enables the productive assimilation of the past. (13) In line with Bloch's ideas, Brecht considered that the task was not to draw up a catalog of what could be inherited but to draw on all means, old and new, tried and untried, derived from art and elsewhere, to put human beings in a position of control with regard to reality. (15)

Meanwhile, in the 1930s and 1940s, Lukács, in fact fulfilling the wish expressed by Becher, delivered a series of studies on central aspects of the German literary inheritance: Kleist, Eichendorff, Büchner, Heine, Keller, Raabe, and Fontane. In addition, the studies published in *Goethe and his Age*, written during the 1930s and first published in 1947, were to have, as we shall see, a monumental influence on Goethe reception in East Germany.

When, in 1945, the exiles returned home from Moscow, they came equipped with a definite cultural program: Weimar and Weimar Classicism were to form the center of focus as the basis for building up "another, a better Germany." (16) Under the guidance of Johannes R. Becher, a new union of German intellectuals was set up as a means of continuing the Popular Front strategy. The elements of the tradition to be taken on had already been defined by Lukács's studies, and the decision to leave aside the more revolutionary tradition and the works closely associated with modernity was only later to be recognized as a serious omission. Only when it became clear that the anti-fascist campaign was a purely temporary phase did the SED start to realize what was implicit in Lukács's position: that the need to stress the middle-class democratic tradition would continue. Because Lukács envisaged a long and gradual process of historical development before a fully socialist form of society could be achieved, his position came under fire as non-revolutionary.

The bi-centenary of Goethe's birth in 1949 became a focal point for the establishment of a cultural policy in East Germany. A central task was identified: the creation of a new and realistic image of Goethe with a view to using the classical heritage as a tool to renew the intellectual and moral life of the German people.

The formalism discussion (1951) and the *Faustus* debate (1952–1953)

In 1947–1948 there had been an anti-formalism campaign in the Soviet Union. In 1951, when, with Weimar as a foundation, Ulbricht's regime was intent on finding an authentic German national identity, formalism was shunned because of the danger of infiltration by cosmopolitanism in the form of American imperialist ideology. There was the added risk of Germany succumbing to the barbarism of "boogie-woogie" culture! Most relevant to our theme here is that formalism strove to develop something entirely new — and thus risked causing a break with the classical cultural heritage. At the time, this was to be avoided at all costs. A new democratic German culture was to be developed, but in strict continuity with the classical past.

This intention was cemented in 1953 with the establishment of the National Research Center[2] and then further, in 1955, through celebrations of the 150th anniversary of Schiller's death. A propos Schiller, Becher pleaded for the development of a literature which would first of all need to catch up with the classical writers — and orientate itself exclusively on the narrowly conceived classical canon.

Bitterfeld 1959

The process of developing a new socialist national culture was seen to need the involvement of the working classes in creating literature. Even this venture was to be closely linked with Weimar classicism. Alexander Abusch, who took over as Minister for culture on the death of Becher in 1958, declared:

> Weimar, where the great writers of the middle-class humanist tradition lived and worked, and Bitterfeld, where the working people of our day are creating new standards and values as they begin to work, learn and live in a socialist way — these two concepts are united in the concept of socialist humanism and in the striving for its broadest radiation into life. (24)

In an essay written in 1961, Alfred Kurella modified Lenin's theory of the two cultures. Rather than having a balance between the established culture and revolutionary trends, Kurella insisted that the revolutionary strands should take second place. While it was good to acknowledge the contributions of less established writers of the left wing like Georg Forster, Georg Weerth, and Georg Herwegh, these writers were by no means to be put on a par with writers like Goethe, Schiller, Heine, Hölderlin, Eichendorff or Lenau.

Executors of the inheritance
(*Vollstreckungstheorie*)

Both Alexander Abusch (Minister for Culture 1958–61) in a speech in December 1961 and Walter Ulbricht in a speech in March 1962 use the same passage out of *Faust Part Two* to articulate the "Vollstreckungstheorie":

> I see how
> To give those millions a new living-space:
> They'll not be safe, but active, free at least

---

[2] "Nationale Forschungs- und Gedenkstätten der klassischen deutschen Literatur in Weimar."

I see green fields, so fertile: man and beast
At once shall settle that new pleasant earth,
Bastioned by great embankments that will rise
About them, by bold labour brought to birth.
Here there shall be an inland paradise:
Outside, the sea, as high as it can reach
May rage and gnaw; and yet a common will,
Should it intrude, will act to close the breach.
Yes! to this vision I am wedded still,
And this as wisdom's final word I teach:
Only that man earns freedom, merits life,
Who must reconquer both in constant daily strife.
In such a place, by danger still surrounded,
Youth, manhood, age, their brave new world have founded.
I long to see that multitude, and stand
With a free people on free land![3]

The workers of the GDR, it was maintained, laid claim to the inheritance and were fulfilling the plan inherent in it. Goethe's vision of a free people on free land was already seen as beginning its realization in the socialist state of the GDR. In continuing the fight for peace and for freedom, the people of the GDR were, it was claimed, "writing" *Faust Part Three*! The same quotation, especially the last line ("freies Volk auf freiem Grund"), was used regularly between 1961 and 1971 in the speeches of East German politicians.

The combination of Weimar and Bitterfeld was seen as a bulwark against more liberal developments, such as those accompanying the attempted 1968 revolution in Czechoslovakia which the Soviet forces put down. Between the glorious Faust and the dung-beetle Gregor Samsa there was no contest.

Not until 1969 were there serious signs of opposition to the tight focus on Weimar Classicism, which was seen as deriving from Lukács. In 1970, Werner Mittenzwei, Director of the Central Institute for Literary History (founded in 1969) in the *Akademie der Wissenschaften* and later to become a distinguished Brecht scholar, said that one of the most pressing tasks of the Institute was to work out a revolutionary theory of inheritance. The result was the focus of attention on numerous new editions of the German Jacobins and the Vormärz[4] authors. Here was an important change of accent but not the end of the Weimar/Bitterfeld idea.

[3] David Luke, *Faust Part Two* 223.

[4] Vormärz is the term preferred by the Marxists in this tradition to designate the period 1830–1848, i.e. the period preceding the 1848 revolution. Scholars in other traditions refer to the whole period 1815–1848 either as the Restoration or the Biedermeier period. For the Marxists, the value of the Vormärz designation is that

With the withdrawal from office of Ulbricht on May 3, 1971, a less rigid regime made it no longer necessary to speak about the "socialist human community." Kurt Hager, a member of the Politbüro, was able to refer to the term as scientifically inexact: it gave the false impression that a harmony which in fact did not yet exist was already in place. With the possibility of pointing out contradictions between theory and practice it was possible to *develop* the inheritance theory. Harking back to Marxism-Leninism, Hager spoke out against too narrow a view of what can be inherited. Inheritance must be achieved critically, which means that the great works of the past have to be seen in the context of the social conditions in which they were produced. Thus the elements of contradiction inherent in their production were to be studied. Finally, the socialist course had to be more than what is implied in the "executors" (Vollstreckung) theory. Berlin, understood by Honecker as the proletarian, revolutionary and socialist capital, was to have new importance in the creative search for new forms. By taking up hitherto neglected traditions, it was to provide a counterpoise to Weimar and its focus on Weimar Classicism.

Plenzdorf (1934–)

In a sensational way, Ulrich Plenzdorf's *The New Sufferings of Young W.*, first printed in *Sinn und Form*, March 1972, showed a new method of inheriting the classics. The hero is dissatisfied with the social reality he has to live with in the GDR. As if this were not shocking enough in Honecker's state, the author communicates young W.'s feelings through the use of a parody of Goethe's novel. W. reads (without realizing what it is) *Werther*, warms to it and even begins to quote it and model his life (and death) on what he reads. This is a most striking departure from the executor attitudes of the past. The enthusiasm with which the public responded to this play showed that the heritage was capable of being developed rather than just being simply preserved. It was now possible to have heroes who were not models incarnating the best in socialism.

The irreverent handling of Goethe by Plenzdorf was not unlike that practiced by Brecht. It was time for a new discussion of Brecht's and (Lukács') treatment of the classical heritage. This came about as a response to the book by Reinhold Grimm and Jost Hermand, *Die Klassik-Legende*, published in 1971. In the GDR, the response of Helmut Holtzhauer re-

---

it highlights the revolutionary aspects of the later phase, whereas Restoration is seen as an essentially reactionary term and Biedermeier has connotations of resigned acceptance, from below, of a Restoration imposed from above. Cf. K. Böttcher and H.-J. Geerdts. *Kurze Geschichte der deutschen Literatur*. Berlin: Volk und Wissen, Volkseigener Verlag, 1981, 350–372.

flected the established executor view, and the more progressive view was represented by Werner Mittenzwei, who was calling for a re-examination of Brecht's relationship to Weimar classicism — especially to Goethe. According to Mittenzwei, Brecht had been prepared to correct mistakes in his view of Goethe and had in his latter years sought a fruitful relationship to the classical works. Brecht recognized that Goethe's own attitude to Weimar was not simple. It was even contradictory — which left room for interpreters like Brecht to depart from the harmonizing interpretations required by East German officialdom.

If this development in the early 1970s led to a partial rehabilitation of Brecht, Georg Lukács enjoyed a similar revival. Not least through the conciliatory influence of Mittenzwei, by 1980 Lukács's early contributions (in the 1930s) were being treated as an essential enrichment of Marxist aesthetic thinking. With a view to moving forward, the Marxists were now prepared to draw on the seemingly contradictory strands of their tradition.

At this same time, in 1978, Bernd Leistner's book, *Unruhe um einen Klassiker,* not only opposed the complacent executor theory but also highlighted the fact that Lukács was not to be associated with it. He went further and found much to criticize in the monumental volumes of the *Geschichte der deutschen Literatur,*[5] which, according to him, tended to smooth out problems of interpretation instead of confronting them.

The rehabilitation of Brecht around 1973 brought with it (through Mittenzwei) a new appreciation of Hanns Eisler's opera libretto, *Johann Faustus,* which after a long period of planning, was eventually staged as a play in 1982 and published in book form in 1983.

Even the work on the German heritage represented by Goethe was not properly completed. In 1980, Hans Kaufmann was able to claim[6] that despite the unceasing official quotations from *Faust Part Two,* there were vast tracts of the work which had been entirely neglected. This, too, had still to be claimed!

---

[5] By a collective of authors. Berlin: Volk und Wissen, Volkseigener Verlag, 1978–79.

[6] *Versuch über das Erbe.* Leipzig: Reclam, 1980, 119.

3: Writing the History

Out of the post-war situation the new tradition began to build. It developed through a number of phases over a period of forty years. After around twenty years of endeavor, East German scholars were aware that a unified tradition was emerging. After thirty years, there was a move to record the beginnings of this era of East German Marxist "Literaturwissenschaft"[1] while prominent participants in the beginnings and the development of the tradition were still alive. The Humboldt University journal *Zeitschrift für Germanistik* published the record of a series of important interviews with the still-surviving scholars who were the first products of the founding generation. Thus the first interview is with Ursula Wertheim, one of the earliest pupils of Gerhard Scholz, whom several of the interviewed scholars refer to as one of the crucial formative influences of those founder years. In 1969, in a volume called *Positionen* Wertheim had already written a lengthy article outlining the importance of Scholz's contribution to the new kind of Marxist literary history.

Between January 1982 and March 1985, *Zeitschrift für Germanistik* published the following pieces under the title "Materialien zur Geschichte der marxistischen germanistischen Literaturwissenschaft in der DDR."

January 1982	Preliminary remarks by Hans Kaufmann
	Lisa Lemke — conversation with Ursula Wertheim
February 1982	Therese Hörnigk — conversation with Hans Kaufmann
March 1982	Hans-Ulrich Kühl — conversation with Hans-Günther Thalheim
January 1983	Reinhard Hillich — conversation with Hans Jürgen Geerdts
February 1983	Leonore Krenzlin — conversation with Claus Träger
March 1983	Gudrun Klatt — conversation with Inge Diersen
April 1983	Lisa Lemke — conversation with Alfred Klein
January 1984	Klaus-Dieter Hähnel — conversation with Siegfried Streller

---

[1] This term has no simple English equivalent. A literal translation would be: the "science of literature." The "study of literature as a human science" defines the term better, but, since the expression is unwieldy, it seems advisable to retain the German term.

March 1984   Ulrich Kaufmann — conversation with Hans Richter

January 1985   Lisa Lemke — conversation with Horst Haase

March 1985   Ursula Heukenkamp — conversation with
              Hans-Georg Werner

In his introduction to the series, Hans Kaufmann makes it abundantly clear that a definitive history of this subject is no simple matter. The concept of Marxist Literaturwissenschaft refers to what is common to a variety of Marxist scholars; yet, while what they have in common separates them distinctly from other philosophies and Weltanschauungen, it is not feasible to reduce Marxist Literaturwissenschaft to a closed system of definitions and fixed conclusions. If this were the case, the writing of the history would have such a strong a priori character as to present few problems of historical complexity. But Kaufmann maintains that a purely systematic account of this tradition would be inadequate. The systematic should be wedded to an historical component, so that the scientific advances would not only be shown for their own sake but would be seen with their limitations or even with their errors. Furthermore, the history should make clear what conditions were responsible for producing such results, limitations and errors. Kaufmann maintained in 1982:

> That is a difficult target. The fact that it cannot be achieved easily and quickly should not be a reason for not aiming at it at all. Rather, it would seem fitting to collect the building materials for such an edifice — if only to draw attention to the problem.[2]

If it is true to say that in 1982 the time was not ripe to write a history of the tradition, it is equally true of the present time. Still more material could and should be gathered from the generation interviewed if a comprehensive account of the beginnings is to be achieved. The progress of the tradition into the late 1980s, including an inside view of the shared hopes and aims of Marxist Germanistik,[3] would best be gained from interviews with the newer generation of scholars produced by the generation already interviewed. But this would lead us beyond the scope of the present book.

I had discussions with East German colleagues about how to tackle this project: whether to treat both Goethe and Schiller equally as playing a twin role in the cultural policy of the GDR. This question I answered in favor of concentration on Goethe, since this limitation would allow a sharper focus on detail and hence give a more concrete idea of the Marxist approach. The more general the treatment the greater the danger there would be of missing

[2] *Zeitschrift für Germanistik* (hereafter *Z.f.G.*) 1982: 6.

[3] For the sake of brevity, this term, meaning the "scholarly study of German language and literature," can be retained in this text.

the individuality of the contributions and thus re-inforcing the false expecta-
tion that the Marxists would all toe the party line and all say much the same
thing.

Another useful suggestion, which, however, I decided not yet to follow
up, was to look at the various centers where the new Marxist Literaturwissen-
schaft was gradually developed. Weimar itself, with the setting up of the Na-
tional Research Center, needs to be studied as an important center of
growth. It produced a series of fine young scholars who, because Weimar
had no university, needed to go elsewhere to acquire their scholarly qualifi-
cations and to pursue an academic career. Hence, while developing its own
key function as a world-renowned cultural center, Weimar spread its influ-
ence to the neighboring university of Jena, to Berlin, and from Berlin to
Rostock and Greifswald. Each of these university centers would reward a
separate study. The university in Leipzig developed in relative independence
of Weimar, having its own dominant forces in the world-famous Germanist
Hermann August Korff (1882–1963) — whose scholarship seemed above all
the ideologies (whether of the Weimar Republic, National Socialism, or of
the GDR); and in the Romanist, Werner Krauss (1900–1976), who contrib-
uted to the development of a genuinely Marxist approach to Literaturwissen-
schaft with his analyses of the relationships between literature and history;
and in the colorful, individualistic figure of Hans Mayer (1907-).

Berlin is significant, not just because it manifests some of the impulses
originating from Weimar and combines these with other forces, but also be-
cause of the dominant influence of the Akademie der Wissenschaften cen-
tered in Berlin and staffed mainly by outstanding scholars.

To do justice to the achievement of each of these centers would demand
detailed and comprehensive studies, to which this volume can only act as an
introduction. The aim of this work is, first, to focus on the Marxist Litera-
turwissenschaft in so far as it deals with Goethe. Second, particular attention
will be paid to some important influences on the tradition which are per-
ceived by the Marxists themselves as relatively foreign to them: for instance,
earlier scholars like H. A. Korff, whose methods they largely discredited, and
Georg Lukács, the Marxist whose approach they eventually rejected for en-
tirely different reasons. Third, the aim is to use the two volumes of the *GDL*
as a basis for analyzing the Goethe reception. Because of the enormous
wealth of the material to be dealt with, attention will be limited mainly, but
not entirely, to the discussion of *Werther*, *Wilhelm Meister's Apprenticeship*,
Faust, and *Elective Affinities*. Only particularly significant works of secondary
literature will be considered in addition to the widely representative volumes
six and seven of the *GDL*. Above all, it is at the same time important not to
lose sight of the fact that within the context of Marxist Literaturwissenschaft
in East Germany the role played by individual scholars is of great importance.

While the larger achievements of the tradition are products of highly organized collectives (the volumes of the *GDL*, for example), individual scholars with their particular gifts, insights, backgrounds play a highly significant part. This applies particularly to the beginnings.

When Germany in the Soviet occupied sector began its economic and cultural recovery after 1945 there was, of course, no officially established Marxist Literaturwissenschaft. Nor was it simply a question of a Marxist takeover of the University faculties. Even what, in the context, was a relatively basic step — the introduction of Marxism-Leninism as a compulsory subject for all students — did not happen until the "Hochschulreform" in 1951 which had as its aim to give a Marxist foundation to all the University disciplines. In German studies there were hardly any Marxist professors, and students in the Soviet zone, who, like Ursula Wertheim (later to become a leading Marxist Germanist and Goethe specialist) for racial reasons and others for political reasons, had had no access to normal pre-university education in Hitler's Germany, experienced difficulty in having their matriculation — based on studies done in the "Vorstudienanstalt"[4] — recognized by the universities.

The children of working-class people or of farmers, whose educational development had been handicapped under the Fascist regime, were not to be admitted to the universities; or at least admission was to be made as hard as possible. (1982: 9)

In Berlin, Ursula Wertheim came under the influence of Professor Wolfgang Heise in the Pedagogical Faculty, who had started a circle studying literature from a sociological angle, applying historical materialism to Literaturwissenschaft. In her interview, Wertheim also mentions her first contact with the work of Georg Lukács, whose *Goethe and his Age* first appeared (in the German original) towards the end of the 1940s.

What was new for me was this kind of link between literary history and social history. At first, I was uncomfortable with this, because the arguments seemed to be imposed on literature from the outside. (1982: 8)

The fortunes of Georg Lukács in the GDR were not simply dictated by the official rejection of him for his part in the Hungarian uprising of 1956. There were misgivings about his particular method of using Marxism in interpreting literature. While it is true that the debt of East German Germanistik to the works of Lukács was underplayed by officialdom, it is important to be aware of its limitations — which should emerge from discussions in later chapters.

A major step forward in the development of Marxist Literaturwissenschaft in East Germany was taken when, in 1950, a group of young Germanists was delegated to take part in a semester-long course in Weimar. This

---

[4]   A special institution designed to prepare students for university study.

was seen as preparation for the Hochschulreform of 1951. At the center of this course, which was to begin to provide a Marxist foundation for German studies, was the preoccupation with Storm and Stress and with German Classicism. The focus on these two phases of German literature is not to be taken as originating from a plan thought out a priori. But it does have an historical foundation — as part of the "Forderung des Tages" (demands of the current situation). In setting out to establish a Marxist foundation for Germanistik, they had to choose a starting point. The choice was largely dictated by the classical jubilees: 1954 Lessing, 1955 and 1959 Schiller. (1982: 10) The cultural policy of the time demanded a response to these occasions. It provided an opportunity to refute the thesis that Goethe was like a lonely Olympian God on his throne above the clouds by showing him to have been a contemporary and champion of the revolutionary Storm and Stress movement in which his early work was rooted.

The "Materialien"

The nature of the "Materialien" as a series of personal interviews giving an account of personal experiences of GDR beginnings in "Literaturgeschichte" is not a chance phenomenon. Both the beginnings and the development of this tradition depended to an extraordinarily high degree on two things: firstly, on the impact of individual personalities, and secondly, on the growing willingness of the individuals to collaborate in teams or collectives.

The role of Georg Lukács
(1885–1971)

In the interview in March 1985 with Hans-Georg Werner, Ursula Heukenkamp (of the Humboldt University in Berlin) said that the younger generations of Marxist scholars could not comprehend why Lukács had been considered so important for the development of Literaturwissenschaft in the GDR. More than likely, the official East German disapproval of Lukács after his expression of solidarity with the Hungarian uprising of 1956 had had, to a large extent, the desired effect, so that for the younger generations the names of Scholz and even Hans Mayer (despite his "defection" to the West) loomed much larger than that of Lukács. But Hans-Georg Werner insisted that for them, "Georg Lukács was at least as important as Gerhard Scholz or Hans Mayer." (Z.f.G. 1985: 277) Horst Haase, in his interview, insisted that his education as a Marxist Germanist was influenced essentially by his writings. (1985: 5) He describes himself as an enthusiastic pupil of Lukács and is not prepared to deny the positive influence Georg Lukács had on his development. (5) Ursula Wertheim, referring to herself and her colleagues around the mid-1950s, says that all the young Assistants were deeply influenced by the publications of Lukács. Claus Träger speaks of the enormous influence of Lukács on all of that older generation. (1983: 145) Similarly, H. J. Geerdts speaks of Lukács's works as sources of their formation (1983: 45), both with regard to content and method, of several scholars of his generation. Why?

Lukács provided, for all practical purposes, the most important contributions (and, in some cases, the only contributions) to a Marxist interpretation of particular literary periods. (45)

Contemporary relevance

What, then, made Lukács so attractive to the young Marxists of the 1950s? His radical commitment to Marxism was obvious from his involvement in the Volksfront (Popular Front) movement formed partly at the instigation of leading German writers (Heinrich Mann included) who had been forced to emigrate after Hitler's take-over in Germany in 1933.[5] (Many people opposed to Hitler — like the Social Democrats, official members of the communist party and others, like Brecht, aligned with them — were prepared to bury their differences in order to present a united front in opposition to National Socialism). He had been able to tackle, with a high level of criticism, reactionary traditions which had interpreted the Enlightenment as foreign to German culture and had seen classical German philosophy as a reaction against European Enlightenment. His approach appealed to the intelligentsia and won many of them over to more progressive ideas: such as the interpretation of Forster, Hölderlin, and Heine as belonging to the progressive strands in German history. (1982: 265) Then, on the one hand, he attacked what he called the capitalist imperialist society for the way it deformed and degraded human existence, and, on the other hand, his writings gave strong evidence of a utopian optimism to be found in what Hans-Günther Thalheim (one of the early generation of Marxist Germanists who went on to play a leading role in his field — especially at the Humboldt University in Berlin and later at the Akademie der Wissenschaften der DDR) calls an enlightened, pre-revolutionary "Demokratismus" (270), an optimism which was to become the criterion for his "literature of the great forms." Works of this kind (for example, *Werther*, and later: *Wilhelm Meister's Apprenticeship* and *Faust*) reflected

---

[5] Cf. Hans-Jürgen Schmitt. *Die Expressionismusdebatte. Materialien zu einer marxistischen Realismuskonzeption.* Frankfurt am Main: Suhrkamp, 1973, 7–28.

the general democratic vision of a utopia based on perfected human development and served, in their turn, as criteria for judging the level of a twentieth century writer's progressiveness in outlook. (270)

Especially valuable to the young East German Marxists was the link they found in Lukács's writings between literature on the one hand and politics and society on the other. This was all the more helpful at a time when the younger generation had not even the beginnings of a really socialist society on which to base their thinking and theory. Werner mentions Franz Fühmann as one of their leading writers who developed his Marxist social theory and arrived at a new concept of history with the help of Lukács's writings. In this, Fühmann's experience was, *mutatis mutandis*, similar to that of a whole series of scholars. (1985: 277) This dependence on Lukács's writings is further illustrated by the statement of H. J. Geerdts who claims that his own book on *Die Wahlverwandtschaften* — written in 1958 and probably one of the most durable of GDR products of its kind — was strongly influenced by Lukács's method. (1983: 45) What Geerdts found particularly enlightening was Lukács's ability to find historical events and developments reflected not just in the background but in the whole structure of classical works. Lukács gave them a method for tackling works which had hardly, if at all, been handled by earlier Marxist writers. Furthermore, his work introduced them into territory which was not only new to them as Marxists but which also had not been explored by their rivals in the West. (45)

Apart from the general timeliness of Lukács for the new Marxist beginnings in the GDR, it is important to consider the basis of the personal impact he had made on the early East German scholars in his subject. Thalheim refers to Lukács's own personal stature as a scholar, claiming that his importance is based on the high level of his culture as a philosopher. (1982: 265) Werner obviously admired him as really outstanding mind with a great breadth of understanding. On the basis of his great culture he was able to pass on a rich variety of insights. (1985: 227) Because of his sovereign grasp of the great artistic works of the past, he was in a position to present them as belonging to a genuine Marxist heritage. (1982: 159) With his breadth of vision, he could write with critical authority about how Germany went astray. Furthermore, because of his political experience he was able to operate virtually as an educator of the new generation, offering them a Weltanschauung which was enlightening for them in various spheres of study. (1985: 227) Ursula Wertheim speaks of the connection Lukács made between literature and social history (1982: 8) — a connection she was at first uneasy with but from which she learned new approaches. It would never have occurred to her previously to look at the role played by any contemporary social circumstances in the shaping of any work of art (or literature). Referring to the same phenomenon, Werner says Lukács combined a feel for politics with a feel for literature (though within certain limits). (1985: 277)

Geerdts's testimony is similar. From Lukács he learned, in his study of Goethe, not to treat social history merely as background but to read the social background from the figures Goethe created in his works. (1983: 45) None of this seemed artificial to Geerdts:

> The relationship between literature and history as seen by Lukács was not schematic in the way which was true of Paul Reimann's book on the *Geschichte der deutschen Literatur*. (45)

With one of his central comments on Lukács, Thalheim leads us into a crucial issue of the time: according to Thalheim, Lukács was opposed to the idea of the later middle-class conception of philosophy and literary history which falsely interpreted the Enlightenment as something foreign to the German tradition. He rejected the tendency to see classical German philosophy and literature as the expression of an autonomous, superior German Geist and as a counter to the Enlightenment. Against this, Lukács upheld the continuity between the Enlightenment and Weimar Classicism and impressed his readers with a progressive and comprehensive grasp of the basic lines of cultural and intellectual development in Germany in the last two centuries. (1982: 265) Lukács's personal contribution to cultural developments in the GDR was due in no small measure to the strong philosophical component of his work, since, as Werner claimed, the development of a Marxist Literaturwissenschaft was first and foremost a process of philosophical thinking. (1985: 227)

Criticism of Lukács

But despite all the positive aspects highlighted in the interviews, the fact remains that, for later generations of Marxists, Lukács had faded into the background. This is, as mentioned above, not entirely due to the official cloud which descended on him after his role in the events in Hungary in 1956.

Part of the Lukács heritage which lasted well into the late 1970s in the GDR was his particular interpretation of German Romanticism. According to Claus Träger, Lukács's view of the Romantic movement remained virtually unchallenged for nearly three decades in the GDR. In this view, accepted by all of Träger's generation, Romanticism represented the failure of the middle-class mind, which had lost its way — as if there were such a thing as the "middle-class mind!" (1983: 150) In this, Lukács is seen to be still a prisoner of his past. He is still not free from his early rootedness in the movement of Geistesgeschichte. Thus he is revealed eventually, in his analyses of classical and Romantic literature in Germany, as a negative version of Korff. (1983: 150)

Furthermore, in yet other respects Lukács was to appear as belonging to the past. According to Hans Kaufmann his analyses left the great works of European literature in a kind of splendid isolation. This problem is expressed differently by Thalheim. For Lukács, the literary works appear to be, to a high degree, purely individual works standing alone as isolated creations. (1982: 268) Comparing Lukács's approach to that of Scholz, Thalheim claims that, from Scholz's point of view, Lukács abstracted too severely from the actual process by which literature came into being. Träger refers to the dogmatic and too classical treatment of certain questions — an approach which leads precisely away from history. (1983: 148)

Lukács's opposition to Brecht and his incomprehension of Brecht's achievements and aims highlighted a short-coming for which Lukács was to be severely criticized, namely, that his Literaturwissenschaft was divorced from praxis. (Interview with Werner, 1985: 278) This opinion is reinforced by the statement of Hans Kaufmann that

> Lukács's indifference to Storm and Stress and to literary forms of a political kind — for example, those of the Vormärz, were in line, methodically, with his criticism of proletarian revolutionary literature and of Brecht. (1982: 161)

Lukács was too rigidly preoccupied with the best classical models to find room for innovation. Most damning of all was his inability to react to the new situation for literature and Literaturwissenschaft presented by the new socialist society. (1985: 277) Geerdts expresses his final reservation about the great Hungarian scholar when he lists the things Lukács was *not* able to do: he gave no encouragement to disciples and admirers to study the specifics of literature, like symbolism, irony, and the techniques of literary writing which Goethe used and developed. (1983: 45)

Eventually Lukács had had his day; but it will be worth observing in later pages to what extent his influence contributed to some important chapters in the writing of German literary history in the GDR.

The role of Gerhard Scholz

Further incisive developments were due to the concrete personality of Gerhard Scholz. It was his particular brand of enthusiasm and his particular set of talents and convictions which were to put the stamp on at least two generations of Germanists, especially on Goethe scholars.

There can be no doubt that the beginnings and development of Marxist Literaturwissenschaft in the GDR mirror the gifts and qualities of Gerhard

Scholz as an individual. Several of the interviewees had direct experience of an important winter semester course given by Scholz in Weimar in 1950 and 1951. The purpose of the course was to prepare the way for the Hochschulreform of the same year through which Marxism-Leninism made its entry into the universities as a compulsory subject and which had as its goal to provide the individual disciplines with a Marxist foundation. (1982: 10)

Hans Kaufmann writes of Scholz:

> When I met Scholz in 1948, he was Director of a Goethe Workshop in Berlin in the context of the "Kulturbund" (League of Culture). Afterwards, he went to Weimar where, in the winter of 1950–51, this course was organized under his direction. He had come back after being exiled as an anti-fascist and was one of the few proponents of Marxism in this discipline. From Scholz we learned to deal intensively with historical material as well as with literary history. We learned to take the texts seriously and to approach them from a Marxist angle. (1982: 18)

In these early days, the Marxists were concerned with eradicating the fascist influences left in their society and culture, and, as an exile from fascist Germany, Scholz had impressive credentials. Furthermore, from his Marxist stand-point he was able to analyze and criticize the thrust of the established middle class Germanistik, showing what political and social interests he thought it served. In a sense, he wanted to disinherit the middle classes. His aim was to have the working class take over the heritage. It was not feasible to shut oneself away. It was necessary to live with the day-to-day political reality. (161) In his whole approach, Scholz showed himself to be a man of the people. According to Ursula Wertheim, there were often intensive discussions aimed at clarifying concepts such as "Volksverbundenheit" and "Volkstümlichkeit." Thus they arrived at the definition of "volksverbunden" (committed to the people) as a particular attitude of authors to the producers of material goods, which meant, in the eighteenth century, the farmers (Bauern). The concept "volkstümlich" was applied to subjects and subject material which either originated in a folk tradition or were accessible and comprehensible to a broad public. Thus Goethe's *Iphigenie* gives testimony that the attitude of the author is volksverbunden, committed to the people, whereas the subject of the play is not volkstümlich because it presupposes a level of education not accessible to the general public. (1982: 11)

Scholz's interest in the ordinary people was manifested in the way he studied relevant social and economic processes and the economic theories (e.g. of the eighteenth century). Of vital importance for Scholz was the way the plebeian and peasant classes were depicted in what was essentially a middle-class literature. He unearthed, for example, documentary evidence of peasants' complaints against their feudal lords and then he investigated what resonance these complaints had in the literature of the time — specifically in the Storm and Stress period. (161)

Closely allied to this carefully guided and minute examination of the actual literary texts is Scholz's preoccupation with the way the texts themselves came into being. By contrast with Lukács, who treated the great works of literature as standing there absolutely in their finished state, Scholz saw them as the result of a long development which he was interested in tracing in detail. They were not simply the products of a particular set of historical circumstances or the fine literary expression of the author's ideas, opinions and intentions. According to Hans-Günther Thalheim:

> What interests Scholz is the way a literary work emerges, with all the vital problems it deals with, from the often difficult and sometimes interrupted process of class struggle and from the poet's encounters with the human and social reality of his age. To tackle a literary work and to understand it in the light of the relationships between the writer and his or her social reality, one has to begin with the oldest parts of the work, the poetic elements, levels, and forms, in which the earliest individual and social experiences are contained. (267)

These older, archaic elements of the great works, "these operative genres or small forms," are identified by Thalheim as aphorisms, epigrams, fables, farces, small comedies, autobiographical sketches etc. These small individual forms have at first a life of their own, representing both the poet's earlier assimilation of reality and his attempts to deal with contemporary society; but afterwards these smaller forms are capable of assimilation into a greater work with much broader human and social perspectives. Scholz applied this method to his *Faust* interpretation, but as Thalheim points out, he applied it also to the analysis of twentieth century socialist literature:

> Thus, battle songs, the new types of political poems, the agitprop plays, journalistic reportage, sketches, reports, etc — notwithstanding their own individual social and literary function — provided the foundations both for more comprehensive poetic works of socialist literature and for its development and rise in importance. (268)

As an educator, Scholz taught his charges to learn by doing. The postwar situation of many of his students did not find them equipped with the sound Bildung of their more privileged middle-class counterparts. They had to fill in the gaps as they went. Scholz himself, unlike the traditional type of German university professor, did not exercise his main influence through his publications. Much of what Scholz achieved was in his work groups, in the discussions which arose out of concrete situations: what Ursula Wertheim constantly refers to as the Forderung des Tages.

With the aid of his young collective, he organized exhibitions based on materials gathered in the Weimar archives. In this way he was able to interest people in literary subjects which, if they had depended on traditional academic channels, would be almost entirely inaccessible to them. He made Weimar into a center which attracted people from the most far-off and foreign cultures, and because he was so tuned-in to concrete reality he was able to cater for their interests. Instead of working with fixed notions about a German Olympian Goethe, Scholz and his collective were flexible enough to build on and to enrich the interests the visitors brought with them.

The immediate influence of Scholz and his methods was obviously due in no small degree to the impact of his own strong personality. No doubt, he had the right kind of experience and expertise for the historical moment. But in the context of Germanistik in Germany he was in no way an established figure. As Thalheim points out:

> Gerhard Scholz always felt like an outsider in Germanistik. He was clearly suspicious of academic Germanists, who then, on their part, saw him as an outsider. (265)

Also in his more narrowly academic methods he made an unconventional impression:

> Scholz presented his ideas most effectively in the context of discussions. He operated with association of ideas and with images rather than systematically and was therefore sometimes difficult to follow; but at the same time he was able to conjure up for his audience a sharply focused historical world which made an extraordinarily dynamic and lively impression. (266)

How could the influence of such an individualistic man survive? Why were Scholz's attitudes and influences not restricted to a "school" in Weimar?

Paradoxically, since there was no university in Weimar — a fact which should have limited the scope of Scholz's influence — his protégés had to move on, as mentioned above, to universities like Jena and Berlin, where they could equip themselves with the formal academic qualifications they needed, and from there to other university centers such as Rostock and Greifswald. Naturally, as people moved on they were subjected to other influences, but the contact with Scholz was for many (like Edith Braemer, Ursula Wertheim, Hans Kaufmann and Hans-Günther Thalheim) quite unforgettable, and a younger generation of scholars like Hans-Dietrich Dahnke, Peter Müller, Wolfgang Stellmacher and Peter Weber remain very conscious of their debt to Scholz. For the visitor to the former GDR one of the most striking impressions made by these scholars was their collegiality amongst themselves — though this was often in the form of tough, even ruthless debate. They also exhibited a natural respect for Germanists coming from a non-German tradition. No doubt their ease in dealing with foreign approaches to Germanistik was fostered by the experience of collaborating with Germanists in other East Block Socialist countries — from the Soviet Union to Poland, Hungary, Czechoslovakia, Romania, Bulgaria, etc., not to mention Cuba and Asian countries like China and Korea. The fact that the Western countries were almost totally closed off meant a considerable isolation for the GDR. But this led to the search for and development of contacts near and far — contacts which were to be fostered by academic exchanges and conferences that built up a far-flung network. In the West, itself closed off in its own "system," it was easy to underestimate the value and richness of this broad network.

Krauss (1900–1976)

Another serious influence on the development of GDR Literaturwissenschaft came from a relatively unexpected source. The interviewees speak highly of Werner Krauss, the Romanist in Leipzig. When he began teaching in Leipzig (1947–1958), Krauss, along with the historian Walter Markov, brought about changes. According to Thalheim, the new GDR Marxist approach to writing literary history was influenced by the struggle to eradicate Fascism in Germany and to set up a new socialist democracy. This entailed also the countering of inhuman elements in middle-class ideology, coming to grips with the problems of intellectual apathy, establishing an anti-imperialist democracy and an active humanism, while at the same time giving a real function to the ideas of Marx and Lenin.

The Marxists were so preoccupied with the stark realities of their historical situation that, in laying the foundations for the development of a Marxist romance studies, it is not surprising that they opposed what Thalheim refers to as the "later middle-class turning aside from history," which resulted in treating its processes as irrational. By contrast, Krauss stressed the link between literary creation and concrete social life. Furthermore, the broadly European horizon of his studies — stretching way beyond the limits of his own "subject" — gave a new orientation to the writing of literary history.

Claus Träger, who, though a Germanist, for several years worked as an assistant to Krauss, speaks of the benefits accruing to his subject from the application of Krauss's ideas. He stresses the importance of Krauss's striving

> not to re-interpret literary history but to see the texts as consolidation of literary history, to understand them in their historical function and, in this way, to achieve a new understanding of literature as history. (1983: 145)

The focus on literary texts as functioning in the historical situation and thus the understanding of literature precisely as history stands in direct contrast to the approach of a Western scholar like Emil Staiger with his art of interpretation which, according to Träger

> depends, — apart from its basic Weltanschauung — to a large extent on chance: the ability of the interpreter to respond to something in the text or to read something into it. (146)

Whatever about Staiger's fundamental Weltanschauung, for Träger any approach to interpreting literary texts which is not founded in — and is not seen as related to — a clear concept of historical processes is misleading.

The very nature of Krauss's preoccupation with literature inoculated him a priori against such a temptation. The Enlightenment period — the center of his interest — was not strong on belletristic literature. Its interests lay elsewhere, so that a scholar in this field would naturally have a broader concept of literature than that represented by Staiger.

Träger highlights a further influence of Krauss which opposed him to ahistorical approaches to literary interpretation. Claiming that Krauss was the first in their tradition to observe that literature is only complete as literature when it is read, when it is "received," Träger says: "That was between 1950 and 1960, long before reception research came into vogue." (149) This led to Manfred Naumann, with the same literary presuppositions and methodology, undertaking to investigate the role of the reader.

Hans Mayer (1907–)

Hans Mayer's role in the development of Marxist Literaturwissenschaft is discussed in detail in the interview with Claus Träger. The fact that he eventually left the GDR for the West was obviously a great loss, but his role as a Germanist in Leipzig was no doubt of extreme importance. In exile, he had written an important book on Büchner, had had some radio experience in Frankfurt, and had then joined the Gesellschaftswissenschaftliche Fakultät[6] in 1948. From 1951 he occupied the chair, specially created for him, for the history of national literatures. Although his formal academic training was as a lawyer, he had responsibility now for lecturing on German literature. Given the presence in Leipzig of such world-renowned Germanists as Theodor Frings and Hermann August Korff, who were not prepared to acknowledge him as their peer, life was not made easy for Mayer. But this did not deter him or lessen his influence. One obvious advantage he enjoyed was that his lectures were the only ones in Leipzig which offered anything resembling a

---

[6] This is a rough equivalent of the Social Sciences Faculty. The conscious subsuming of the study of literature under the study of society — rather than considering it as a Geisteswissenschaft — is a Marxist statement about the primary importance of society; it also considerably broadens the category of Social Science.

Marxist-Leninist approach to interpreting literature. The enormous breadth and depth of his knowledge — encompassing not only law but also literature, art, music, and philosophy — was obviously impressive; and, politically, he did what Korff was far less likely to do: he furthered the careers of the young Marxists.

As a student in Leipzig, Siegfried Streller had experience of both the old and the new: Korff and Frings on the one hand and Mayer on the other. It is clear that Mayer stretched his net far too wide for scholars of the old school. His approach could broadly be described as sociological. Using Marxist categories, he examined the interaction between social and aesthetic processes. He drew a sharp distinction between real history (Realgeschichte) and history of literature, but, according to Streller, he lacked the requisite methodology to come to grips with such questions. In his presentation of his material he was essayistic, making it easy for his adversaries to write him off as a journalist. Frings looked on him as a charlatan, and Mayer looked on Frings as a relic of by-gone days. "Frings is a monument," he often said. (1984: 10) Whatever the relative validity of the criticism of Mayer as a literary journalist, he brought into Germanistik in Leipzig a flexibility and openness which was new. He achieved this without creating a school comparable to that of Scholz in Weimar. Although he did not develop a fundamental theoretical or methodological conception which could be handed on to disciples, the scholars who went through his hands gave evidence of a much greater variety of approaches than did those directly influenced by Scholz.

Thalheim underlines the significance of Mayer's contribution to Marxist Germanistik:

> He represented, in relationship to middle-class reactionary Germanistik, a progressive counter position which was strongly influenced by the traditions of the Enlightenment, of "Vormärz," and, in general, of middle-class humanism. One of the merits of his activity was that he was able to pass on his insights into international literature. This provided a stark contrast to the narrowness of traditional Germanistik. In addition, Mayer was much more open to the literature of the twentieth century — in all its breadth and differentiation — than, for example, was Lukács. He also had a positive impact on the development of East German research on Brecht.
>
> (1982: 264)

By contrast with Lukács, Hans Mayer also turned his attention to contemporary socialist writing in the GDR in the 1950s. He could hardly be said to have promoted it, but, where others ignored it, he gave it a critical airing, criticizing it for too schematic a representation of reality. Countering Lukács's approach, he maintained that it was not possible to deal artistically with the modern world by confining oneself to forms used by Balzac and Tolstoi. It was more appropriate to learn from twentieth century writers. By this he meant not just Heinrich and Thomas Mann, but also Trakl, Heym, Joyce and Kafka. If these were left aside, the result would be stagnation and sterility. (270)

What Streller appreciated was that Mayer's lectures dealt with the newest literature and promoted the conviction that Literaturwissenschaft was not to be understood as the study of literature purely from an historical perspective but as something which is directly concerned with the development of contemporary social processes. Streller also appreciated his openness: Mayer invited many contemporary writers to the university as guests, among them Brecht, Becher, Leonard Frank, Anna Seghers, Hermlin, Huchel, Bachmann, and Enzensberger.

As with Lukács, one of the main criticisms levelled at Hans Mayer was his adherence to a form of Geistesgeschichte in his approach to understanding literature. Behind this approach was the implied conviction that there was a Zeitgeist evolving from period to period and leaving its print on the fundamental as well as on contemporary experiences of the writers and their heroes. According to Thalheim, this idealistic presupposition

> already contains within itself the potential — which was later realized — for interpreting the deeply-rooted contrasts and contradictions between the literary fronts in the twentieth century (the time of transition from capitalism to socialism) as mere inner tensions within a more or less homogeneously structured epoch. (264f.)

This internalizing of the conflicts ran counter to the then current Marxist tendency to focus on the specifics of contemporary conflicts. In fact, for the Marxists it emerged that Hans Mayer eventually showed little sympathy for their cause. He had failed to make allowances for the fact that the new socialist literature was in its infancy. They found his judgments too abstract and too sweeping and too remote from the facts of the class struggle. His sympathy for the modern literature in the West resulted, in fact, in a withdrawal of his sympathy both from socialist writing and from the socialist orientation it represented. According to Thalheim, his change of allegiance led him to sharply anti-socialist positions. (271)

Korff (1882–1963)

Hermann August Korff proved to be a central figure in Leipzig Germanistik even after the arrival of Marxism. He had not disgraced himself under the Hitler regime and, while not compromising himself simply to curry favor with the new regime, he learned to live with it and to show it a fundamental loyalty. While the "Materialien" (the series of interviews) show a nuanced reaction to Korff on the part of the Marxists, the picture painted has a certain clear unity.

On the practical level, the young Marxists had the problem of dealing with an enormously weighty, internationally famous scholar who had been writing important books since the 1920s, and they were only too aware that their own (in many cases) interrupted education and lack of experience put them at a grave disadvantage in coping with him. Thalheim and Streller both refer to Korff's confrontation with the Marxist positions in a special seminar. In the context of explaining the lengths to which Korff would go to deal with his young opposition, Thalheim reports:

> Korff came up with the grotesque idea of preventing awkward questions and criticisms by having entry to his seminar checked by officials . . . He went a step further and decided to give a seminar on socialist Literaturwissenschaft himself. (263)

According to Thalheim, Korff thought it was enough to read a few little Marxist brochures on basic philosophical questions. The intention was to show the unscientific and primitive nature of the sociological approach to literature and to show that it was totally inappropriate for studying literature. Not surprisingly the seminar was no success, but Korff's position was not thereby affected. He was enormously popular with the majority of the students and could always be sure of applause when he entered the lecture theater and held his lectures, which were both pedagogically effective and intelligible.

If Thalheim's account is not really antagonistic, Streller's version of the same incident could be described as more conciliatory. He sees this seminar as a genuine offer of debate with the Marxists. But, "in the acute and severe situation of the class struggle, it could only be misunderstood." (1984: 7) The young Marxists had an axe to grind, and Streller relates how his own behaviour was so aggressive that Korff had him removed from the auditorium. But Korff bore him no grudge. In fact when called upon to assess the merits of Streller's first doctoral thesis, Korff recommended that Streller's academic career be vigorously promoted. In all fairness to Korff, Streller says:

> I would like to stress that, as a middle-class scholar, Korff endeavored to work along with the new regime. But this is not to withdraw anything said in the objective context of evaluating his theoretical position. (7)

The contrast between Korff's theoretical position and that of the Marxists with regard to Literaturwissenschaft is perhaps most aptly expressed by the contrast between Geisteswissenschaft (mental sciences) and Gesellschaftswissenschaft (social sciences). For Korff, Literaturwissenschaft belonged, in the Dilthey tradition which had wrested the discipline from the grasp of the positivist scholars, to the realm of Geisteswissenschaft. Thalheim's criticism of the corresponding method was that it treated literature as if it belonged to a timeless sphere, that it pretended to be apolitical and that it would not condescend to dwell on its relationship to any social dimension. (1982: 262)

In his massive five-volume work on *Der Geist der Goethezeit* (The Spirit of the Age of Goethe), written between 1923 and 1954, Korff was engaged in writing Geistesgeschichte, which, as a method, has been criticized for implying that a particular age has its own "Geist" (Mind) whose evolution can be traced in the great works of literature and in the personality of their creator. Here, for example, the Geist finds expression in the life and personality of Goethe as well as in the figure of his main creation: Faust. Here there is the double problem: first, that stressing the importance of the ruthless Faust character was hardly acceptable after the events of the Third Reich, whether in Germany or elsewhere; and second, in a society like the GDR, which was undergoing radical transformation towards socialism, a Literaturwissenschaft with insufficient focus on society made itself irrelevant.

Criticism of *Geistesgeschichte*

It is interesting that, when the time came to criticize both Lukács and Mayer, the attack came from a similar direction. As we saw above, Claus Träger saw the limitations in Lukács's method reflected above all in his interpretation of the Romantic movement as a failure of the middle-class mind. (1983: 150) Commenting on this interpretation, which he claims held sway in Marxist circles for about thirty years and which his own generation grew up with, Träger says it was essentially a reversal of the view represented by Geistesgeschichte ("im wesentlichen eine Umkehrung der geistesgeschichtlichen Auffassung"). So, what was once called the "Spirit of Goethe's Age," had now become the "Spirit of the Middle-Class Era." Lukács's important book *Die Theorie des Romans,* (The Theory of the Novel) first published in 1920, was the work of a writer still manifesting tendencies towards Geisteswissenschaftliche, as Lukács himself points out in his Preface to the 1962 edition.[7] Although the terms geisteswissenschaftlich and geistesgeschichtlich are not simply synonymous, the latter comes under the umbrella of the former. In referring to Dilthey's *Das Erlebnis und die Dichtung,*[8] Lukács says it "appeared to us then as a world of comprehensive syntheses of both a theoretical and an *historical* kind." (*Theorie des Romans.* 7)

This positive comment is flanked by a two-fold criticism: first, though he and his contemporaries did not realize it at the time, they were overlooking how little this new method really represented a defeat of positivism, how lit-

---

[7] Cited in: *Theorie des Romans.* Neuwied and Berlin: Luchterhand, 1971: 6.

[8] Leipzig, 1905.

tle these fine syntheses were founded in reality; and second: it became cus-
tomary to form general concepts from purely intuitively grasped characteris-
tics of a trend or of a period, and to apply these deductively to concrete phe-
nomena and thus to arrive at a grandiose synthesis. (7) The criticism outlined
here is not essentially different from that generally levelled against Geistes-
geschichte, and Lukács says of his own book: "That was also the method of
the *Theory of the Novel.*" (7)

In a similar way, when it came to a criticism of Hans Mayer, Thalheim
stresses:

> But to a large extent he remained a prisoner of a liberally conceived Geist-
> esgeschichte. The dominant principle is a Zeitgeist taken from Vormärz
> ideology.[9] This Geist changes from period to period and determines both
> the fundamental experiences of poet and hero as well as their experiences of
> the epoch. (1982: 264f.)

The close affinity with Korff's methods and with his interpretation of the
significance of the idealist philosophy of the Goethe period is evident.

---

[9]   See above, chapter two, footnote 4.

4: Religion versus Society:
Transcendence versus Immanence

Spinoza (1632–77)

While it became increasingly obvious that the method based on Geistes-geschichte, with its stress on the history of ideas to the near exclusion of the social dimension, was not compatible with the Marxist view that the history of literature belonged to the Social Sciences, it is nevertheless fascinating to study the attention the Marxists devoted to the ideas of a figure like Spinoza. To the student of the history of philosophy who has not been particularly exposed to Marxism it would come as a surprise to see how important a role is played by Spinoza in the Marxist interpretation of the Goethe Period.

Clearly, since Spinoza loomed large for Lessing, Herder and then Goethe and was central to the pantheism debate of the 1780s, this was a figure which could hardly be ignored; but that he should have been such a key figure for the Marxists themselves needs some explanation. From the early years of the GDR till its very final stages the Marxists found a place for Spinoza. From the hard-line, doctrinaire approach of the early writers like Lindner and Girnus, through the more moderate contributions of those who wrote the *GDL*, to the wide-open views represented by Jürgen Teller and Günther Mieth, Spinoza continued to be a focal point. For those who remember Goethe's admiring references to Spinoza in *Dichtung und Wahrheit* as the "theissimum und christianissimum der Menschen," the Marxist interest in him is puzzling. In fact, Spinoza is given a central role in the Marxist polemic against the traditional interpretations of Goethe, according to which, despite all highlighting of certain anti-Christian stances on Goethe's part — especially before 1800 — , it is still feasible to see Goethe as a fundamentally religious man. Goethe's early and then continued interest in Spinoza seemed to offer the Marxists a striking way of refuting or disarming this traditional view.

Referring back to the treatment meted out to Spinoza by the orthodox forces of his own time — which saw him as a materialist and an atheist — the Marxists like Lindner, Girnus and some of the authors of the *GDL* and even the later and more critical interpreter within the Marxist tradition, Heinz Hamm, saw Spinoza essentially as a figure who opposed the theistic views shared by the Churches in seventeenth century Europe. In seeing Goethe as Spinozist in attitude, the Marxists were then able to find an equivalent to Spinozism in Goethe's own thinking. There is no doubt that Goethe was opposed, in theory and in practice, to the established Churches of his time. We would have to agree that he rejected what the Marxists call the "kirchlich-theistisch" elements of his time. We know, for example, that he shunned the drab, joyless form of pietism as he found it in Straßburg — which does not necessarily mean that he rejected pietism out of hand, especially in the form he knew at close hand through his friend Susanna von Klettenberg. We know that he thought contemptuously of the "Pfaffen" — the Church-men with their particular brand of theism. We know, in particular, what uncomfortable relationships he had with the Protestant pastor Lavater — despite his personal admiration for the man — and with Friedrich Jakobi and later with the Romantics because of dogmatic Catholicizing tendencies which he could not abide.

But Goethe's views, over a period of time, are rarely black and white. If he rejects various forms of Church theism — or even *all* forms of Church theism — it does not follow that he rejects theism as such. Goethe's fierce independence with regard to the established Churches does not force him into a form of atheism. What Goethe rejects is precisely a Church monopoly of religion. He was well aware that Spinoza was not only rejected by the Jewish synagogue but was persecuted by the Christian authorities as an atheist. Yet Goethe, in calling him "theissimum" and "christianissimum" is maintaining that there are intrinsic religious qualities which a person can have to an extraordinarily high degree even when outlawed by the established Church authorities. It is not justifiable to argue simply from Spinoza's (and Goethe's) oppositional stance to an assertion of their atheism. Finding oneself in agreement with the seventeenth century dogmatic establishment view of Spinoza as materialist and atheist should sound an alarm bell.

As Marxists, the new generation of Literaturwissenschaftler in the 1950s and 1960s needed to establish their Weltanschauung on as firm a basis as possible. Goethe and Schiller, as two of the most central and broadly acceptable writers in the history of modern German literature, could be seen as incarnating the progressive, democratic views of the pre-Marxist generation. Quite strikingly, at a time when some thinkers in the West had the tendency to do down Goethe as the Olympian figure with his head in the clouds or even as the writer who curried favor with the nobility, the Marxists set out to show Goethe as a man of the people, representing in his early Storm and Stress years the best in the rising middle class. Goethe was seen in this context as a protagonist, both artistically and socially, of a revolutionary movement which rebelled against the status quo. The merits of this view can be studied in the wealth of literature devoted to Goethe interpretation in the GDR.

Not surprisingly, the Marxists' tasks present them with some difficult problems. Claiming Goethe as a fore-runner to the Marxist materialist philosophy required more than highlighting his seemingly atheistic outbursts. In an unending series of places in his writings Goethe is found referring with great enthusiasm to "Gott" or "das Göttliche." This is so obvious that we hardly need to dwell on it. But to solve this problem the general solution to hand was the "deus sive natura"[1] formula of Spinoza. Once it can be shown that Goethe is Spinozist in outlook, it seems clearly possible to solve the problem of Goethe's religion by substituting "nature" for God and thus proceeding with the materialist idea of the primacy of matter over spirit. Nature, seen as material, is the object of the physical sciences and, as such, can be submitted to a never-ending human scrutiny. There is no longer the need to be silenced by the profound mysteries proclaimed by religion. It is an interesting study to follow the various Marxist attempts at explaining key Goethe texts such as the "Prolog in Heaven" and the concluding scene of *Faust Part Two*.

Pietism

A similar problem arises with the subject of pietism. This fundamentally religious movement is described, in the *GDL*, in a surprisingly positive light. It is seen, firstly, as an oppositional movement within the established Lutheran Church, the Brethren having little concern for the dogmatic aspects of Christianity and for the hierarchical structure, which, within the Lutheran Church, mirrored the hierarchical political structure of contemporary feudal society; and, secondly, as a movement concerned with crucial social issues — like setting up orphanages and institutions to help the destitute:

> Pietism, which was specially wide-spread in the Protestant territories of Central and West Germany, was symptomatic of the situation and attitude of broad sectors of the German middle class. In a most contradictory way, Pietism combined religious ardor directed towards the "other world" — accompanied by an intensely religious inner life — with elements of sharp protest against the rigid orthodoxy of the established Church with its remoteness from life and from the people. Pietism was also characterized by its practical social involvement with the poor, the oppressed, and the un-

---

[1] "god or, alternatively, nature" — sometimes rendered in German: "Gott gleich Natur."

educated . . . The pietist phase left its trace on Goethe's development, as numerous of his works testify.[2]

Against this background, it is surprising that no new interpretation of Goethe's "Confessions of a 'schöne Seele'" in *Wilhelm Meister's Apprenticeship* emerges. The *GDL* interpretation of the novel seems completely to lose contact with its historical interpretation of pietism and represents hardly any advance on the truncated Lukács interpretation of the "schöne Seele" figure. The interpretation of Sperata's religion is no more differentiated than that offered by earlier critics, whether in the East or the West. As we shall see below, a similar problem arises with the interpretation of *Elective Affinities,* in particular of the religious aspect of Ottilie's experience.

Immanence and transcendence

The eighteenth century seems to have presented a special challenge to Marxist literary historians. It is at once an age where, in Germany even in the first half of the century, there is at least a strong undercurrent of resistance to the political status quo: the feudal society in its absolutist form. With regard to the orthodox religious ideas, the situation is much more radical. Following in the wake of the Renaissance, the Reformation, and the Thirty Years War, the eighteenth century is the continuation of a well-established process of secularization. The ever-increasing onslaught against the once generally accepted ideas about a transcendent God and against the religious preoccupation with the "other" world (Jenseits) eventually finds utterance in an open atheistic stance and a glorification of "this" world (Diesseits). For the Marxist literary historians there is much in the eighteenth century to explore. Secularization of a once predominantly religious society, with a predominantly religious literary readership, proved to be a very exciting phenomenon. While it is clear that the process of secularization was painfully obvious even to Church men of the eighteenth century who felt the Church was losing its grip, and while twentieth century scholarship in general has discussed the phenomenon fully, it took on a special meaning for a literary-historical trend which looked to the eighteenth century as a basis for validating its own ideological position. Secularization in its various forms was not just another issue. It was a particular aspect of German culture with which the Marxist literary historians could identify and which they could exploit to show that some of the basic concerns of Storm and Stress and of Weimar Classicism had greater affinity to their own theoretical position than to that of their

---

[2] *Geschichte der deutschen Literatur von den Anfängen bis zur Gegenwart. Berlin: Volk und Wissen, Volkseigener Verlag, 1978–1979.* Volume 6: 498. Hereafter referred to as *GDL.*

counterparts in the West. Hence, when they set out to show Goethe as a people's poet — and even more so: his commitment to the people (his "Volksverbundenheit") — they are not simply highlighting some of Goethe's better characteristics, but, much more, they are claiming that Goethe has more in common with them than with scholars supported by a capitalist society which has no sympathy with the people. And when they highlight, as many scholars in the West have also done, the anti-ecclesiastical utterances and attitudes of Goethe, they are not simply recording interesting phenomena in literary history, but rather they are trying to wrest Goethe from links with a religious establishment which they consider (rightly!) is foreign to him as well as to themselves and to interpret his works in isolation from the then (and still) current ideas of transcendence and from the then (and still) current cult of a religion of transcendence.

Hence we witness the effort to interpret the "Prolog in Heaven" not merely as a somewhat secularized, half-Christian, Goethean idea of Heaven, but as a set of traditional, biblical — and therefore partly Christian — images, *through* which Goethe is expressing a *totally non-Christian* idea about the constitution of the world. The Lord is not seen as the transcendent God of the Bible or of Christianity, nor even as the dominant, ordering aspect of the cosmos, but as one important but immanent part of the whole cosmos.

Korff and secularization

The explanation of how the East German Marxists came so quickly to use Spinoza and his pantheism as a basis for highlighting Goethe's materialism is paradoxically given, at least in part, by the influence of H. A. Korff. Although his particular approach seemed, in principle, to be at odds with the materialist approach of the Marxists, his ideas provided a platform which, when converted, could support the "new" Marxist interpretation of Goethe's work.

Perhaps the most fundamental intellectual link between Korff and the East German Marxists is to be found in the Hegelian basis of both systems. There is no need to stress the Hegelian pedigree of much in Marxist thinking (whatever about the materialist conversion from Hegel's "Geist"). It is, however, important to realize that the fundamental approach which characterizes Korff's work (the Geistesgeschichte method) is profoundly influenced by Hegelian thinking.

Characteristics of Korff's
Geistesgeschichte

As the title of Korff's book (*Geist der Goethezeit*) suggests, Korff sees the Go-
ethe period as having its own Geist. In his introduction to volume one he
refers to the "innerste Wesen dieser Epoche" (the innermost essence of the
period) as being represented by Goethe, the author of *Faust*.[3] This is not
simply a manner of speaking but is closely related to the Hegelian idea of Ab-
solute Mind evolving and developing with the unfolding of human history.
Korff sees the rebellion of the individual subject against the objective law — a
phenomenon which in so many literary works of the period is interpreted in
purely social terms — as at last being presented in Goethe's *Faust* as a prob-
lem of *metaphysical* proportions. (287) All the political, social, and moral
problems which preoccupy the authors of the *Storm and Stress* period are
now seen as foreground problems. The metaphysics of Goethe's *Faust* draws
back the curtain to reveal the deeper background to these problems. (288)

Within Faust himself a similar structure is to be found. Just as within the
foreground of human history an inner metaphysical spirit is at work, so in the
individual Faust with his own personal concrete history there is an inner
God. When Faust summons up the Earth Spirit he summons up, according
to Korff, the new God. This is the God of nature. Then, when Faust estab-
lishes his bond with the devil, this means, according to Korff that "trusting in
the new God within him, whose image he has conjured up in the Earth
Spirit, he makes the daring step of overturning the tables of the law of the
old God and of finally rejecting faith in the old God and his ethical world.
(290)

How is this new God to be characterized? In a sense, Faust's conflicts re-
veal the God's own inner conflicts. When the Earth Spirit appears to Faust,
this is not an objective apparition but rather the external manifestation of
Faust's inner God, "the unknown God who for a long time now has been
raging in his bosom with inexplicable pain." (295)

The traditional conflict between an *objective* good and evil is now re-
placed by a different struggle. Faust's pantheism allows for conflict between
those who are filled with the pantheist god and those who are not. These are
the new good and evil. Then, within the individual self, there are times when
the person is fulfilled or destitute of fulfilment — depending on the presence
or absence of this unknown god. (296) In the fulfilled moments the individ-
ual feels raised above "this" world only to experience the inevitable crash
down into the humdrum world of ordinary human existence.

---

[3]   *Geist der Goethezeit*. Volume 1. Leipzig: J. J. Weber, 1923: 2.

In this alternation of high and low, the individual becomes aware of an unlimited horizon of possibilities but all too soon is confronted with the reality of human limitation. Korff sees the unlimited god-like nature of Faust leading to his exaltation, and the limitation of his human form leading to profound disappointment. But even this inner conflict, which in itself implies a metaphysical structure, is seen by Korff as having a further metaphysical implication: the problem of the individual for whom death means liberation from this conflict (note that the German word Erlösung used here has religious overtones like those associated with the word "redemption") amounts to the liberation (redemption) of a god from the torture of his finiteness; or it amounts to God's return to the metaphysical form of his infinite self. (303)

At this point we can ask ourselves what, in this interpretation of important aspects of the Goethe period, could be of interest to the Marxist scholars.

The first volume of Korff's *Geist der Goethezeit*, published in 1923, is full of confrontations between the old and the new beliefs. He speaks of the emancipation of modern man from the personal God of the ethical world. Thus, belief in the personal God of Christianity to whom the whole system of ethical strictures is traditionally ascribed is replaced by a belief in the "new" pantheistic god. The central figure representing the emancipation of modern man is precisely one in league with the devil in rebellion against God. (288) This, of course, conforms also with the East German Marxist view of the eighteenth century phenomenon of secularization. Korff, like many of the Marxists, interprets Faust as a Columbus figure. For Korff, he is a religious Columbus who paradoxically is led to God precisely by the devil. [For the Marxists, Faust is naturally interpreted as a more secularized figure who in no way seeks God.] Furthermore, there is a fundamental similarity where Korff speaks of the intimate relationship between good and evil. In the pantheist system to which also many of the Marxists subscribed — despite their problems with the theist elements! — good and evil do not have two relatively independent sources (as in the Christian God and the devil) but are two necessary, opposite aspects of one and the same reality. When Korff says that the world in which these opposites exist can metaphysically be understood only as divine (291), he is close in meaning to what the Marxists understand in their use of Spinozist pantheism, even though they only ever use the word metaphysical in a pejorative sense implying reference to a totally other world (Jenseits) which they reject; yet it seems philosophically quite appropriate to apply the term metaphysical to denote the relationship between the two intrinsically related aspects of pantheism: the *natura naturans* and the *natura naturata*.[4]

The inclusion, in a pantheistic interpretation of Goethe's *Faust*, of good and evil as necessary opposites, involves a dialectic which, in the context both of Korff and of East German Marxism, derives ultimately from Hegelian thinking. The dialectical thinking is further revealed where Korff writes about the relationship between error and truth. Error is seen in Korff's interpretation of *Faust* as part of the very structure of life ("Gesetzmäßigkeit des Lebens"). Error and truth are not seen as mutually exclusive. Instead of these being alternatives, we are confronted in *Faust* with the idea: through error to truth.[5]

Going on to characterize Faustian humanity by contrast with what he calls "classical" humanity he says:

> The balance between the opposite poles of human life is in classical humanity an achieved state, whereas in Faustian humanity it is dynamic . . . This balance is not a possession but a task, not something enjoyed in the present but a process. Only this latter corresponds to the truth, to the true idea of life. (421)

In a final point worth noting here, there is a partial overlap between the positions of Korff and the East German Marxists: the challenge to the accepted code of middle-class morality. In both positions the code is relativized by something more profound: for the Marxists, by the historical process; and, for Korff, by the individual's relationship to the ultimate structures of life. (416) But the further characterization of these ultimate structures indicates a radical difference between the two positions. What counts in Korff's interpretation of *Faust* is the individual's direct relationship to God. Even if this view represents a large measure of secularization, the language clearly shows its Christian pedigree. The parting of the ways could not be clearer than where Korff goes on to speak of Faust as a man with a personal destiny, an individual law, a man subject to inner necessity and a real fate.

> He is not to be guided, not to be educated, he resists every general law and obeys only the "Dämon" in his own bosom. He is, in a word, the daemonic individual. He too finally becomes active for his community and eventually wishes to be integrated, with his whole personality, into society as a whole. (417)

---

[4] *natura naturata* and *natura naturans* are terms used in the context of pantheistic philosophy. *natura naturata* designates nature *constituted* as nature (=the passive aspect, in so far as nature is *produced*); and *natura naturans* designates the force by which nature *constitutes* itself (=the active aspect which *produces* nature).

[5] *Geist der Goethezeit.* Volume 2: 421.

Within the spectrum of East German *Faust* interpretations there is little overlap with this notion of Faust as an extreme individualist, who in his last moments, enjoys the profoundest awareness of himself as a dominating personality with a totally unfettered freedom. Where the Marxists would have room for this interpretation of the final moments of Faust's life, they would have to see it in connection with his situation as a capitalist entrepreneur. This brings with it the complication that the final moments can hardly be dissociated from the rest of Faust's life, so that the whole course of his existence would have to be seen as largely egotistical and destructive — which does not accord with most East German interpretations.

Part Two: Interpretations

5: Introduction

The following chapters will attempt, in a concrete and detailed discussion of actual Marxist interpretations, to study with what success the Marxist criteria and methods have been applied to an understanding of particular Goethe texts.

In the important volume two of his *Goethe in Deutschland*, Karl Robert Mandelkow aims, among other things, at situating the Marxist tradition in the general context of Goethe interpretations since 1945. It is clear that he is concerned first and foremost with outlining and contrasting the way the different traditions developed in the two Germanies and in Switzerland after World War Two. It is not his purpose to look at detailed Marxist studies with a view to assessing their "validity" or to measuring their power to convince the reader.

What is particularly striking in a context where Mandelkow stresses the excellence of some histories of German Literature concerning the Goethe Period (among them that of Gerhard Schulz) is that he passes over in a mere six lines[1] the volumes six and seven of the *GDL*, which comprise nearly two thousand pages. In his chapter three, where he discusses the general lines of Faust interpretations in the various traditions after 1945, there is no mention of the *GDL* volume seven at all, though, as will be seen below, the ideas warrant detailed discussion. When he does refer to the *GDL* in another context, it is to point out what he sees as a major short-coming in the GDR: "the ignoring, the undervaluing and the neutralizing of Goethe as a thinker about nature." (263) If it is true that the *GDL* volume seven gives only scant attention to Goethe's scientific work — referring, for instance, only to the "historical" part of the Farbenlehre — Goethe's preoccupation with nature is a recurring theme in the *GDL*, especially in conjunction with Spinozist pantheism, and is seen to be of central importance. The category nature, used time and again by the Marxists to cope with the continuously recurring references to Gott and das Göttliche, is so dominant in the *GDL* interpretations that credence cannot be given to Mandelkow's claim that, since Lukács, the GDR image of Goethe stood completely under the primacy of the category history. (263)

Two reviews in the important international review journal *Germanistik* (one on volume six in 1981 and the other on volume seven in 1984) did

---

[1] Karl Robert Mandelkow. *Goethe in Deutschland. Rezeptionsgeschichte eines Klassikers*, volume 2, 1918–1982. Munich: Beck, 1989: 263.

nothing to arouse interest in the two *GDL* volumes which concern us here.
Of course, the relatively short amount of space — reviews of one page in
length — devoted to works each of nearly one thousand pages makes full
discussion impossible. Christoph Siegrist's review[2] of volume six contains not
one sentence of a positive kind, and Gerhard Schulz, himself the author of a
history of German Literature of the same period, writes in a somewhat nega-
tive vein. He does note[3] a welcome advance on Lukács's schematic catego-
rizing of progressive and reactionary tendencies and acknowledges that the
GDL does not so readily dismiss the Romantic movement as obscurantist.
(494) Schulz acknowledges that the decision to orientate the History on
wider historical data was a good one, but regrets that it was in fact not fol-
lowed through in the structuring of the volume. Apart from his final words
("There is no bibliography") his concluding remarks are positive:

> The value of the volume lies in some of its material on literary and artistic
> theory; in the fullness of the material presented and especially in the accom-
> panying material ("Beilagen") — in the form of numerous illustrations,
> maps and charts. (495)

In his introductory paragraph he notes that the volume is not falsely centered
on German Classicism, that it takes account of political literature, Pam-
phletistik, and popular literature; and that it deals with a wealth of names and
works. He cites instances of what is missing in the volume, and he cites one
instance (representing more) of unreliability on the part of the collective of
authors. Finally, his reference to *Wilhelm Meister's Apprenticeship* is to show
how the volume limits itself to a consideration of the relationship between
Wilhelm and the Tower to the exclusion of his important relationships with
the other characters — for example, Mariane, Natalie, and Therese.

Since much of the discussion in the following pages relates to the Marxist
views expressed in volumes six and seven of the *GDL*, especially the latter, it
is important to stress the representative character of these volumes, which
appeared (in reverse order) in 1978 and 1979. They represent the views not
just of a small number of scholars expressing their own individual readings of
Goethe — which could be interesting in itself but would be too narrow as a
basis for the study of East German Goethe scholarship — but, as Wolfgang
Stellmacher points out in his review[4] of the nearly one thousand page long
volume seven, this massive work was the result of many years of work by a
great number of authors. It is an interesting example of how productive the
sustained collaborative efforts of collectives working in the field of literary
history could be. The work of two collectives was organized under the direc-

[2] *Germanistik. Internationales Referatenorgan.* 22 (1981), 726.

[3] *Germanistik* 25 (1984), 494.

[4] *Weimarer Beiträge* 26 (1980) no. 6, 171–183.

tion of main authors: Hans-Dietrich Dahnke, who was responsible for the period 1789–1806, and Thomas Höhle and Hans-Georg Werner, who were responsible for the period 1806–1830. These "main" authors drew on the expertise of scholars from the following institutions: the Humboldt University in East Berlin; the Martin Luther University of Halle-Wittenberg; the Friedrich Schiller University of Jena; the Academy of Sciences (Wissenschaften) of the GDR; the Academy of Social Sciences of the Central Committee of the SED; and the College of Education (Pädagogische Hochschule) of Erfurt-Mühlhausen.

The importance of this undertaking was seen as two-fold: first, it dealt with an outstanding period of German literature; and second, the period of German literature under discussion was an important center of focus, now, as in the nineteenth century, for international scholarly and ideological discussion (Meinungsstreit). The result is that this volume seven (and the same applies, *mutatis mutandis*, to volume six) — with its assimilation and presentation of the period — has great importance both by virtue of its scholarship and because of its reflection of cultural policy.

Stellmacher is acutely aware of the controversy surrounding the decision to divide literary history into periods determined by more general historical events — like the French Revolution in 1789. But he defends this decision in so far as it highlights the Marxist concern to focus on the close links between society and literature. Thus volume seven, in Stellmacher's judgment, offers an impressive analysis of society and literature between 1789 and 1830 and of the manifold relationships between developments in society on one hand and developments in literature on the other. Some of these relationships are more obvious than others, but, according to Stellmacher, the treatment is so differentiated that no handle is given to the view that the Marxists deal with such relationships too mechanically.

A further salient feature of the volume, according to Stellmacher, is its broad concept of literature which includes not only *belles lettres* but a wider spectrum including trivial, popular, and journalistic literature. The highly differentiated image of the epoch, which took account not only of the work of the German Democrats and supporters of revolution but also of the phenomenon of mass literature, provided a new and more fruitful framework for understanding the conditions under which Classical and Romantic German literature was produced and received. According to Stellmacher, this contribution alone would have been enough to justify the existence of volume seven.

Another striking feature of the volume is the concern of the writers to show how the writing of Goethe (and Schiller) is pre-occupied with contemporary issues; how precisely these authors sought to reach as broad a readership as possible. This is the East German response to the modern criticism by the extreme left, which was trying to write off Weimar Classicism as esoteric. While imbedding the study of Goethe and Schiller in the broader context of the period which included the democratic and politically operative literature, the East German scholars strove, according to Stellmacher, for an aesthetic evaluation of works of the period which avoided what he calls a "conception-less, positivistic summation which left all movements and tendencies on a par with one another." (174)

Given the complexity and the diversity of the works of the period which needed to be discussed, the authors had to devote much space to the analysis of individual works. Without going into a discussion of these individual analyses, Stellmacher finds that too many of these analyses are already (at the time he is writing) in need of revision or have already been overhauled by individual studies. Those which most concern us here are the sections devoted to *Wilhelm Meister's Apprenticeship* and *Faust*. With regard to *Wilhelm Meister* he finds problems on the level of Weltanschauung and with the treatment of the symbolic structure of the novel. These are problems which will be reflected in the relevant chapter below. With regard to the *Faust* section he finds fault with aspects which do not concern us directly here. He realizes that, as in any book of its kind, people will find much more to criticize — which, of course, does not detract from the overall usefulness of the book.

Stellmacher is critical of some aspects of volume seven which concern the later Goethe, where his remoteness from contemporary problems is not convincingly dealt with and where there is no satisfactory explanation for the fact that his fame rested on the works of his early years rather than on those written when his fame was already established.

Volume seven is not to be seen as a definitive work, but Stellmacher claims that, without exaggeration, it could be seen as a standard work which should not be ignored by anyone involved in studying the period. One of its special virtues is that it gives a basis from which Western interpretations of the Classical Period can be criticized. Undoubtedly, the volume has been used in this way by many people in the former socialist countries of Eastern Europe and — in Western countries — by some scholars with Marxist leanings. Its value today rests on what it can tell us about the largely ignored East German contribution to scholarship relating to the Goethe period.

6: Early Poems: Subjectivity/Objectivity

In respect both to Shakespeare and Spinoza, Goethe's attitudes and thinking owed much to the influence of Herder. The *GDL* highlights a pantheistic element in Goethe's poem "Maifest," which dates from the period of early contact with Herder in Straßburg:

> In rapturous exclamations is manifested a pantheistic feeling for the world. Optimistic affirmation of life is combined with an unbroken and joyous harmony with nature, which is awakened to its own life. (6 507)

Soon (1772) Goethe uses this awareness of nature to confront the restrictions his generation experienced in contemporary society. Where he writes:

> As soon as a nation is cultivated, it immediately has to think, act, and feel in conventional ways; it immediately ceases to have character (511f.)

the *GDL* points up the contrast between the freedom which nature allows and the situation with religion and — closely bound up with it — the bourgeois relationships, the pressure of the laws and the still greater pressure of social ties. (512) The dimensions Goethe experienced in the world of Shakespeare and Spinoza are interpreted as a liberating force from the shackles of religion, civil law, and social convention. The famous speech "Zum Shäkespears Tag," in which Goethe exclaims: "Nature! Nature! Nothing so natural as Shakespeare's people!" contains the statement:

> I knew, I felt my existence infinitely expanded in the most palpable way; everything was new to me, unknown . . . Gradually I learnt to see.[1]

Rightly the *GDL* recognizes in this context the importance of the idea to which they often return: that of the

> secret point in which what is peculiar to the self — the freedom of will we lay claim to — collides with the essential, unfree movement of the whole. (6 519 and HA 12 225)

Perhaps this can be seen as a first attempt on Goethe's part to formulate the problem which becomes central to his thinking: the relationship between in-

---

[1] Goethe. *Werke.* Hamburger Ausgabe, volume 12. Munich: Beck, 1981: 225. The edition used for quoting Goethe is, where possible, the Hamburger Ausgabe, referred to hereafter as HA.

dividual freedom on the one hand and the recognition and acceptance of a binding and necessitating system of laws in the universe on the other. As his first exposure to Spinoza through Herder becomes reinforced in 1774 by his contact with Friedrich Jakobi, Goethe's early subjectivism is provided with the safeguard which rescues him from the dangers confronting Werther. Whereas Werther always ran the risk of collapsing into his own subjectivity, never able to come to terms with an objective world with its objective structures, Goethe, in the course of his life, survived such crises. It is at first sight paradoxical that a poet like Goethe could find much to attract him in a work like the *Ethics* of Spinoza, with its arid-seeming geometric logic. Eventually Goethe's insistence on the self-assertion of the individual, the non-absorption of the individual into the One, guaranteed that he was not totally pantheist. At the same time, while retaining a strong grip on individuality and refusing also to accept the shackles of orthodox religion and social convention, he found in Spinoza's work a system of laws which bound and necessitated on a much deeper level. He could devote his life to exploring the objective world, and he became a master of living in it. This has nothing to do with shallow compromise or opportunism. Instead, it reflects the acknowledgment of a sphere of objectivity, which, however flawed and in need of radical change, constitutes the only reality of which we are part, the only alternative to Werther's suicide and opting out. As the late poem "An Werther" (1824) suggests, Goethe was conscious of the two alternatives. In the depths of his depression at having to break off the relationship with Ulrike von Levetzov, he wrote:

> I destined to remain and you to part
> You went ahead and didn't lose a lot.   (HA 1 380)

But, despite the misgivings about Werther's possibly having chosen the better part, to live and confront life was Goethe's choice and it provided him with the possibility of unfolding and developing the rich talents he was endowed with; and the poem "Aussöhnung" expresses the rewards which balance up the sorrows experienced by the Werther in him: the world of art and music mediated for him on this occasion by the Polish pianist, Madame Szymanovska, gives him "the double joy of music and of love." (HA 1 386)

Goethe's method of coping with objective reality became fundamentally established at a relatively early stage. As Eckermann records, his poetry depends essentially on his contact with reality:

All my poems are based on actual occasions; they are stimulated by reality and are firmly embedded in it. Poems taken out of thin air have no value for me. Reality should yield up the motifs and the points that need expression — the real kernel; but it is for the poet to make a beautiful living whole out of it.[2]

The *GDL* highlights this statement not only as evidence of Goethe's orientation towards objective reality but, further, as evidence of his opposition to the practice of using traditional and accepted material, themes, and motifs. Instead of drawing on the conventional models and traditional subjects, he drew on his individual and private experience. He also found that this kind of writing reached a much broader audience. As he showed when he wrote the short poem "The Author" in 1773, he was conscious that his new approach to writing depended much on reaching a new readership — without which his feeling would be conversation with himself and his joy would be silent.

There is no lack of emphasis on effusive subjectivity in the *GDL* presentation of Goethe's poetry in this phase. "The Artist's Morning Song" (1776) is seen as a manifesto of the young middle-class literary movement. The joyful and conscious discovery of human personality and its right to assert itself against all the conventions is the experience of a whole progressive generation. It is described by the *GDL* as their

> passionate urge. It was their inspired feeling that, in a newly won freedom, they had a broad field of activity which seemed unrestricted (unbedingt).
>
> (6 545)

The word "seemed" is of course important here. Goethe will learn that no activity is completely "unbedingt." But the emphasis on subjectivity, though it will be modified and offset by the necessitating aspect of the world — its system of laws — will never be retracted. The balance will be established and retained with a struggle throughout his long life.

The *GDL* sees an advance in two further poems: "To Connoisseurs and Lovers" and "The Artist's Evening Song," which seem to be the first poems in which Goethe formulated his thoughts on the work of the artist. Here the productive activity of the artist is seen in close relationship to that of nature. Shortly before writing these two poems, Goethe had gained closer knowledge of Spinoza's teaching. With regard to the latter, the *GDL* claims:

> The foundation of Spinoza's thinking — God equal to nature — served as a theoretical underpinning of the general relationships between God, nature, man, and artist. (546)

Since nature in this context does not simply contain the landscape and the world of plants and animals but is seen as identified with the cosmos as a whole, the creativity of the poet is not simply similar to that of nature but partakes in the creative process of nature itself. This gives added significance to the poet's creative activity and to his role with regard to his fellow men. It

---

[2] 6 545; *Gespräche mit Goethe.* September 18, 1823: 36.

also explains Goethe's preoccupation with nature as the only sphere where the divine is to be encountered. It explains his relativization of orthodox religion in favor of a religion which is at once more private and more universal; and it explains the tendency (at least in the Storm and Stress phase) to identify the creative person himself with das Göttliche. (Cf. Faust: "Am I a God? There is so much light!")

The theme of love, so central to the Sesenheim poems, becomes complicated through the experience of conflict on a social level. The emancipation of the individual through love is seen as conditioned by the conflicting social ties of each of the lovers. The glittering social environment of the wealthy banker's daughter, Lili Schönemann, was problematic for Goethe, and the *GDL* interprets the Lili poems as reflecting, on the one hand, the elemental experience of the love relationship between the pair and, on the other hand, the tensions generated by the conflict of social environment. The social aspect of the problem is highlighted all the more because Lili appeared to Goethe as virtually the perfect woman for him. The fact that she led too public a life seems, on the surface, to be the only factor which led to his breaking off the engagement. This social emphasis is insisted on by the *GDL*. The more recent work of Nicholas Boyle[3] interprets Goethe's flight from the oppressive Frankfurt as based on fear that his creative urge might otherwise be stifled. In Boyle's interpretation, the bond with Lili would shackle Goethe to Frankfurt and thus seriously hinder his development as an artist. This slightly different slant is seemingly not far removed from the view of the *GDL*. Both interpretations take no account of the earlier work of Kurt Eissler,[4] who insists that, because Goethe's intimate bond with his sister Cornelia is at this stage still dominant, he is not capable of marrying her or any other woman in any other place.

The "Hymnen"

With the next group of poems to be mentioned, the great "Hymnen," Goethe responds, according to the *GDL*, to the great questions concerning the self and the world. (6 548) After analyzing the lesser poems in this group — "Wandrers Sturmlied" and "Der Wandrer" eventually being summed up as merely preparation and Intermezzo — the *GDL* comes to "Mahomets-Gesang," "Ganymed," "Prometheus" and "An Schwager Kronos," four poems which are seen as forming a tightly-knit group of complementary po-

---

[3]   *Goethe. The Poet and the Age.* Oxford: Clarendon, 1991: 199.

[4]   Goethe. *A Psychoanalytic Study, 1775–1786.* Detroit: Wayne State UP, 1963. This work of Eissler was also largely neglected in West Germany until the late 1980s.

ems. Here nature is seen as a cosmos which has an intrinsic system of laws and into which the human person is entirely integrated. At the same time the poems manifest the dialectical relationship between individual and society. Not that the objective conditioning of the individual by a developing social reality is a constantly recurring phenomenon in these poems. But, on the one hand, the rebellious self-assertion of the individual is central and, on the other hand, there is strong emphasis on the individual's subjection to a ne-cessitating factor.

It is not surprising, given the well-known Marxist premises, that the surging of the water down to the sea is interpreted as a symbol of human, so-cial progression. (549) Perhaps this interpretation is a shock — and appears tendentious — to readers accustomed to reading this symbol metaphysically as the course of man's return to his divine origins. But, by setting as the goal of this social and human progression the ultimate union "with the All of the world sea," the *GDL* is comfortably and worthily back with the pantheistic reading of Goethe's poetry.

Naturally "Prometheus," with the extremely rebellious tone, stands in stark contrast to the unificatory character of "Mahomets-Gesang." If in the latter the creative Genie is seen as a leader and inspirer of a whole generation of young contemporaries, the Prometheus poem highlights the idea that the creativity of the Genie owes nothing to the gods in so far as these might be seen as transcending man's immediate world. Prometheus is seen as rejecting all relationship to the gods — and there are clear overtones in the poem which suggest that the same rejection applies to the God as manifested in the Christian orthodox religions — and setting himself up as an independent creator. But religion returns at the point where Prometheus acknowledges time and fate as cosmic powers to which everything — not only himself but the gods as well — is subordinate. Time and fate represent the system of laws which are binding on and intrinsic to all reality — personal, social and oth-erwise. The *GDL* quotes in this context the statement of Goethe which many years later sums up the philosophical content of the poem:

> Nature operates according to eternal and necessary laws which are so divine that not even the divinity itself can modify them. (551)

The message contained in "Prometheus," in diametrical opposition to or-thodox Christian teaching, was explosive indeed.

In "Ganymed" the reader is confronted with an attitude to the gods which is entirely conciliatory and unquestioning. The problem of how to reconcile "Prometheus" and "Ganymed" has naturally exercised the inter-preters. Readers who have accepted the now traditional interpretation in terms of Verselbsten and Entselbstigung — offered by Trunz (HA 1 486) — will be surprised to find that for the *GDL* the Spinozist formula *deus sive na-*

tura is called on to explain the connection. The all-loving Father so fervently sought by Ganymed is not a god as such but the totality of the unlimited universe. This, with its universal, necessitating laws, which Prometheus claimed held sway over the gods themselves, contains everything and encompasses all reality with the same laws. The identical application of this same Spinozist formula will be used later in *Faust* to explain the relation between the Lord and the rest of his creation.

The last poem of the group is seen by the *GDL* as the corner-stone of the cycle. (6 552) Gone is the distance created by the use of mythological figures. Focus is directly on the present, which is to be grasped, affirmed and enjoyed. Here "An Schwager Kronos," with the headlong journey through day into the night of death, confronts the phenomenon of death in a way which the other poems do not, and, according to the *GDL*, sets up the theme of earthly fulfilment on the sound foundation required for this theme to become central to all of Goethe's future writing. The *GDL* sees in the "Strebend und hoffend hinan" of "An Schwager Kronos" the merging of Ganymed — with his unearthly ("zeitentrückt) longing — and Prometheus — with his ties to time and to the earth. Thus is formed the union which will constitute the heart of the *Faust* drama.

At this point it is meaningful briefly to compare the *GDL* account of "Prometheus" with the pre-war work of Korff. A brief consideration of what Korff writes on the Prometheus poem will indicate an affinity which even the most positive aspects of the Marxist appraisal of Korff's contribution would not lead us to suspect.

In his first volume of *Geist der Goethezeit* Korff deals vigorously with the attack by the Storm and Stress generation on traditional religion. This attack is seen as furthering the work of the Enlightenment, yet no longer in the name of reason but rather in the name of a new feeling for religion. Man is no longer to be seen as godless, a heathen, but as finding the divine within himself. Thus Prometheus — and, after him, Faust — achieves what Korff calls his metaphysical freedom. This does not imply any belief in a metaphysical order but rather it implies for Korff the rejection of any transcendent world which might be deemed to exist beyond the world of which we are directly a part. By denying the world of the gods — and, above all, of the Christian God — Goethe is, according to Korff, expressing not an atheistic view but a new kind of religious feeling, in which man experiences his affinity with the divine in a pantheistically understood cosmos. For Korff this is the new religion, but it *is* religion. In this he does not go as far as the Marxists, who make the shift from God to nature, and, expressing a new kind of atheism, are not happy to retain the aspect God in the Spinozist formula but prefer to let it lapse completely in favor of nature.

Possibly the most significant distinction between the Korff and the *GDL* interpretation is that Korff stresses the aspect of feeling in the new religion without claiming for it any theoretical or strictly philosophical underpinning, whereas the Marxists are interested in highlighting a new philosophical view which interprets these feelings within a system which in fact categorically denies the existence of the divine. Even to refer to man as the divine, or to the cosmos as divine, reflects for them old habits which need to be overcome.

7:   The Sorrows of Young Werther

In considering the *GDL* treatment of *The Sorrows of Young Werther*, the reader might well be struck by the almost complete absence of the pantheistic interpretation of nature (and life!). Whereas Korff, with his consideration of Werther's Weltschmerz, which he sees as a broader experience than the conflict with society, uses the pantheistic categories to explain the significance of Werther's suicide as a search for unity with the God=Nature, the *GDL* is intensely preoccupied with Werther's rejection of the social bonds virtually to the exclusion of nature as part of a solution. More strongly than either Lukács or Peter Müller, whose contributions we shall soon discuss, the *GDL* accentuates the over-riding subjectivity which Werther is not able to keep under control. This is seen by the *GDL* as a significant weakness in Werther's make-up, and the collective makes no attempt to explain it away in terms of pantheism. Korff too sees Werther's opting out of "this" life as a stage which Goethe ultimately supersedes. Goethe also has his Faust survive the temptation to suicide and live on to confront the constraints of earthly existence. Korff sees both Werther and Faust as dealing with a metaphysical problem: that of man's radical unhappiness with his very existence. The solutions are both metaphysical: Werther's in that he escapes from the physical in favor of a deeper-lying reality of which the physical is inextricably a part; and Faust's in that he learns to live and *to view* his life in the context of this same all-embracing (and deeper-lying) reality. Though the term metaphysical may not be acceptable to the Marxists because they take it essentially to imply the existence of some extra-terrestrial, transcendent reality, Korff does not use it in this sense, but in a sense which is compatible with the immanence implied in pantheistic philosophy, which arguably is itself a particular brand of metaphysics. In any case, the real factor separating the two views is the status of social reality: for Korff there are two possible solutions — Werther's and Faust's — both compatible with the pantheistic conception which Korff attributes to Goethe at the time; but, for the *GDL*, opting out of society because of the deplorable contemporary social circumstances is not acceptable. The focus must be put clearly on the ills of society, and these must be tackled. There must be no suggestion of becoming reconciled with them in the name of some higher unity. Thus the irreducibility of the social factor makes the full application of the Spinozist or pantheistic theory impossible. Perhaps this is why in the context of *Werther* we find this theory underplayed.

This sudden omission of the pantheist theme in the treatment of a work where there is so much enthusiastic involvement with nature and the divine is all the more striking when we find the *GDL* returns to pantheism in dealing with the some of Goethe's early Weimar poems, such as "The Divine" and "Human limits."

Marxist Werther Interpretations

In the GDR, much attention was shown to the Werther novel. Because written in Goethe's relatively revolutionary phase, it attracted the GDR Marxists as they tried to define their identity vis-à-vis their capitalist neighbors in the West.

Georg Lukács's chapter on *Werther* in his *Goethe und seine Zeit*[1] (Goethe and his Age) laid the foundations for later studies by East German Marxist scholars. Within the GDR tradition itself, the most important early contribution is undoubtedly Peter Müller's book: *Zeitkritik und Utopie in Goethes "Werther,"* which appeared in Berlin in 1969.[2] Next in importance is volume six of the *GDL*. This volume offers us a *Werther* interpretation which it is fair to characterize as a well thought-out GDR Marxist view. Since the appearance of this volume 6 of the *GDL*, Peter Müller's book, which came under fire from other GDR Marxists in the early seventies, appeared again in a second edition in 1983.[3] I intend to restrict myself here to this *inner*-GDR controversy without discussing its extension into the "Westberliner Projekt" of 1974.[4]

The question to be posed here is whether the East German works mentioned above — together with the work of Lukács — yield up a clear and specifically East German Marxist interpretation of *Werther* with characteristic methods and characteristic results. If so, are we in a position, on the basis of our reading of the *Werther* text itself, to measure the success of the methods and to test the accuracy of the results?

Lukács treats the Werther figure as the embodiment of the new middle class man trying to achieve the ideal of a fully developed personality. Underlining the link between this Goethean ideal and that of the early Marxist tradition, he quotes Feuerbach:

[1] Bern: Francke Verlag, 1947.

[2] Peter Müller, *Zeitkritik und Utopie in Goethes "Werther."* Berlin: Rütten und Loening, 1969.

[3] References here will be to the 1983 edition.

[4] Gert Mattenklott, Klaus R. Scherpe (Editors). *Westberliner Projekt: Grundkurs 18. Jahrhundert.* Kronburg: Taunus, 1974.

> Our ideal is not that of a castrated, disembodied imitation, but a whole, real, rounded, perfectly developed human being.[5]

It is important to note that Lukács understands the emergence of this type of character dialectically: Werther belongs to the kind of middle class which, on the one hand, formulates this ideal as an expression of its own needs, but which, on the other hand, precisely because of its nature as middle class, gradually develops a social system that, instead of furthering the total development of the many sides of the human personality, reduces it through the capitalist division of labor to a state of lifeless specialization.

In Lukács's view, Werther has problems not only with the class structure of feudal society but equally with the tensions present in the emerging middle-class society. Addressing the question whether Werther is to be understood as a novel about love, Lukács writes:

> First of all, Goethe made Werther's love for Lotte into an artistically heightened expression of the hero's popular, anti-feudal way of life.
>
> (24/46)

In a further passage he writes positively about both Werther and Lotte and *negatively* about the social circumstances:

> Thus the tragedy of Werther is not only the tragedy of unhappy love, but the perfect expression of the inner contradiction of bourgeois marriage: based on individual love, with which it emerged historically, bourgeois marriage, by virtue of its socio-economic character, stands in insoluble contradiction to individual love. (28/46)

Finally, Lukács refers, at the end of the essay, to the later Tasso figure in Goethe's play and to the many other characters of fiction seen as more acute cases of Werther (gesteigerte Werther) — from the novels of Balzac down to those of our own day — all of whom *founder* when confronted with the same problems as Werther:

> But their downfall is less heroic, more abject, more sullied by compromise and capitulations. Werther commits suicide precisely because he will relinquish nothing of his humanistic revolutionary ideals, because he knows no compromise in these questions. This straightforwardness and consistency endows his tragedy with that radiant beauty which even today constitutes the imperishable charm of this book. (29/48)

Zeitkritik und Utopie, while providing a much-needed textual analysis of the novel, repeated some of Lukács's ideas. The Werther figure was interpreted by Peter Müller in an extremely positive sense; the theme of totality, many-sidedness and perfection of the human personality took on an even

---

[5] Ibid. 21/39. The first page number refers to the German edition and the second refers to the English translation.

more central role than in Lukács's essay. Müller, like Lukács, also strongly highlighted the elements of *social criticism* embodied in the novel, although here the target was more squarely the *feudal absolutist* elements, whereas Lukács divided his critical attention fairly evenly between the feudal system on the one hand and the new capitalist middle-class system on the other.

Despite the Marxist thrust of the work, *Zeitkritik und Utopie* met with radical criticism in the GDR. Hans Kortum and Reinhard Weisbach[6] found Müller's treatment of the dialectical relationship between *individual and society* to be unsatisfactory: the question of the individual's place in society had been seen by Müller too much out of context. He had not taken into consideration the fact that in Germany there was as yet no general middle-class movement, so that the individual's aspirations to fulfill his whole personality could only take place *outside of society* and to this extent could only be an illusion. This led, according to Kortum and Weisbach, to Müller's laying undue emphasis on the problems of the individual. (217)

Next, Hans-Georg Werner's review of *Zeitkritik und Utopie* stressed, first, that Werther's withdrawal from society was interpreted as a real possibility for self-development;[7] and second, that for Peter Müller Werther was "at least temporarily a completely developed individual," and third, that the whole individual was to be found existing in the original state of nature, and that, finally, for Müller Werther's morality had the status of an objective category claiming absolute validity. As opposed to this view, Hans-Georg Werner, representing what he held presumably to be a more orthodox Marxist view, considered that the formation of an harmonious society and of totality in the individual was only possible as a result of massive social change. Furthermore, whereas Müller focuses continually on the *positive* aspect of deep, pure feeling and real insight,[8] Werner refers to the socially caused deformation of his nature through the one-sided exaggerated development of his affective life and maintains that Werther is in *no* phase of his development a total individual. Werner does not even admit that Werther finds genuine happiness in nature. According to Werner's view, then, Werther's individuality turns out to be vulnerable and needs to be handled with extreme care.

Werner further criticizes Müller's interpretation of Werther as a Prometheus figure. Far from being a highly active character in the mold of Prometheus, Werther is for Werner a person with no taste for action:

[6] Kortum und Weisbach, "Unser Verhältnis zum literarischen Erbe. Bemerkungen zu Peter Müllers Zeitkritik und Utopie in Goethes *Werther.*" In: *Weimarer Beiträge* 16 (1970) no. 5, 214–9.

[7] Hans-Georg Werner, "Peter Müller, *Zeitkritik und Utopie in Goethes 'Werther.'* In: *Weimarer Beiträge* no.7, 195.

[8] Cf. for example, *Zeitkritik und Utopie*: 62, 69, and 92.

Werther's personality and fate are conditioned by the fact that he is not able to see any possibility of a meaningful social function for himself and thus comes to terms with his own lack of external, social influence. (197)

A final criticism levelled by Hans-Georg Werner against Peter Müller's book concerns Werther's love relationship with Lotte and the ethical questions connected with this. According to Werner, Müller characterizes the moral categories which prevent the fulfilment of Werther's love to a large extent as feudalistic. Against this view, Werner maintains (and in this he is close to Lukács's interpretation):

Werther's expectations of love do come into conflict with feudal morality but above all with laws of bourgeois society. Müller's statement that Werther, "from the point of view of middle-class morality, had first claim on Lotte, is simply not true." (198)

Omitting consideration of Hans-Heinrich Reuter's article in the *Goethe-Jahrbuch* of 1972 (86–115) which, in all its essentials, was absorbed into volume six of the *GDL* and formed the kernel of the section on *Werther*, we can look directly at the pertinent section in volume six. Despite some variations, this section reflects the influence of Peter Müller's work: here, too, we find "Zeitkritik" and also "Utopie"; here, too, there is the focus on middle-class consciousness with the emphasis on self-development and totality which we have already seen highlighted by Müller and Lukács:

To an extraordinary degree, Werther represented this self-consciousness, including the tendency within him to develop his human personality in every direction. (6 566)

As with Müller, here, too, the notion of personal development is not clouded by any suspicion of illusion:

A picture of reality emerged in which any analytic characteristics corresponding to contemporary reality were overlaid by a vision of the future.
(6 566)

As with Müller, Werther's nearness to the people is again stressed. We read also of Werther's overwhelming awareness of nature which Müller had interpreted as philosophically close to pantheism. (Müller: 167) Here, too, we encounter the highly positive interpretation of the productive and active sides to Werther's character:

despite all his sensibility, he is neither unpractical nor lazy; he is not weak-willed or indecisive, but, rather, genuinely filled with a striving after a meaningful and responsible social function. He thus has a strict concept of activity. (*GDL*: 566)

Every hint of an active tendency on Werther's part is picked up. But, by comparison with Müller, there is a new interpretation of Werther's reactions (ultimately suicide) when he finds that his new social circumstances at court allow him no possibilities for personal development: whereas Müller sees in Werther's suicide a meaningful, heroic rejection of the unalterable oppressive social conditions, (Müller: 182f.) the collective offers the interpretation that social pressure leads to boundless cultivation of subjectivity; this leads to a flight from reality. The act of suicide is then seen not merely as Werther's fate — given the basic bourgeois situation — but also as a logical result of his own extreme subjectivity and flight from reality — both being forms of a sickness which can lead to death. (*GDL* 568)

A further divergence from Müller's *Werther* interpretation concerns the love relationship between Werther and Lotte:

> the plot carries through *ad absurdum* the attempt (forced on Werther by circumstances) at one-sided self-fulfilment through love — to which everything is more and more exclusively related, whether it be a question of nature and art, or society and the life of the plain people. (569)

All this is much more negatively critical than in Peter Müller's interpretation. The collective shows that the love story between Werther and Lotte, conditioned by Werther's one-sidedness and extreme subjectivity, unfolds against the back-drop of the reality of the middle-class marriage which binds Lotte to her partner Albert. According to the collective:

> By his rejection of it, the hero — unconsciously — revolts against, in general, the concept of property of a class-ridden society, and, in particular, both against the transformation of love into a ware and against the humiliation of woman. (569)

Whereas for Peter Müller Werther is to be understood as a "Bürger," as a representative of a new revolutionary middle class over against feudal society, the collective sees Werther as rebelling against elements which are intrinsic to middle-class society itself. Here the reader is reminded of Lukács's interpretation.

From this brief survey of East German opinion about Werther, it is clear that we are dealing with a *spectrum* of views rather than with *the* East German Marxist view.

Author's point of view

Not surprisingly, the whole debate is focused on the specifically social aspects of the *Werther* novel. The text of the novel — except perhaps in the case of Lukács — was always under scrutiny. One important criticism, suggesting the limits of the debate, is that little attempt was made to get beyond the horizon of Werther's own consciousness to *discover the author's point of view*.

In analyzing the 1774 version of this text, Müller seems to identify the horizon of the novel with that of the Werther figure himself; and it is typical of the whole debate centered on Peter Müller's book that there was no systematic attempt to get *beyond* this horizon to arrive at the author's point of view, no full discussion of the *narrator's* relationship to the text, no attempt to discuss Werther's *own* role as a narrator in the text. But this raises a problem which scholars in the West also could not claim to be finished with: namely, how does a study of the narrative perspective in this novel help us to arrive at a surer knowledge of Goethe's own position with regard to his Werther figure?

Towards the end of his book Peter Müller indicates that, in the 1787 version of the novel, Goethe tries to historicize his Werther experience: to show his now more critical attitude towards it. Despite the close relationship between the early author and the Werther figure, the later Goethe leaves his Werther stage behind him and attempts to "lift himself out of the dust and to gain a new and meaningful perspective on life." (209)

Thus, according to Peter Müller, the second version of the Werther novel includes two main areas of change: 1) the inclusion of the farmhand (Bauerbursch) episode and 2) changes to the conclusion of the novel.

The inclusion of the new episode shows the limits of Werther's chances of fulfilment in love and general happiness if he tries to live a life of withdrawal from the conditions of feudal society: the farm-hand episode shows that, even for the man of nature, fulfilment is not possible — neither within nor outside of feudal society is there any future for Werther. (214)

Through this same insertion we see Werther as now having a broader horizon: his perspective widens to include the problems of another man belonging to a totally different stratum of society, so that this second version could be interpreted as Goethe's *criticism* of the self-centeredness of his hero of the first version. (215)

With regard to the conclusion of the novel: whereas Goethe had, in the first version, shown the marriage between Lotte and Albert as problematic within itself, his second version shows it as having no intrinsic seeds of conflict, so that Werther has no excuse for interfering. (219) Peter Müller rightly interprets this revision as an attempt on Goethe's part to show Werther in a negative light.

A further insertion which Peter Müller highlights is the diary entry:

> I am amazed how *knowingly* I went into all of this, step by step; how I was so clear about my situation and yet acted like a child; how I *now* see so clearly and there is still no sign of improvement.[9]

[9] Goethe, *Die Leiden des jungen Werthers*. Erste und Zweite Fassung. Edited by Erna Merker. Berlin: Akademie-Verlag, 1954: 50.

Peter Müller points out that we have here a clear distinction drawn between the narrator's judgment and that of the hero. Thus

> with the stress on the illusory in Werther's behaviour, partially comical characteristics are attributed to him which at least inhibit identification with him if they don't exclude it altogether. (218)

This 1787 version is, then, a far cry from the Werther of the 1774 version, which is the basis of Peter Müller's analysis. Yet here we may ask whether this distancing of the narrator from his hero figure is not already clearly traceable in the 1774 version. In the whole GDR Werther discussion the relationship between author, narrator and Werther figure is only briefly touched on (and then only by Peter Müller); in fact, even Müller does not look at the problem in his analysis of the 1774 version. Yet the role played by Goethe's 1787 insertions indicates to us the presence of an authorial hand in this later version and perhaps invites the question whether there is not a similar presence in the early version.

If we are justified in distinguishing between the Werther figure's point of view on the one hand and the narrator's point of view on the other, we need to question further the link between the narrator's point of view and that of the author.

Hannelore Link, in *Rezeptionsforschung*, distinguishes between authors 1, 2 and 3 and the corresponding readers 1, 2 and 3. To illustrate and explain these categories with reference to Goethe's writing of *Werther*: author 1 is not immanent to the text but is the historical, concrete person who wrote the novel.[10] Author 3 is the author *in* the book who writes the letters. This is Werther, the narrator of his own story, and, along with him, the editor (Herausgeber) — the fictitious character in the novel who claims to have collected Werther's letters and to have filled in the story where Werther — on the point of collapse — was not able to do it himself. These narrators, both Werther and the editor, are fictions of the author. Author 2 is the author, immanent to the text, *functioning as* author. (40) He is not fictional. He manipulates his fictional characters, makes them tell their story, gives them their style of speaking, *creates* the situations they encounter, defines the country and century they live in, juxtaposes one scene or one encounter with another and thus, by his very structuring of the story, has the tools in his hand for commenting on his characters. This implicit or abstract author is present not only in the 1787 version but also already in that of 1774. His presence is the condition of possibility of Goethe being able to relativize his hero from within the text.

---

[10] *Rezeptionsforschung: eine Einführung in Methoden und Probleme.* Stuttgart: Kohlhammer, 1976: 39.

What of *reader* 1, 2 and 3? Reader 1 is the de facto reader (42), the concrete historical person who picks up the book and reads it, perhaps with enjoyment but not necessarily with discernment. Reader 3 is the fictitious reader (41) to whom, in the novel, most of Werther's letters are addressed, namely Wilhelm. Reader 2 is the adequate reader, (41) the one who is able to pick up author 2's signals, tune in to him and recognize his comments on his central figures. The real communication which takes place through the writing and reading of the novel is that between author 2 and reader 2.

Focusing now on author 2, we can show that the kinds of alienation of Werther attributed to Goethe by Peter Müller with reference to the 1787 version are — contrary to Peter Müller's view — already to be found in the 1774 version.

In his reference to the diary entry, Müller has, as we have seen, highlighted that Werther is seen to be guilty of a naive but conscious self-deception. Certainly Goethe inserts this passage into his later version to cast a shadow over Werther's behaviour. But has he not done this already in the first version?

Even in this first version, when Werther first hears about Lotte, he is already warned about the fact that she is "already accounted for." At the ball itself he was already no longer indifferent. The forewarning he had received was reinforced at the ball when, in the middle of a dance with Lotte, Werther noticed a warning finger raised by an onlooker who also mentioned the name of Albert in his hearing. From having forgotten about Albert, Werther is now forced to think about him and about the implications for his relationship to Lotte. He has not only been forewarned, but warned again, and yet on the way home from the ball he makes arrangements to meet Lotte again *that very day*. Despite his knowledge of the situation he plunges on straight into disaster: knowingly. His unwillingness to *act* according to his knowledge of the real situation is perceived by the reader 2 as a clear weakness in Werther's make-up. We don't really need the later inclusion of the farmhand episode to draw our attention to Werther's indecisiveness, his tendency to dither. Goethe's criticism of his Werther figure is amply clear from the way he, as author 2, manipulates the text.

The inner-Marxist controversy proves to be largely a continuation of the same kind of discussion which Peter Müller presents in the opening chapters of his book. To all intents and purposes, Goethe's critics (Lessing, Nicolai, Goeze) and his defenders (Wieland and Lenz), while representing on the one hand a spectrum of different responses to the Werther figure, all coincide, on the other hand, in one important respect: they do not find evidence of Goethe's distance from his hero, they find no authorial *criticism* of Werther. Hence their differences consist in whether they find Werther *acceptable* or not as a hero. For Lessing he is *not* acceptable, because he does not measure up to classical standards for heroes: his weakness is virtually contemptible. For Nicolai and Goeze he is *not* acceptable, because, with his personal demands and hatred of the *status quo*, he represents a threat to the foundations of feudal society. For Wieland he is acceptable, because, according to Peter Müller, Wieland is not aware of the political implications of Werther's new morality; and for Lenz he is acceptable, precisely because Lenz is aware of these implications and celebrates the arrival of a new morality which encompasses the whole person and gives sense and sensibility its due prominence.

The Marxist discussion, from Lukács through to the volume six of *GDL*, functions, to my mind, on the same plane, making adjustments in the light of the Marxist ideology and revealing differences of point of view from one Marxist to another, but essentially operating on the same terrain as the early critics of the novel. Werther's own horizon remains the main one and, even where Werther is criticized, there is no systematic attempt to show *how* the author communicates this criticism.

If the Werther figure is judged by each reader applying his own set of standards or criteria, the author's own standards or criteria are apt to be forgotten. Thus the reader comes to grips with the *figure* and then there are as many interpretations as there are readers or as there are degrees of acceptance or rejection of the figure. But the more comprehensive reading of the novel includes the attempt to respond not just to the Werther figure but to the *author* as *presenter* of the Werther figure. Reading becomes a communication between author 2 and a reader 2. If we do not attempt to isolate the author 2, as Peter Müller virtually does for parts of the 1787 version, a valuable instrument for finding the sense of the book lies idle.

8: *Egmont, Iphigenie,* and *Tasso*

The section in the *GDL* dealing with these three plays is somewhat para-doxical. Goethe's transition from an unsettled life, centered largely on Frankfurt and associated with his Storm and Stress period, to a more settled and secure existence at the court of Karl August in Weimar, associated with his maturing to the so-called classical phase of his life and work, is interpreted in a fashion which, at first sight, might seem untypical of Marxist writers. Some of the post-war interpretations of Goethe as aloof, unconcerned about the social plight of Karl August's subjects while drawing one of the very biggest salaries in the Duchy, are surprisingly contradicted by the *GDL* inter-pretation of his works. Goethe is seen as a writer fully aware both of historical processes and of how the individual's personal development is to be under-stood — not in isolation and for its own sake, but as dialectically related to the necessary course of the whole (notwendigen Gang des Ganzen). The *GDL* interpretation of Egmont, for example, stresses that here the hero, by contrast with Götz, is a representative of the nobility caught up in the early stages of a revolutionary national movement. Far from identifying with the nobility, Goethe shows that Egmont's downfall is brought about by his clinging to a dream, to the illusion that, what is in fact an irrelevant and out-dated regime, has a future. But in the midst of his downfall he is shown, in the vision of the revolution, as correcting his error. (6 724)

Furthermore, the *GDL* interpretation stresses the important role played by the people, represented by Vansen and, above all, Klärchen. At the begin-ning, the people are seen to be at odds with one another in their opinions and attitudes. In the final vision, these differences are overcome so that the way is paved for a revolutionary victory. The Goddess of Victory has Klär-chen's features. The *GDL* interpretation of this reads:

> One of the most lively and most lovely of figures in the entire works of Go-ethe is elevated to become a representative of the energies of the people —
> in so far as they are geared towards the future and are prepared to fight. She
> is glorified as a heroine. (725)

According to the *GDL,* some aspects of the play owe much to Goethe's experience in Weimar:

> The poet weighs up the last decade of his existence in Weimar. Alba's
> negative attitudes towards progress and towards the people open the hero's
> eyes once and for all and lead him to a genuine awareness of history. (725)

In his own context in Weimar, prior to the French Revolution, Goethe has to be seen as a progressive figure. It is thus not surprising that the German public at the time was not ready for a play like *Egmont*. When, at Goethe's request, Schiller edited the play for the Weimar stage in 1796, he left out the final Vision. Only in 1814 could the play be presented in the full version, this time accompanied by Beethoven's revolutionary music. In this combination Goethe's *Egmont* was assured a permanent place in the German stage repertoire.

If *Egmont* represented for Goethe to some extent a transition stage from Frankfurt (where he had already written a substantial part of the play) to Weimar where his experience, according to the *GDL*, provided him with the basis to finish the work, *Iphigenie* and *Tasso* were more wholly products of the Weimar and Italy experience. If part of the inspiration for the harmonious Iphigenie and Princess Leonore figures could arguably be traced back to Goethe's Frankfurt experience of Susanna von Klettenberg, his actual writing of the two plays belongs to the post-Frankfurt period — at a stage where, for Goethe, *Storm and Stress* has been left behind.

Dealing with the new phase, the *GDL* trend is similar to what we have seen of the *Egmont* interpretation. The Weimar in which Goethe started to write his *Iphigenie auf Tauris* was no ivory tower:

> Goethe speaks of the volumes of official documents from which he had to free himself. He wrote his *Iphigenie* in isolation, having just come back from mustering recruits (for the Duke's army). When his work on the play comes to a standstill, he says "it's a curse: the King of Tauris has to make his speech as if none of the stocking-makers in Apolda was starving." (727)

Similarly, the Iphigenie figure, though drawn from the realm of mythology, becomes for Goethe the incarnation of modern, contemporary aspirations. Her victory in resolving the conflict between Thoas and Orestes is for Iphigenie, according to the *GDL*, her explicit self-affirmation as a woman. (728) Here the emancipation of woman is seen as the culmination of a development traceable from figures like Minna von Barnhelm, Emilia Galotti and Luise Millerin. With *Iphigenie*, female emancipation becomes for the first time a structuring principle of an important literary work.

> The positioning of Iphigenie's monolog, in which she comes to the knowledge of her saving function as a woman and thus transcends her role as sister to Orestes, also gives evidence — from the point of view of the structure of the play — of the importance attached to that principle. (728f.)

The importance of Iphigenie's personal function is all the more highlighted if considered against the back-drop of Euripides' play, where the conflict is resolved, not by any personal contribution of Iphigenie, but by the miraculous intervention of the *deus ex machina*. According to the Marxist view, Iphigenie achieves the solution by recognizing her place in the development of human history. The prevailing order of things — the curse on the family handed down from previous generations — is not passively and fatalistically accepted but challenged and overcome. Iphigenie rids Tauris of the barbarous practice of human sacrifice. The distinction between barbarians and the civilized is not accepted; rather, the barbarians become civilized. Goethe's aspirations to solve the problems he sees around him — associated with the feudal society of which he finds himself a part — can easily be seen as mirrored here.

The *GDL* interpretation of Iphigenie's peculiarly modern self-understanding is somewhat daring. Descending from the demi-god, Tantalus, Iphigenie belongs to a dynasty of Titans which rebelled against the Olympian gods and was in the process of becoming more purely human. Thus, at the end of this line, Iphigenie is seen as pure, not just in the moral sense, but in the sense that she is not god or even demi-god but human being. Her achievement is seen as human achievement. The liberation of her family and of the Taurians from the curse of the past is liberation by human hand, not by any divine influence. The tension between individual and fate is no longer seen as a metaphysical necessity but as one which can be resolved by purely human endeavor. (728)

The Marxist preoccupation with the social and political circumstances in which the play is written and which are also mirrored in the play itself is one of the main strengths of the interpretation, doing much to rescue the play from any suspicions of irrelevance either to the issues of Goethe's day or to those of our own contemporary world. But this preoccupation is so strong — though justified as far as it goes — that other issues of at least equal significance are neglected or played down. The important question of the source of Iphigenie's unparalleled strength is not really dealt with, and yet the inner life of Iphigenie is so central to the play as to account for the difficulty experienced in its actual staging. Schiller himself repeatedly expressed his doubts about the specifically dramatic qualities of the play, though he admired it in every other respect.

The justified stress laid on Iphigenie's pure humanity (reine Menschlichkeit) by interpreters will in fact not absolve the reader from examining in what this purity really consists. It is possible to say, in agreement with the Marxist interpreters, that Iphigenie is neither god, nor demi-god. But that does not justify the reader ignoring an issue which is central to Goethe's text: the actual relationship of Iphigenie to the gods. The opening lines show Iphigenie linked with Diana's temple. She enters it "shuddering" (mit schauderndem Gefühl), which is not unlike the feeling that Arkas expressed in Iphigenie's presence. What brought her to Tauris was the initiative of the goddess saving her from being sacrificed at Agamemnon's hand, and it is a divine will which keeps her there. Chafing at the semi-bondage of her present existence, she serves with quiet reluctance the goddess who saved her. Regretting this reluctance, she emphasizes the constancy of her dedication to Diana: not only should her life be devoted freely to the service of Diana,[1] but Iphigenie expresses her profound relationship to Diana based on continued hope and reliance:

> Always have I hoped in you,
> As even now I hope in you, Diana. (39f)

After telling her story to Thoas, Iphigenie emphasizes her relationship to the goddess, referring to herself as belonging to the goddess. (432) Again:

> The goddess — she who saved me —
> Who but she can claim my consecrated life? (438)

Her life had been consecrated to Diana by her father, Agamemnon, and now she awaits a sign from the goddess, indicating what she is to do. Her presumption is that she was being saved up as a consolation to her father in his old age. Certainly, if she were now meant to stay on in Tauris she would need a sign from the goddess. Iphigenie herself quite consciously acknowledges the concrete influence exerted by the gods in making her decision against Thoas's offer of marriage:

> And here I thank the gods who strengthened my resolve
> Against this union of which they disapproved. (490f.)

To Thoas's objection that it is only her heart speaking to her, not the gods, she replies that they only speak to us through our heart. These words are certainly not meant by Iphigenie herself as a simple identification of the gods with the human heart. Nor can we simply claim that Goethe is here annihilating the gods in favor of a human heart emancipated from them. Equally, there are no grounds for supposing that the gods stand here as a metaphor for the Christian God. An interpretative tool we might expect the Marxists to have employed here would be yet again the pantheist and Spinozist categories which they apply not only to the interpretation of the *Storm and Stress* texts but, as we shall see, to later texts as well. Yet here they are not employed.

Torquato Tasso and *Iphigenie auf Tauris*, written virtually contemporaneously with one another, reflect the same immediate social situation of the Weimar court as well as the wider problems of the pre-revolutionary age. The first version of *Tasso*, no longer extant, was written in 1780 and 1781. The play was completed in August 1789 and appeared in volume six of Goethes *Schriften* in 1790. There is no doubt that the conflicts for the middle-

---

[1] HA volume 5, *Iphigenie auf Tauris,* lines 37f.

class individual at a princely court and in particular for the poet amongst practical statesmen directly reflected Goethe's own conflicts. Whereas in *Iphigenie*, according to the *GDL*, and also in *Nathan der Weise*, the reconciliation between the opposing forces came about in an attempt to provide an artistic vision of harmony arising out of the conflicts of the era, in *Tasso* stress is laid on the obviously irreconcilable nature of a deeply disharmonious situation. This disharmony reflected not only the immediate problems of the situation in Weimar but of fundamental historical processes in Europe at the time.

At the center of the conflict is the problem of the artist in society. For the Storm and Stress poet, the role was understood more triumphally. But:

> In *Tasso*, the seventies' conception of the creator and genius was carried further. *Tasso* demonstrated that the meaning of the artist's existence and his task were that of a responsible mediator and proclaimer of pure humanity in the sense in which this term is used in the context of *Iphigenie*.
>
> (6 731)

There is the added important ingredient of the problematic nature of the artist's subjectivity, which, according to the *GDL*, remains subordinate in the play to the over-riding problem of the artist's relationship to society.

The Marxist *a priori* leads here to a short-circuit. As with *Iphigenie*, the extremely *inner* nature of the play is understated in favor of the social concerns. Goethe's exceptionally delicate portrayal of the Princess figure is not referred to. There is one reference made to her:

> At his departure he makes a passionate declaration of his love to the sister of the Duke. She repulses him; also — even especially — in the sphere of intimate human relations the social barriers are seen to be insurmountable.
>
> (732)

It is true that the Princess repels Tasso, just as it is true that Iphigenie repelled the advances of Thoas. The reasons in the latter case were clearly stated and had nothing to do with class distinction. In the case of the Princess and Tasso the reasons need to be examined. It can be shown that the subjective factors referred to above by the *GDL* are here the over-riding ones, and, as far as the Princess is concerned, have nothing to do with class.

The Princess, like Iphigenie, has been formed by an enforced isolation. Both have been the innocent victim of an outside force — Iphigenie was subject to the curse on her family and the Princess was subject to a sickness. Their inner life developed as a result of the isolation involved. Like the heroine of the "Confessions" (Bekenntnisse einer schönen Seele), like Susanna von Klettenberg herself, like Charlotte von Stein, like Goethe himself at various times in his life, the Princess has experienced a deepening of her inner life and a remarkable growth of inner strength through confrontation with sickness and with the possibility of her own death. Before her first meeting with the then young poet, while Tasso himself was drinking-in the external glories of the court festivals in Ferrara, the Princess was, through her sickness, learning in the school of patience.[2] As she emerges from her sickroom and Tasso is introduced to her for the first time, there is a first encounter between two different worlds which the Princess hopes will fuse. Though she has felt the hand of death, her hopes are centered on embarking on a new life with Tasso, who was the first to meet her as she began to "live" again. She says to Tasso, looking back on her attitude at the time, that she had had great hopes for him and herself. (866) She goes on to claim, if with a certain reserve, that her hopes have shown signs of being realized. At this point, the possibility of a union between them remains open, though the cautious way the Princess expresses herself suggests that she sees the need for testing the relationship further. Tasso himself seems to have sensed the same need. In his desire to mean something to her, he has realized that it is not enough to do this merely with words. To cement the kind of relationship they both want, he has to go further:

> In deeds, in life to show you
> How my heart is, deep within itself, alive for you alone.   (909f.)

The Princess analyzes this need in the same way:

> And if it is your wish that I should stay with you,
> Let me see this through your harmony.
> Make life happy for yourself and me.   (1062ff.)

At the end of Act II, Sc.I, she leaves no doubt about how Tasso is to show his readiness for the union. He must show it in more restrained and more controlled behaviour:

> Many things
> We need to grasp with vigor:
> But other things are only for the moderate,
> For those who learn in fact to do without.
> Virtue, they say, is of this kind, and so is love,
> Its close relation. Bear this in mind!   (1119ff.)

In this context it must be said that the Marxist interpretation of Tasso's subjectivity as attributed to him by Goethe is not adequate. Goethe does not merely give more space and importance to the poet's subjectivity. He shows, in fact, that in Tasso's case subjectivity amounts to a most destructive neuroticism which would destroy any relationship. It is precisely this subjectivity which is seen as causing the breakdown of the relationship. The Princess and

[2]   HA volume 5, *Torquato Tasso* 849ff.

Tasso (in his saner moments) never see their differing social rank as a barrier. Peacock's summary of his interpretation of Tasso's disposition, quoted here for the sake of brevity, reflects a well-established view which cannot be simply ignored:

> Goethe shows every possible negative trait, overlooking nothing. The impetuous, self-centered, wilful, impatient character fails in its blindness to establish a decent human relationship, exhibiting a striking lack of any tact or diplomacy or simple intelligent appreciation of other persons and their feelings. There follows the loss of restraint and dignity, and then, when mistakes, high temper, and quarrelling have occurred, appear the still uglier symptoms of the neurotic's vicious circle . . . The climax is reached in persecution mania and a general chaotic state of the judgement.[3]

In his final encounter with the Princess, Tasso at first explains, with an air of objectivity, his plans for Rome, then adopts the tragic pose of one who expects to fail where people blessed with better health would succeed, and he then produces an imaginary picture of himself visiting his home town of Naples where his life would be in danger. Selfishly he wraps himself in these romantic images as if his friends and their anxiety for his well-being did not exist. The sorrow expressed in the Princess's words at the thought of his parting is enough to change the colour of his dreams. This time he is able to see himself in the romantic role of a gardener caring for the trees and the plants and keeping everything in order so that no stone or brick or blade of grass would be out of place. The Princess realizes how unreal all his notions are and how impossible it is for the two of them to build a future together. Encouraged by her concern, he shows that he is back where he started by asking: "O tell me, what am I to do?" (3229) The Princess's answer serves as an interpretation of Tasso's behaviour since the last time she had advised him what to do:

> It is very little, what we ask of you,
> And still it seems to be too much.   (3234f.)

The Princess is not trying to mold Tasso into a shape which would be foreign to his inner self:

> We want nothing of you that is not yourself,
> If only you could first accept yourself.   (3237f.)

Her earlier advice was geared towards helping him to find his own identity; and this same attitude is expressed in her wish that he become the sort of person who is acceptable to himself. Here she is touching, however implicitly, on something which is quite essential to the relationship: their future to-

---

[3] Ronald Peacock. *Goethe's Major Plays*. Manchester: Manchester UP, 1959, 108f.

gether depends on Tasso's ability to find himself and to establish his inner identity.

When at the end of the play his final tempestuous advance has been rejected by the Princess and he sees the carriage taking his friends away from Belriguardo, he feels that another meeting with the Princess would perhaps cure him. But then he concludes:

> No,
> I am rejected, I am banished,
> I have brought about this banishment myself.   (3398ff.)

This speech highlights a theme which Goethe is deliberately underlining at the close of the play: namely, Tasso's own responsibility for his particular plight. In a most important passage he asks:

> Are all my forces spent
> Which gave me inner life? Have I become now nothing,
> Nothing at all?   (3414f.)

His answer is plain:

> No, I am what I am, and yet it's nothing.
> From myself I am estranged and she from me!   (3417ff.)

If he is turned away from himself, alienated from himself, this means loss of his own identity; and simultaneously the Princess is alienated from him; loss of his own identity implies loss of the very basis required for a profound relationship with other persons.

9: *Wilhelm Meister's Apprenticeship*

Georg Lukács's essay on *Wilhelm Meisters Lehrjahre* in *Goethe und seine Zeit* is a cornerstone for the development of the East German approach to interpreting the classical Goethe. He makes great claims for the novel, reminiscent of those made by Friedrich Schlegel. For Lukács, this novel is

> the most important product of the literary transition from the eighteenth to the nineteenth century. It has the characteristics, ideological as well as artistic, of both periods in the development of the modern novel. It is no accident, as we shall see, that the definitive edition was written during the years 1793–95, the period during which the revolutionary crisis of transition between the two eras reached its apex in France. (31/50)

Thus his interpretation will have ideological, political and artistic features. These will be repeated, though with significant variations, in the *GDL* interpretation.

Lukács refers to the earlier version, *Wilhelm Meister's Vocation to the Theater*, in which the theater means the liberation of a poetic soul from the impoverished narrowness of the bourgeois world. In the later work, the *Apprenticeship*, the problem is no longer seen as that of the poet but concerns the human development of the whole personality in the framework of modern bourgeois society. Lukács highlights how Goethe attacks the narrowness of the bourgeois society in which Wilhelm is reared and expected to live his life. Lukács also shows how, in the first five books of the novel, Goethe portrays the aristocracy in a very negative light, though Wilhelm recognizes the value of their status for the opportunities it presents for personal development. Lukács is careful to distinguish from this group the aristocracy which figures in the last three books and emphasizes Lothario's concern to break down the system of privilege typical of feudal society.

Central to Goethe's novel is the human being and the development of his personality. This theme, which dates back to the Renaissance, is treated in a particular way by Goethe, in as much as he depicts the full development as occurring in a real society. Though books seven and eight have utopian characteristics, since an aristocracy like the one depicted there did not exist in Germany, the society out of which Goethe makes this aristocracy develop is not a utopia but is real, concrete German society. It is an idea based in, and evolving out of a real situation rather than a fancifully invented one.

When it comes to interpreting the artistic organization of the novel, Lukács works with broad, abstract categories. One main division he employs is the distinction between "Subjektivismus" and "Praktizismus." In the first category he includes the "schöne Seele" of Book Six:

> The canoness is as extreme in her subjectiveness and pure inwardness as most of the questing characters in the first part, like Aurelia or Wilhelm Meister himself. This subjectivist quest, which takes refuge in pure inwardness, forms there the relatively, but only relatively justified counterpart of the empty and fragmented pragmatism of Werner, Laertes, and even Serlo.
>
> (38/57f.)

This rejection of the two extremes amounts at the same time to an attack on Romantic attitudes which are characterized by an inability to put down roots in bourgeois life. According to Lukács:

> The overcoming of sterile Romanticism fills the whole novel. Wilhelm's yearning for the theater is the first phase of this struggle; the religious Romanticism of the "Confessions of a Beautiful Soul" is the second. And the homeless Romantic and poetic figures of Mignon and the harpist wander through the novel as the highest poetic personifications of Romanticism.
>
> (39/58)

Enlightening as some of these statements may be, it is inevitable that such broad categories violate the text to a greater or lesser degree. But even leaving aside here the details which could be cited to show the need of a radical modification of Lukács's interpretation of the "schöne Seele," it is worth while challenging the validity of Lukács's use of Hegel as an authority in this context. This is all the more necessary as Hans Schmeer's[1] work on the "schöne Seele" has not been directly challenged with regard to his use of Hegel, so that the authority attributed to Hegel is used not only in the West in an anti-"schöne Seele" essay by Beharriell in 1970 at least indirectly,[2] but also quite explicitly by the *GDL* authors later in the same decade.

Lukács claims:

> The turning-point in the education of Wilhelm Meister consists precisely in his turning away from this pure inwardness which Goethe, like Hegel later, in the *Phenomenology of Mind*, condemned as empty and abstract. (38/58)

---

[1] Hans Schmeer. *Der Begriff der schönen Seele bei Wieland und in der deutschen Literatur des 18. Jahrhunderts.* Series: *Germanische Studien* 44. Liechtenstein: Nendeln, Klaus Reprint, 1967.

[2] Frederick Beharriell. "The hidden Meaning of Goethe's 'Bekenntnisse einer schönen Seele.'" In: *Festschrift für H. Henel.* Edited by J. L. Sammons. Munich: Fink, 1971: 39.

This view is reflected in the reference in the *GDL* to Hegel's *Phänomenologie des Geistes (Phenomenology of Mind)*.[3] Hegel's polemic involved a criticism of the Romantic tendency to turn away from the present and from concrete reality. He sought to establish scientific rigor and to support clear conceptuality and rationality. Consistently with this

> Hegel, following the whole thrust of Goethe's *Apprenticeship* novel, criticized the idealization of the existence of "beautiful souls," rejected out of hand both the subjective irony of the early Romantics which relativized everything and the Romantic and subjective twist given to Spinozist philosophy. (7 145f.)

Here the acceptance by the *GDL* writers of the Lukács and Hegel interpretation of the "beautiful soul"[4] is apparent. Their interpretation of this aspect of the novel is dictated by the same presuppositions:

> She has developed herself as a personality in tune with itself, but only inwardly. She is almost hermetically closed off from the outside world and leads a *vita contemplativa* . . . The Uncle's maxims envisage a *vita activa* — a life of activity and effectiveness. (7 172f.)

It should be fruitful at this point to examine what exactly Hegel said and meant in the appropriate passage of the *Phenomenology of Mind*.

Hegel (1770–1831) and the *schöne Seele*

In the section on "Mind" in the *Phenomenology of Mind* Hegel deals with "Morality: the Mind as sure of itself" under the following headings: a) the moral Weltanschauung; b) pretense; c) conscience; d) the "schöne Seele"; e) evil and its forgiveness.

In 1926 Hans Schmeer wrote a history of the development of the concept of "schöne Seele" with particular reference to the work of Christoph Martin Wieland. While he deals at length with Wieland's works — which is the main object of his book — he treats in summary fashion the concept of "schöne Seele" as it is found in the works of Schiller, Goethe, the Romantics, Hegel and Theodor Mundt. Schmeer writes:

> Let us summarize Hegel's concept of the schöne Seele, which is the last step in the development of the concept and is also its burial: the schöne Seele is the unhappy consciousness. Self-reflection, unworldliness, inability

[3] Georg Wilhelm Friedrich Hegel, *Phänomenologie des Geistes*, Frankfurt am Main: Suhrkamp, 1977. The English translations below are my own.

[4] Hereafter: "schöne Seele," to avoid the insipid connotations of the English term.

to comprehend evil, insubstantiality. To sum up: in empirical terms, it is the yearning of an ego bound up in itself. (73)

Without going into an immediate discussion of the validity or otherwise of applying this definition to Goethe's Susanna[5] figure — it is, in any case, only a summary definition — it is worth establishing as precisely as possible exactly what Hegel means by the term schöne Seele and what particular status the schöne Seele has within the process of the development of Mind.

Referring to the schöne Seele as "unhappy consciousness," Hegel writes:

> Es fehlt ihm (dem unglücklichen Bewußtsein) die Kraft der Entäußerung, die Kraft sich zum Dinge zu machen und das Sein zu ertragen. Es lebt in der Angst, die Herrlichkeit seines Innern durch Handlung und Dasein zu beflecken; und um die Reinheit seines Herzens zu bewahren, flieht es die Berührung der Wirklichkeit und beharrt in der eigensinnigen Kraftlosigkeit, seinem zur letzten Abstraktion zugespitzten Selbst zu entsagen und sich Substantialität zu geben oder sein Denken in Sein zu verwandeln und sich dem absoluten Unterschiede anzuvertrauen. Der hohle Gegenstand, den es sich erzeugt, erfüllt es daher nun mit dem Bewußtsein der Leerheit; sein Tun ist das Sehnen, das in dem Werden seiner selbst zum wesenlosen Gegenstande sich nur verliert und über diesen Verlust hinaus und zurück zu sich fallend, sich nur als verlorenes findet; — in dieser durchsichtigen Reinheit seiner Momente eine unglückliche sogenannte *schöne Seele*, verglimmt sie in sich und schwindet als ein gestaltloser Dunst, der sich in Luft auflöst. (*Phänomenologie*. 483f.)

Some of the main ideas for consideration here are:

1. What is lacking to the unhappy consciousness is the strength to empty itself (kenosis), the strength to make itself into a thing and to bear (cope with) being.

2. It lives in fear of sullying the glory of its inner self through action and existence;

3. and in order to retain the purity of its heart it flees contact with reality

4. and persists stubbornly in its own powerlessness to give up its purely abstract self and to give itself substantiality

5. or to transform its thinking into being and to entrust itself to the absolute distinction.

[5] It should make for clarity in this chapter to refer to the Aunt figure — the central figure of the "Confessions of a schöne Seele" — as Susanna. In this way, confusion with the "schöne Seele" in the broader discussion of Hegel and Schmeer can most easily be avoided, as can the unnecessary repetition, in reference to her, of terms like the German schöne Seele and "the Aunt." The choice of "Susanna" seems to be acceptable because of the connection of this figure with Goethe's friend, Susanna von Klettenberg.

6. The empty object which it produces for itself fills it accordingly now with the consciousness of emptiness;

7. its activity consists in longing, which loses itself in the process of becoming an object without essence,

8. and over and beyond this loss and falling back on itself only finds itself as something lost.

9. In this transparent purity of its moments an unhappy so-called schöne Seele it burns itself out and disappears as a shapeless vapor which dissolves itself into the air.

Some of the phrases in Hegel's text may seem puzzling. The type of harmony which Hegel describes in this passage, looked at in general terms, is not altogether unfamiliar in terms of ordinary every-day experience. (A "phenomenology" is going to reflect how we encounter in ordinary reality the object of our investigation.) We may think perhaps of a rather withdrawn person neatly barricaded off from surrounding society so that, without being a recluse, he organizes his existence to suit his inner demands and allows nothing to interfere with his inner peace. He keeps children out of reach, insulates his house against noisy neighbors, either doesn't marry at all or finds a partner who is unlikely to cause any disturbance. He is never likely to fall foul of the law. This kind of harmony is seen as paying a high price: lack of contact with reality. This kind of person is seen as harmless, ineffectual, outwardly conformist (for the sake of peace), insipid, lacking in energy and vitality: an unhappy consciousness.

When Hegel says, in the first sentence quoted, that the unhappy consciousness has not the strength to "empty" itself, he means that it cannot let down the barricades, open up his inner space for the invasion of external reality — in general in the form of the world of persons or of society — in so far as this latter claims attention for its own sake and not just as a function of the individual's own inner private concerns. When Hegel says, again in the first sentence, that the unhappy consciousness lacks the strength to make itself into a thing and to cope with being, he is referring to the individual's inability to give up his claims to virtual isolation, his inability to see himself as part of a totality — a thing amongst other things.

Bearing being, coping with being, is achieved by avoiding the closing off of the self in a futile attempt to be separate from the rest of being.

When dealing with Goethe's novel as a novel about educating the individual for reality, Lukács claims that Hegel, in his *Aesthetics*, was to put this theme at the very center of his theory of the novel:

The chance aspects of external existence, belonging for instance to the age of Cervantes, have been turned into a fixed and secure order of things based on civil society and the state, so that now the police, the courts, the army, the government replace the illusory goals which the knights set themselves, who, as individuals having their subjective goals of love, honour, glory or their ideals of changing the world, are now confronted with this fixed order and prosaic reality which impedes them at every step.

(40/59–60)

From this text it is clear that Hegel has quite concrete notions of the kind of social reality that the individual must come to terms with to avoid the danger of self-loss. In the same context Hegel continues, showing that the novel he has in mind is in fact *Wilhelm Meister's Apprenticeship*:

These struggles in the modern world are none other than the apprenticeship years, the education of the individual by exposure to concrete reality, and derive from this education their meaning. Then the end of such years of apprenticeship consists in the subject knocking the corners off himself, with his wishes and intentions fitting in with the prevailing circumstances and the rationale behind them, entering the network of the world and gaining a suitable place in it for himself. (40/59–60)

Hegel obviously has in mind here the general theme of Goethe's novel.

To return to the main ideas listed above for consideration: the implication of the second sentence, which refers to the fear of sullying the glory of its inner self, is that the individual seems proud of its narrowly restricted form of harmony as an achievement. This more or less deliberately withdrawn person betrays a smug, self-satisfied attitude. It is better (in its own mind) than the imperfect external world. The superior stance it adopts is referred to by Hegel as "Verstellung," which implies the adoption of a stance of pretended superiority, which however is really only a cover-up for the fact that the person is afraid of confronting the real world. It flees contact with reality (3).

The incompatibility of this harmony with reality is seen in the threat posed by action and existence: action implies not just decisions which assert your control over your inner life but, above all, decisions which bring you into contact and conflict with aspects of external, social and political reality where you are not totally sure of being right or wrong — where you have to decide on a course of action without any guarantees that you are doing the right thing.

In (4) Hegel says it persists stubbornly in its own powerlessness to give up its purely abstract self and to give itself substantiality. How does one persist stubbornly in powerlessness? Persisting stubbornly implies here that, without this persistence, powerlessness could be overcome, the abstract self could give itself up and give itself substantiality. What is the source of the person's powerlessness in this respect? Obviously nothing outside the self has this power. The blockage has to be within the self. Presumably it is fear of not being able to cope with the external world. Then how does the self give up the purely abstract self and give itself substantiality? It must be by the decision to acknowledge society as the real sphere in which one must operate, stand one's ground, and develop.

Another form this powerlessness takes is the inability to transform its thinking into being (5) and to entrust itself to the absolute distinction.

In (6) Hegel refers to the empty object the unhappy consciousness produces for itself. Because it refuses to open to the world of real objects, the "world" it does know is empty of reality, unrelated to existence, and is therefore an empty object. Had the consciousness been able to open itself, to empty itself and make room within itself for reality, it would be filled with the reality of a real object; instead, it is now aware of the emptiness of its own reality.

(7) Its activity is not engaged with anything real and can only consist in longing; the object it stretches out to has no real essence but is the self. There is no distinction between the self that seeks and the object that is found. Hegel refers to this in the equation "Ich=Ich," which is for him an expression of the Romantic subjectivism he rejects. The subjectivism of the equation "Ich=Ich" is a short cut which eliminates, for Hegel, the necessary acknowledgment of the negation, the non-self. Ultimately the absolute Mind will, after the distinction between self and the negation has been acknowledged (5), overcome the difference and unite the opposites into a higher unity of the absolute Mind in a higher stage of its development.

If we were to think that Hegel is here preoccupied with the psychology of a relatively insipid kind of individual we would in fact be far from the truth. He is really talking about a development of the Absolute Mind at an advanced stage of its course towards total fulfilment. The stage of the unhappy consciousness has to be passed through for the Mind to reach the final stage of Absolute Knowledge, as this is outlined in the final chapter of the book. Mind manifests itself in our everyday experience — in its various stages. It is important in this context to realize that this unhappy consciousness, this schöne Seele, even with all its shortcomings, is raised by Hegel's *Phenomenology* to an exalted plane — as part of the Absolute Mind's Becoming. It is itself a manifestation of the Absolute Mind at a particular, and presumably necessary, stage of its development. If Hegel does recognize in the Susanna figure the unhappy consciousness (and if he is right in doing so), then the critic is not justified in quoting Hegel's authority in underlining her limitations without explaining the corresponding positive aspect of his theory — namely, as he sees it, the elevating link of her existence with Absolute Mind.

Just how elevated a status this schöne Seele enjoys can be seen from the passage where Hegel identifies this phase of the Absolute Mind's development as the phase of conscience. He writes:

So conscience, in its majestic sovereignty with regard to any specific law and every specific content of duty, inserts any specific content of law and duty into its knowing and willing; morally ingenious, it knows the inner voice of its immediate knowing as the divine voice and while it knows (in this knowing) existence just as immediately, it is the divine creative power, which has in its conception life itself (die Lebendigkeit). It is within itself divine service (Gottesdienst), for its activity is the beholding of its own divinity. (481)

It comes perhaps as a shock to find, a few pages later, that precisely this exalted, seemingly god-like level of consciousness is identified as the *unhappy* consciousness!

What becomes increasingly clear is that Hegel, in all he says, is tracing the manifestation of Absolute Mind through the various stages of its gradual development. In his concluding section (580), Hegel writes of an aspect of conscience, i.e. of the Mind certain of itself: he says it stops short at the concept of itself (and is what he has referred to as the schöne Seele). This Mind consists in knowledge of itself in the pure, transparent unity of the self, the self-consciousness that knows that this pure knowledge of the self is Mind; this knowledge is not just the beholding of the divine but the self-contemplation of the divine. Deliberate tarrying in this stage of self-consciousness results in one-sidedness which dissipates into empty vapor. But this one-sidedness, in a next stage, is overcome, on the one hand, by religion, where the divine is seen no longer as simply one with the self (without any element of otherness) but precisely as the other; and, on the other hand, the one-sidedness is overcome by the action ("Handeln") of conscience presumably in the real world. By giving up the simple unity of itself with the eternal being, it has existence, it is in the real world.

Writers like Hans Schmeer, Georg Lukács, and others who call on the authority of Hegel in this matter, fail to draw attention to two important facts: first, that Goethe's Susanna figure, even if she were as subjective as they claim, still has a far loftier place in the Hegelian scheme of things than they indicate; and second, it is agreed in *Wilhelm Meister's Apprenticeship* that there is a still loftier schöne Seele figure in the novel: Susanna's niece, Natalie, who is seen as the schöne Seele par excellence and who, while religious in a certain way, is never accused of excessive subjectivity and whose whole orientation is towards altruistic activity. Hegel is not an authority who can be used to demolish Goethe's schöne Seelen; but rather, in so far as he has them in mind at all, his phenomenology attributes to Susanna a relatively exalted status in the development of Mind and, by implication, to Natalie almost a status of *non plus ultra*.

Lukács's profound suspicion of the Susanna figure's inwardness (Innerlichkeit) and the negative evaluation which seemed prompted by Hegel's interpretation partly explain his under-playing of the inner harmony, strength, and resolve which are characteristic of Natalie — who is very close in many respects to her Aunt — and which account for her particular impact as a person and as an educator. This neglect is all the more surprising considering the excellent post-war essay written by Lukács precisely on "The Ideal of the Harmonious Man in Bourgeois Aesthetics." Tracing what he sees as the liberation of the individual from the shackles of the medieval period to the entanglement of the individual in the new shackles of an emerging capitalist system, Lukács situates Goethe and Schiller at a point where the individual has not yet lost the battle against capitalist fragmentation of the individual through division of labor. Unable to

> foresee the displacement of capitalism by socialism, . . . they are forced to seek these (idealistic) solutions in order to preserve the ideal of the integrated man.[6]

He continues:

> This aesthetic utopia does not merely avoid dealing with actual labour as it exists but also seeks utopian solutions in a general sense. Goethe and Schiller believed that small groups could achieve the ideal of the integrated individual among themselves and provide nuclei for a general diffusion of this ideal — rather after the model of Fourier, who hoped that from the establishment of a phalanstery a gradual transformation of all society to socialism, as he understood it, might be achieved. The educational philosophy in *Wilhelm Meister* is based on a theory of this kind; similar utopianism is echoed in Schiller's *On the Aesthetic Education of Man.* (95)

The reference to the nucleus as a center from which the ideal of the integrated individual could be radiated out obviously includes Natalie and Lothario as part of the Tower, the "island" of educators in the novel, but the inward aspect of their harmony is never subjected to scrutiny — neither here nor in the *Wilhelm Meister* essay.

To return to the point made above: Lukács's interpretation will have ideological, political, and artistic features. These will be repeated, though with significant variations, in the *GDL* interpretation. The broad ideological and political features of Lukács's interpretation of the novel are largely shared by the *GDL* interpretation: the significance of the French revolution is common to both; Goethe's largely positive attitude to the French revolution and his reflection of it in the novel are interpreted in both accounts in a similar light; the tension for the young middle-class hero arising, on the one hand, from the effects of feudal society and, on the other hand, from the newly ex-

---

[6] *Writer and Critic and Other Essays.* Edited and translated by A. Kahn. London: Merlin Press, 1970: 95.

perienced effects of a developing capitalism in society is also common to both.

On the level of artistic interpretation, Lukács's essay is interesting for the broader sweep which allows him to align Goethe's work with that of Cervantes — both being seen as works of a transition period, the novel in each case being distinguished from those that precede and those that follow it precisely by not belonging entirely to one or the other distinct period it spans — and with the great realist works of the nineteenth century. By comparison with these latter, Goethe has, so far as the *Apprenticeship* is concerned, both strengths and limitations:

> Before *Wilhelm Meister*, and especially after it, the totality of society was expressed by a realism more comprehensive in scope and more passionately probing in depth. (46/66)

Here Lukács is referring to the works of Balzac and Stendhal. Over against this limitation, he characterizes the positive achievement of Goethe's novel as follows:

> Goethe's mastery resides in his profound comprehension of the most essential characteristics of human beings, his elaboration of their typically common and distinctively individual characteristics, his consistently thought-out systematization of these relationships, contrasts and nuances, and his ability to transform all these features into a vivid plot which can characterize them. The persons in this novel are grouped almost exclusively around the struggle for the ideal of humanism, around the problem of two false extremes: enrapturement (Schwärmerei) and practicality... This manner of writing, which the modern novel has never equaled, although some of its later representatives surpassed Goethe in several respects, constitutes an imperishable heritage for us. (46/66)

With this reference to heritage Lukács is pointing the way forward for the socialists of the future:

> It is a very topical heritage, for one of the great tasks of socialist realism is to portray important spiritual and emotional developments in a way which is both calmly harmonious yet sensuously vivid form. (47/67)

When, more than two decades later, the Goethe scholars of the GDR were in a position to work systematically on this inheritance, they could do so from a stand-point which, at least from the literary critical angle, was more advanced. The *GDL* interpretation of *Wilhelm Meister's Apprenticeship* focuses very sharply on the role of the new narrator and is thus able to give a better founded account of Goethe's ironical treatment of his characters and of his material. The world is not seen from the hero's point of view. Instead the hero is integrated into a much greater totality. (7 170) Through the hero, the reader's attention is focused on "the decisive — because determining factors in life's processes" (170), and the hero is seen as not capable of meeting the demands of the concrete social situation. His subjective attitudes and views have to be changed by confrontation with concrete reality. By contrast with the *Werther* novel, according to the *GDL*, the change of con-temporary social structure must be matched by the hero's attempt to under-stand the world around him and to adapt his activity to the realities of his situation. (171)

When it comes to analyzing how Wilhelm is brought to this under-standing, Lukács's relatively abstract methods are still invoked:

> If the Tower Society represents a collective subject of education, the whole of reality serves as a medium for education. Thus it is clear that the writer has built up a broad spectrum of figures which, both in a positive and in a negative way, answer the central question of how people have to shape their lives. Special weight is given to some of them — like Mignon, the Harpist and the canoness. (172)

These neat abstractions serve, as they did with Lukács (cf. his positive and negative polarization), to simplify some of the complexities of the novel. They reflect Lukács's negative judgment of the Romantic figures. Mignon and the Harpist both remain, for the *GDL* writers, "unconsciously and inac-tively in the iron grip of fate." (172) The barbaric circumstances under which they had to live contribute to their fate, but so equally does their inability to deal with the consequences of their initial situation. They have not achieved the synthesis between subject and object, human being and world. This criti-cism of Romanticism is then aligned with the criticism of the Susanna figure of the "Confessions." Here the equivalent polarization is expressed in the contrast between the *vita contemplativa* and the *vita activa*. While Susanna has achieved great unity within herself, she is interpreted as having developed only inwardly. By contrast there is the world of the Uncle, already intro-duced to the reader in the "Confessions": the maxims of the Uncle are geared to a *vita activa*, to the practical side of life and the exercise of influ-ence. Out of this world is produced the Tower, a society whose activities are played off against the more contemplative world of Susanna. A by-product of this polarizing tendency on the part of both Lukács and the *GDL* authors is the extreme contrast set up between Susanna and Natalie. Susanna's life functions for Wilhelm as a caution (Bedenkbeispiel) in his crisis situation (169), while Natalie, as a member of the progressive and productive new so-ciety, represents the mastery which Wilhelm aspires to.

What this polarization overlooks is the much more organic integration of the Susanna figure into the "new" society. Without launching into a detailed discussion of Goethe's presentation of the Susanna figure of the "Confessions,"[7] suffice it here to draw attention to two considerations: first, Goethe's deliberate attempts to forge links between Susanna and her niece Natalie; and second, Susanna's place within the series of generations which form an important part of Goethe's portrayal of society in the *Lehrjahre*.

The fact that the Marxist literature does not look closely enough at Natalie partly explains the fact that their image of the Susanna figure has in no way been revised, for Goethe makes deliberate attempts to forge close links between the two women. A fuller, more detailed understanding of Natalie would lead to a more accurate understanding of her aunt. The first important link is to be found in the title schöne Seele. When it is taken by Lothario from his aunt and conferred on Natalie, this is done not with a view to discrediting their aunt but as a way of emphasizing the high degree of inner harmony achieved by Natalie — an even greater degree than is found in the aunt. Furthermore, this shift of the title to Natalie confirms for the reader — if such confirmation were necessary — that the title confers a distinction on its bearer.

Another point which the Marxist writers would have no interest in studying is that the schöne Seele link is further established by a definite, if diverse kind of religiosity in the case of both women. The inner harmony achieved by Susanna, it can easily be shown, is intrinsically bound up with her openness to what she identifies as a divine sphere. Naturally the case of Natalie is different. She has no clearly defined attachment to any public form of religion, nor is she openly religious. Yet Goethe takes pains to link her with the sphere of the Holy (das Heilige). Where Natalie first appears to Wilhelm she is referred to as "die Heilige," and her sudden appearance and disappearance take a form similar to the religious epiphanies of the Old Testament. The rather sober Therese says of Natalie: "her beauty, her goodness make her worthy of the adoration of a whole world." (HA 459) When Wilhelm enters Natalie's house for the first time we read:

> He entered the house and found himself in the most serious and — according to his own feeling — the holiest milieu he had ever been in. (512)

This impression has to be seen as a sober one — i.e. not one inspired by his admiration for Natalie — , because he has no idea he is in Natalie's house, but instead expects it to be that of the baroness he had met in the Countess' company. The next day, when he already knows that it is Natalie's house, he says of it:

> It is not a house, it is a temple, and she is the worthy priestess; she is herself the genius of the house. (519)

---

[7] Cf. Daniel Farrelly. *Goethe and Inner Harmony*. Shannon: Irish UP, 1973.

A further link is given where, on the morning after his arrival Wilhelm discovers a portrait which he had to take to be one of Natalie." It is, in fact, not Natalie, but it is obviously equally important to Goethe to underline both the similarity and the difference. Although the picture is a good likeness of Natalie, it is not a total likeness, and when she enters the room "the similarity seemed totally to disappear" (519); yet "seemed" is not strong enough to deny the basic similarity, to confirm which Natalie is wearing on her bodice the cross of a religious order like the one in the picture — a point which also hints that they have some kind of religiosity in common. The similarity between the aunt and Natalie is further stressed by the fact that the picture was painted when she was the same age as Natalie is now. General confirmation of the likeness is offered where Natalie says that everyone thinks it is she when they first see it.

There follows a discussion of Susanna's qualities between Natalie and Wilhelm, who has read the "Confessions." Whatever about the shortcomings Natalie finds in her aunt, the overwhelming impression is one of gratitude for the positive influence the aunt has had on her. Natalie refers to her as an excellent (treffliche) Person and says "I owe her a great deal . . . She was a light that shone for only a few people and for me in particular." (519) No aspect of the aunt's experience is fully discredited. It was, after all, the educators who tried to keep the children away from their aunt, and Natalie makes it clear to Wilhelm that her own ideas about education are quite different from theirs:

> "So" (says Wilhelm), "your methods are completely different from those of our friends?" "Yes!" said Natalie. (527)

It must be admitted that, despite the fundamental affinity, a considerable measure of secularization distinguishes the niece's world from that of the aunt. The whole religious dimension tends to be more implicit than explicit. Thus, in Therese's letter to Natalie, faith, hope and charity, known in technical terms as the three theological virtues, are referred to as "the three fine qualities" (die drei schönen Eigenschaften). Therese's language, which reflects the mental climate she shares with Natalie, implies secularization; but at the same time, her way of speaking of these qualities reflects a structure identical with that of the theological virtues. Certainly, each of these qualities suggests reference to a higher order of things than that referred to by Therese's own set of contrasting qualities. Jarno says that

> instead of faith Therese has insight, instead of love stamina (Beharrlichkeit), and instead of hope confidence (Zutrauen). (531f.)

Contrasting them as educators, he says that Therese trains (dressiert) her charges, Natalie educates (bildet) them. The difference is clear. The set of categories which apply to Natalie and her methods are more in line with the religious categories applicable to the Aunt than with those which apply to Therese. Under these circumstances a polarization which sets the Susanna figure over in stark contrast to Natalie is suspect.

Much has been written high-lighting the conflict in interests between the Susanna figure and the Tower educators. These latter are taken to represent involvement with society, and Goethe's focus is seen to rest either on the remnants of feudal society, or on the ominous beginnings of capitalist society with its destructive division of labor, or on the new aristocracy with its liberal, anti-feudal tendencies. In this context Lukács and the GDR Marxist writers see little significance in the Susanna figure. Yet Goethe presents her not as an abstract type to act as a caution for Wilhelm, but he places her, consciously or otherwise, in a quite clear and significant social context which needs to be examined in its own right.

Susanna's education

In general, critics' attempts to characterize the Susanna figure have been based almost exclusively on interpreting the significance of her religious experience, on the one hand, and — usually in conjunction with this — her physical frailty on the other. This restriction of focus leads to distortions in interpreting Goethe's intentions. While he lets Susanna tell her own story without taking the reins of narration out of her hand,[8] as the author he himself is responsible for creating the elements of the story — which she then relates — and for creating the sequence according to which the various episodes occur, as well as creating the consequences which result for Susanna from these episodes. The elements of her education (Bildung) which form part of the narration but not part of Susanna's invention (indeed, she invents nothing) are part of the author's statement from within the "Confessions." Goethe takes great pains to create a social context in the novel. This refers not only to his depiction of the middle-class world from which Wilhelm originates and which is represented by his friend Werner; not only to the world of the stage and to the aristocracy which figures in the first five books; not only to the world of Natalie and Lothario and the Tower which is adumbrated in the "Confessions" and developed in detail in the final books; but even within the "Confessions" there is a picture of society and social and family structures which belong to still earlier generations than Natalie's: namely, to the world of Susanna and her sisters and, still further back, to that of her father and mother, and, if not in a chronological sense, at least culturally further back, to that of her own aunt and uncle (the Oheim).

---

[8] Cf. Beharriell's opposite thesis.

Thus Susanna's "performance" is not simply to be viewed in the context of her health and religion and a few relationships with men. The context which Goethe creates for her is clearly representative of what young women like Susanna had to expect. Thus she is to be understood within the framework of the generation to which she belonged and of the generation which preceded hers. While Goethe clearly shows her generation as superseded by Natalie's, he equally clearly shows her as a product of an earlier generation, which she quite strikingly reacts against and in dealing with which she shows a degree of autonomy which raised eye-brows in her circle. She becomes aware of the strictures placed upon young women in a man's world and she gets the quiet support of her mother, who herself had not been in a position to behave autonomously, and from her father who treated her as a "son gone wrong" (mißratener Sohn); on the other hand, one of her aunts expects her to behave as contemporary society would seem to dictate.

Goethe clearly intends to highlight the contrast between Susanna and the earlier generation. A dramatic demonstration of this is found at the end of the Narziß episode, where she is determined to make up her own mind about terminating the relationship. "My family noticed it, they asked me about it and expressed surprise." On this occasion she took a stand which she refers to as manly (männlich), i.e. as the kind of stand which was not normal for a woman. But in her own home, at least, she soon prevailed. Her stand is one her mother would like to have made as a young woman: "She rejoiced to see her own unspoken wishes fulfilled through me." (380) But the narrower mental horizon which the mother had secretly transcended still had its prisoners. Of Susanna's aunt we read:

> The reasons she advanced seemed to her irrefutable — and they were, too, because they were quite ordinary. I am not wronging her when I say that she had no sensibility ("kein Gemüt") and that her ideas were very narrow.
>
> (380)

Earlier within the Narziß episode, the reader becomes aware of other handicaps imposed on women of Susanna's generation. From the beginning, the narrator has highlighted her "desire for knowledge" and her openness to all the kinds of knowledge which first her father and then Narziß lay before her. Here Goethe confronts the reader with the problems posed for a woman by the male hierarchy. Of Narziß's behaviour Susanna writes:

> He made fun of learned women as all men do, and yet he worked unceasingly at my education. (374)

Because of the cultural climate, Narziß was convinced that Susanna's intellectual interests should remain a secret:

> While he constantly brought me writings of all kinds, he often repeated the dubious notion that she had to keep her learning a darker secret than a Calvinist his religion in a Catholic country. (374)

This passage indicates a high level of awareness on Susanna's part — much higher than that of Narziß. The severe constraints imposed on women of her generation are evident. Susanna's education is seen as developing, by comparison with that of Natalie a generation later, in an extremely unfavorable climate. When after her break with Narziß she had the courage not to conceal her love for the arts and the various branches of knowledge, she manifested, for a woman of her generation, an impressive degree of autonomy and steadfastness.

Goethe places Susanna in the social context of her time and shows how, faced with the constraints imposed on women, she stands out as an autonomous, clear-headed woman. Her growth in this direction is supported by her father who, from the beginning, saw her enthusiastically as a girl who was interested in "things" in a way that girls in her generation normally were not. Then, when she was trying to assert her independence to decide about her future with Narziß, her father, after cornering her with his purely rational arguments, was able to acknowledge the superiority of her intuition and feelings and thus vindicate her decision.

This support offered by her father is based on a flexibility which the narrator compares favorably with the relatively rigid and uncompromising character of the "Oheim" figure. The patriarchal attitude of the Uncle towards both Susanna and her sister — the plans to make Susanna a "canoness" and to marry her sister "well" were *his* initiatives — reflects another aspect of society which Susanna had to contend with. It is this patriarchal society, of which the Uncle is so much a representative, which creates the social limitations which hem her in and for which the Uncle then criticizes *her!*

The social context outlined and discussed here, far from being foreign to a Marxist concern, is strikingly akin to interests they manifest in other contexts and represents a line along which their Goethe research could eventually have been expected to develop.

10: *Faust*

It is a surprise for non-Germans to find how closely the State in East Germany scrutinized *Faust* productions. This had nothing to do with ordinary censorship but with monitoring the way the State's cultural inheritance was managed. Goethe was long seen in East Germany as Germany's greatest writer and *Faust* as Germany's greatest literary product. In the eyes of officialdom — at least in the early years of the GDR — no other view was tolerated. This fact is instanced by Brecht's own experience of producing his version of *Urfaust* in Potsdam in 1952 and in Berlin with the Berliner Ensemble in 1953. Because his view of the Faust figure was diametrically opposed to the official interpretation, his productions were closed down, and when Hanns Eisler published a libretto for the national Faust opera he was composing, his book aroused the same official opposition for much the same reasons.

The official line of *Faust* interpretation was to become evident in at least two of the *Faust* productions given in East Germany in 1949 to celebrate the bicentenary of Goethe's birth. In her account of the treatment of *Faust* in the GDR, Viëtor-Engländer prefers to focus on the Bortfeldt Weimar production of *Faust*, because it deals with both *Part One* and *Part Two*, whereas Peter Schmitt[1] highlights Wolfgang Langhoff's *Faust Part One* production because it clearly represents a polar opposite to the seemingly negative Faust conception of both Brecht and Eisler. Both need inclusion here.

Hans Robert Bortfeldt

At a time when East Germany was moving from what was understood as a defensive, anti-fascist, democratic stance to a stage where the foundations for a new socialism were to be laid, Bortfeldt sought to create a *Faust* interpretation which owed nothing either to the pre-war "bourgeois" (non-socialist) productions or to the Gründgens productions of 1932–1933 and 1941–1942, which clearly reflected an affinity with National Socialism.

Bortfeldt aimed at presenting Faust as a creative man of action, a model for the new post-war man who could realize the humanist dream of Goethe's (and Schiller's) Weimar. Aiming at fidelity to the Goethe tradition, he in-

[1] *Faust und die "Deutsche Misere." Studien zu Brechts dialektischer Theaterkonzeption.* Erlangen: Palm and Enke, 1980.

tended to let the text speak for itself. (However, his unwillingness to ma-
nipulate the text by too many cuts meant that the play lasted six hours!)
Furthermore, he tried to rescue *Faust* from its museum status and to show it
both as an expression of the living present and as a pointer towards a new
and better future for mankind. Finally, by presenting both *Part One* and Part
Two as a unity he intended to offer *Faust* as a complete picture of humanity.

Not only was the pessimism of *Faust* in earlier non-socialist productions
to be avoided, but, even more so, the National Socialist conception of Faust
as Superman (Übermensch) was to be overcome. A major obstacle to nego-
tiate was the dominance won for Mephistopheles by the powerful acting of
Gründgens in the role. In Bortfeldt's production it was unfortunate that the
actor playing Faust was too young and inexperienced to assert himself against
the powerful presence of a senior actor whose interpretation of Mephi-
stopheles owed much to Gründgens.

Bortfeldt was more successful in his portrayal of Gretchen. Here he was
able to avoid the National Socialist version of her as a blond-haired BDM
girl[2] with a plait. Instead, he followed Lukács's lead and presented her as be-
longing to the people but typical of the lower middle-class: she is seen nei-
ther as a heroine nor as a victim. In his representation of the Gretchen trag-
edy he followed Lukács in highlighting the limitations imposed by middle-
class society on any love relationship.

Wolfgang Langhoff

Langhoff's *Faust Part One* production in Berlin in 1949 came nearer to sat-
isfying the requirements of officialdom. More free of the indirect influence of
Gründgens, he could keep his production plain, simple, and close to the folk
tradition associated with Goethe's work. As an alternative to the mystical
Faust of the National Socialist years, Langhoff presented Faust as a man of
the people. He made much of the Easter Walk, the peasants' dances, etc.
Gretchen was a daughter of the people. A disadvantage in the "simplicity" of
the production was that Faust became typified as good and Mephistopheles
as evil. In response to criticism, Langhoff corrected this trend in a second
production of the play in 1954, laying more emphasis on the intellectual is-
sues as advocated by Lukács, Abusch and Grotewohl. (Schmitt: 25) In this
later version, Faust was seen no longer as merely freeing himself from the
shackles of the medieval period but even more positively: this act of freedom
was a symbol for the break-through into a new age, hinting at the latest pro-
gress towards a better society and a fuller humanity in socialism. (25)

---

[2] "Bund Deutscher Mädchen," or Union of German Girls.

These orthodox Faust interpretations, though not unchallenged, as we shall see, by those like Brecht and Hanns Eisler for whom the classical tradition had an entirely different function, held sway for approximately another twenty years. Between 1965 and 1967, Fritz Bennewitz produced another orthodox version of Faust (Part One and Part Two) in Weimar,[3] in which Faust, in answer to yet another Gründgens version in Hamburg (1961), was seen as representing man in an extremely positive light: man is to be understood, in line with the Feuerbach theses, as creator both of himself and of his own history. Whereas the unorthodox producers focused on the Storm and Stress Faust, Bennewitz stressed his proximity in history to the Renaissance — even earlier than Galileo — in the time of Columbus and Copernicus.

> The central idea of the whole play — from the "Prolog in Heaven" to the final vision at the end of *Part Two* — was to show man as a being who can and must find an answer to his own questions. Though shaped by the social reality around him, Faust is seen, however, as himself capable of effecting change in his world. Instead of devoting himself to contemplation, Faust was to adopt an aggressive stance with a view to activating the audience. Witnessing the presentation of a comprehensive historical process, the audience was to see itself as part of a national historical process. Faust was to be seen as the Columbus of his time: not as a resigned scholar in his ivory tower, but as an explorer, a conqueror and a challenger of the world. He was to be seen as a practical worker whose main task was to assimilate and control this world through the organization of all the creative possibilities he found within himself. This view was to reflect a synthesis between Weimar and Bitterfeld. (156)

Consistently with this portrayal of Faust, Mephistopheles was seen, on the one hand, as an equal companion with Faust, but, on the other hand, his function was largely limited to helping Faust to achieve the good. Gretchen, rather too positively, was to be portrayed as a combination of Shakespeare's Juliet and Joan of Arc — a revolutionary of love.

The other tradition:
Brecht and Eisler

The official, orthodox line — from Bortfeldt through to Bennewitz — was based largely, if not in every detail, on the impressive work of Lukács. But since the early 1930s, within the Marxist ranks, Brecht's outlook on literature had represented a marked contrast to that of Lukács. Not least, their differences were based on a totally different attitude towards tradition. Whereas

---

[3] Viëtor-Engländer: 156.

Lukács had lionized the European canon from Goethe to Balzac and Tolstoi and then to Thomas Mann and had shown himself more skeptical towards the innovators, Brecht had shown scant respect for the established tradition, least of all for Goethe. Thus, when in 1952 with his pupil Egon Monk he worked on a production of *Urfaust* in Potsdam as a preliminary to bringing it to Berlin, it is no wonder that his interpretation was to cause an uproar in orthodox circles. Though well received by the audience and positively reviewed in the local press, it was condemned by officialdom. A similar rejection was experienced in 1953 when Brecht produced *Urfaust* with the Berliner Ensemble in the Deutsches Theater. Within the same time-frame (May, 1953) Hanns Eisler's *Johannes Faustus* opera libretto caused a similar furore within officialdom. One substantial point common to Brecht's and Eisler's work was their historical interpretation of the Faust figure. Even the authorities, represented by Johanna Rudolf, conceded that the historical Faust was a dabbler in black magic, a charlatan, a drunkard and a cheat.[4]

Yet, in the case of Brecht, they objected to the treatment of Goethe's *Urfaust* which identified the Faust figure with the historical Faust; and, in the case of Eisler, they objected to the same historical figure being central to a libretto of what purported to be a national German opera. Of course, for Brecht and Eisler there was more to the historical Faust figure than the scurrilous characteristics just mentioned. In his defense of Eisler's text, Brecht includes an outline of the plot which offers a clear definition of the Faust Figure:

> Faust, the son of a peasant, goes over to the side of the overlords in the Peasants' War. Faust's attempt to develop his personality thereby founders. He is incapable of bringing off a total betrayal. His guilty conscience forces him at the last minute to be so rebellious in carrying out his ambitious plans that he does not achieve success with the overlords. Realization of the truth was to his disadvantage, a poison rather than a salutory potion. When in the end the oppressors of the peasants give him recognition, he breaks down and in a "Confessio" gives expression to his insight into the truth.
>
> (Bunge: 159)

Resurrecting the historical Faust in this fashion ran counter to the official programme, which was much better served by Goethe's re-working of the story.

A further bone of contention was Brecht's public refusal to be intimidated by the classics. His productions of *Urfaust* were seen as a destructive attack on the best of the German literary tradition. These concerns are amply expressed in two documents of the time: one by Johanna Rudolf in the

---

[4] Hans Bunge. *Die Debatte um Hanns Eislers "Johann Faustus."* Berlin: Basis, 1991: 121.

SED's own newspaper (*Neues Deutschland*)[5] and the other by Alexander Abusch from the Central Committee of the SED.

Johanna Rudolf

For a considerable time Goethe's *Urfaust* has been part of the Berliner Ensemble's programme. The basic principle of the production was a concept which in more than one respect bears a striking resemblance to the thrust of Eisler's opera text and its evaluation by Ernst Fischer.[6] The staging of the play must likewise be seen as an attempt to get away from the classical *Faust*, to go back behind it, to withdraw it. If Eisler and Fischer represent Faust as a central figure of the *Deutsche Misere*, the Berliner Ensemble says in its programme notes: "With *Urfaust* it is easier than with the finished play (*Faust Part One*) for the theater to avoid intimidation by the classical." What are we meant to understand by intimidation by the classical? Only the production itself will tell. This production can only be understood as a rejection of the classical traditions of our national culture.

But how is it possible to regard the German classical works, the creative highpoints of the art of the German people, as intimidation? The only possible basis for such a view is necessarily estranged from the German people and anti-national.

The Storm and Stress writer, Maximilian Klinger, wrote a *Faust* novel amounting to a cry of protest against the conditions of decline in a Germany divided into petty princedoms. Klinger's Faust, inventor of the printing press and author of a Bible translation which no one wants to buy from him, is driven by poverty to make a pact with the devil . . . But every human effort is in vain. Hell is the victor. The devil decides everything. Outbursts against the Peasants' Revolt are the other side of the coin to the tendencies to rebellion. Portrayed like this, Faust could serve as a model figure for the German *Misere*. His protest is never more than a negation. There is not a single positive character in the novel. Out of a criticism of the social status quo arose social nihilism, a cul-de-sac which accounted for more than one writer of the *Storm and Stress* period . . . Such a conception of things obviously influences Hanns Eisler's libretto to *Johann Faustus* . . .

In contrast to Klinger, Goethe aimed at an optimistic conception. His Faust is always the man of the German Renaissance who wants to know nature and truth. The linking of the Faust problem with the Gretchen tragedy — which was not to be found in the old folk fable — , its inclusion in *Urfaust*,

---

[5]   27.5.1953 Edition B and 28.5.1953 Edition A.

[6]   Ernst Fischer wrote favorably of Eisler's libretto in an article in *Sinn und Form* 4 (1952) no. 6, 59–73.

the poetic shaping of it showed this early work of Goethe as in touch with the people and full of humanism. The Gretchen figure is essentially the same in all versions of Goethe's *Faust*, although in *Urfaust* she is not explicitly declared saved. She is poetically typified as a girl of the people, the German girl who, with her loving surrender stands for the right to a higher morality in the face of the inhuman standards of the social status quo. It is Gretchen as embodiment of "Eternal Womanhood" — fostering development in life — who in the end brings Faust his redemption in *Part Two*. She it is who leads him on to higher morality.

In the "Gretchen Tragedy," Goethe presented the tragic conflict between the humanistic morality of the common people and the "moral" norms of the ruling class. Because Gretchen defends the higher morality, she perishes. By inspiring the audience to have the deepest empathy with Gretchen, Goethe compels them to be committed to a future opposed to a system which puts to death such a person as Gretchen.

The Gretchen tragedy, as inner core of the *Urfaust* fragment, is one of the essential links to the later versions of Goethe's *Faust*. In any staging of *Urfaust* it must occupy a central place; it must give the disturbing conflict its due prominence and challenge the audience to commitment.

But the Berliner Ensemble's production, in turning away from the classical tradition, functioned more like a puppet show which could not give rise to deep human feelings. The production took up the more dazzling and formless aspects of the story and exaggerated them. The primitiveness of the scenery was meant as a symbol for the German *Misere*. The spirit of the Renaissance, which flowed through the veins also of the *intellectually* creative people of this period, was nowhere in evidence but hovered in the background in the form of symbolic decoration borrowed from the Italian Renaissance, thus giving the impression that the German Renaissance amounted to nothing more than mysticism and that rational clarity and reason were dominant only in the Italian Renaissance. In this context any attempt at realism in the scenery, as, for example, in the scene at the well, could only come across as unsubtle naturalism. (Bunge: 123)

In this production Gretchen was not allowed to *be* Gretchen. She was clearly an intellectual construct showing how a child of the sixteenth century would react when approached by a gentleman of a higher class. The picture of Gretchen's active domestic life, her love for the little sister whom she helped to rear — all evidence of Goethe's profound sympathy with simple people — was glossed over and spoken in a broken, gabbled fashion. Obviously the words were not meant to convey anything except her own feeling of embarrassment. According to the programme notes, Gretchen's innocence stems from the physical, bodily aspect of her being (Sinnlichkeit). Through this interpretation — with its depth-psychology — the socially critical aspect is removed from the Gretchen tragedy. Likewise, the confrontation of views between Faust and Gretchen in the garden —

one of the most important scenes in the whole of German literature — is stripped of its proper value. (Bunge: 124)

We believe that it has to be said that the young colleagues of the Berliner Ensemble, many of whom are very gifted and who, unlike in many another theater, are receiving a thorough training, are being led in a false direction by the use of methodic principles which Brecht, as artistic director of the Berliner Ensemble, applies when producing his version of the classic writers.

Alexander Abusch (1902–1982)

On May 13, in a meeting of the Wednesday Society (Mittwochgesellschaft) in the Akademie der Künste, Alexander Abusch had already read a paper[7] expressing his opposition to Hanns Eisler's *Johann Faustus* libretto. The basic issues are the same as in the Rudolf article, but because of Abusch's authority as an intellectual within the system his stance can be viewed as even more telling than that of Rudolf. It should suffice to quote here some central passages which deal with the problem of principle.

It is completely new to present the immortal figure of the intellectual hero of German classical literature as a 'central figure of the German Misere.' Only if we answer the question whether such a conception is possible and right are we in a position to establish whether Hanns Eisler has succeeded in creating a text for *the* or *a* German national opera.

Goethe and the tragic conflict of Faust

The Faust saga, as it was handed down through the Erfurt Faust stories and then through the first chap-book (Frankfurt, 1587) has only a hint, in primitive form, of the profound human and national substance contained in this German saga. That is due to the historical conditions under which it was handed down.

The saga stems from the first half of the sixteenth century when the feudal society of the Middle Ages was suddenly plunged into a process of dissolution by the new economic developments and early capitalism was exploding the clerics' medieval view of the world. The rising middle class in the German towns was striving to widen its intellectual horizon, was shaking off the authority of Rome and pressing for the enjoyment of its own freedom. This was the time in which the polemical Ulrich von Hutten wrote that "in this century, with the new sciences, it was a joy to live."

---

[7] "Faust — Held oder Renegat in der deutschen Nationalliteratur." In: *Sinn und Form* 5 1953): 179–197.

The tragic conflict of the middle classes in this German Renaissance arose out of the insoluble contradiction that, on the one hand, they were driven by the powerful urge to seek truth and spiritual independence of Rome, to seek a comprehensive grasp of life's problems, the greatest possible involvement in social activity, the best possible enjoyment of life, a new morality; and, on the other hand, at every step they encountered insuperable barriers which belief in the devil and the puritanism of Luther's Reformation erected in front of them. On German soil this conflict was of a particular kind, for here at this time the struggle of the best men for a free country for the German nation suffered defeats with serious consequences. Goethe, with a profound understanding of his people's history, realized that the problems of the Renaissance man in the emerging German middle class were expressed in the saga of Doctor Faust in a specific way which was only feasible under the conditions of national division.

In his *Faust-Studies*, Georg Lukács has shown the historical root of the falsified handing down of the Faust saga: all strands of this tradition originate from "enemy territory" (Feindesland), namely from Lutherans who made of the striving of the tragic hero of the Renaissance a deterring example of religious sinfulness. The sources to which even a middle-class scholar like Ernst Beutler has recourse in his *Faust* commentary (Luther's comments in his *Table Talks*, mention of a sermon by Melanchthon, the Erfurt Faust stories of 1556 etc) confirm Lukács's observation. In the Lutheran tradition, Faust's characteristics as daemonic and mystical, as a magician and a charlatan, were highlighted, and Beutler writes: "Thus for the whole of Protestantism the Faust saga was based on Church dogma about the devil. Using the saga, the Lutherans proved that the evil enemy is still today in our midst, as in the times of the Garden of Eden and the patriarchs."

The tendency is also very strongly mirrored in the English play by Christopher Marlowe, who had taken over the German saga in its distorted form. The later puppet play *Doctor Faustus*, which was derived from Marlowe's work, aims at showing the Christian emerging triumphant from the devil's pact.

The Faust saga also preoccupied Lessing, who was led to solve its problems straightforwardly in the spirit of the Enlightenment. Lukács shows, by contrast, the great achievement of Goethe's play, which is much closer to the original saga than Lessing was and "indeed not only in its much more intimate dependence on aspects of the action but above all in the renewal of the spirit of the Renaissance and of the original, fundamental ideas which had been lost in the Lutheran versions." Lukács shows how this renewal by Goethe took place in a period when the middle class thinking of the Enlightenment was giving way to the idealist dialectic. From these important observations we see, on the one hand, how Goethe went back to the *genuine problems of the Renaissance*, and, on the other hand, how this philosophical development was in line with that of Goethe himself, whose philosophy stretched to the highest peaks of thought which were possible for his class ("das Bürgertum") in that historical period. (Bunge: 49)

Faust as national hero

In Lukács's *Faust-Studies*, to which we owe valuable discoveries about the history of the development of the Faust saga from its origins, about the dialectical relationship between Faust and Mephistopheles and about the human and social meaning of the Gretchen tragedy, emphasis is laid in too generalized a way solely on the drama of the human species. Lukács did not deal sufficiently with the national significance of Goethe's treatment of the Faust material.

In my view (which I have tried to sketch first in my book *Der Irrweg einer Nation* 1944–45 and later in other works), this national aspect consists in the fact that, in *Faust*, Goethe created a mirror image of the contradictions which characterized the inner struggle of the German nation in those centuries — with the daemonic reactionary forces opposed to the enlightened progressive elements, with the rough exterior forces opposed to those of a finer inner life, with the contrast between intellectual repression and the search for genuine science. Goethe achieved this on the basis of his intellectual position at the end of the eighteenth and the beginning of the nineteenth century, where, deeply in touch with the history of the German people, he looked back over more than three centuries. The split in the progressive forces at the beginning of the sixteenth century, together with the national disaster represented by the failure of the great German Peasants' War in 1525, had an important influence on the battles between the enlightened progressive forces allied with the development of the sciences on the one hand, and the dark, mystical and reactionary forces in German society on the other: namely, that these battles came late and in an intensified form. Goethe transposed this struggle from the reality of a divided nation into the Faust legend: into the battle between two souls in Faust's bosom. This hero, deeply divided within himself, is also, as Marietta Schaginjan finely observes, drawn by Goethe "as a contemporary related to himself, as the embodiment of a divided personality from the first half of the nineteenth century."

The fact that Goethe was able to portray the battle between the obscurantists and the scientists, between reaction and progress in the life of the Germans only by recourse to this legendary, romantic flight into an internal sphere was a result of his own position with regard to the German *Misere*. The contradictions he encountered at court in Weimar could also often only be dealt with interiorly. But the genius Goethe, in this Faustian struggle within the breast of his hero, achieved a truly poetic rendering of a Weltanschauung which was the highest possible in his epoch. His work had a lasting effect on a future age because it anticipates so much of it and contains so much objective truth.

Faust embodies Goethe's own struggle: his search for knowledge of the laws of becoming and dissolution in nature and society, his passionate surrender to the enjoyment of life, his painful collisions with the narrow limitations of the world around him, his weaknesses and his maturing in relation to "Eternal Womanhood" (Das Ewig Weibliche), his striving after the highest perfection as an active human being — and, in his advanced old age, his resignation about the fact that definite, insuperable limits are set even to the most progressive thinking of his class. Thus Goethe's Faust is both the Faust of 1520 and 1540 — divided within himself — but he is also the searching Goethe of the period between 1790 and 1830 when the Germans of his class had not yet been able to solve many of the fundamental problems posed by the sixteenth century. (51)

Continuing conflict

The official line, broadly based on Lukács's *Faust* interpretation, and the fundamentally different approach represented by Brecht and Eisler remained in conflict into the 1980s. Of course the level of public awareness of the conflict varied according to the level of official commitment to the suppression of the opposition. The Brecht/Eisler line was efficiently suppressed after its very brief emergence in 1952 and 1953. The continued dominance of the official view was reflected in the Bennewitz production (1965–1967) briefly mentioned above.

The Heinz and Dresen challenge (Berlin)

But this was to be challenged, in the politically charged atmosphere of September 1968, by the *Faust* production of Wolfgang Heinz and Adolf Dresen. August 1968 had seen the Soviet intervention in the Czechoslovakian uprising. In East Germany, Klaus Gysi[8] made a speech on August 28 — in commemoration of Goethe's birthday — in which he played off Faust as a symbol of socialist and humanist ideals in contrast to Kafka's dung beetle figure representing the "shady, shifty figures" of the "counter-revolution" in Czechoslovakia. The Heinz and Dresen *Faust*, in this climate, ran into immediate difficulties, not least because it used the "Walpurgis Night Dream" (more usually omitted from East German *Faust* productions) to criticize the regime for suppressing the work of playwrights like Peter Hacks, Helmut

---

[8] Minister for Culture 1966–1973.

Baierl, and Heiner Müller — a scene which the Minister for Culture ordered
to be cut the following day. In addition, some similarities with the Brechtian
"irreverence" with regard to the classical tradition were noticeable. As
Viëtor-Engländer relates, the Faust figure was a neurotic intellectual. He was
nervous, ascetic, inhibited; he experienced extreme highs and lows and was
plagued by doubt and self-questioning. Instead of being a well-focused indi-
vidual and reminiscent of a renaissance discoverer of a new world, he was a
Storm and Stress middle-class figure in crisis, wearing the blue costume of
Werther, and accompanied by a sensuous, aroused, ordinary small-town
Gretchen — no "revolutionary of love" as the authorities would have her to
be. (159)

Schwerin, 1979

As we have seen above in the outline of the development of cultural policy,
the whole cultural and political climate was to change radically by the mid
1970s. Christoph Schroth's *Faust* production in 1979 was dedicated to the
thirtieth anniversary of the foundation of the German Democratic Republic.
The programme explicitly related the production to the conceptions behind
the Brecht (and Monk) 1952 and 1953 productions and included quota-
tions from Werner Mittenzwei, a known champion of Brecht's cause. This
production was so clearly a search for new ways of seeing and presenting
Faust that, when it was brought to Weimar to the plenary session of the Go-
ethe-Gesellschaft in 1982, it shocked the Germanists from the West. They
did not anticipate that the East German cultural policy had swung around
180 degrees and was now promoting — as typical of the new East German
attitudes — a *Faust* production which highlighted the presence of contra-
dictory aspects not only in the figure of Faust but even in Goethe himself!

Urfaust 1984

When in 1984 the Berliner Ensemble presented *Urfaust* — not a revival of
the Brecht *Urfaust* — the break with the old official attitudes of the past was
complete. Horst Sagert, instead of stressing the renaissance Faust, high-
lighted what was to be seen as the dark, Catholic, mystical side of the Middle
Ages prior to the new cult of rational, scientific knowledge. In the 1960s,
this, as an "alternative" to the renaissance explorer, would have been imme-
diately suppressed by officialdom. But now, centering on Goethe and Wei-
mar Classicism was no longer official policy. It was no longer important to
keep Goethe on his pedestal. The old guard, however, did not vanish. But a
balance between the two contradictory traditions in the East German view of
Goethe and his *Faust* had now been achieved. The whole story of this strug-

gle bears witness to depths of cultural life which the domination of official-
dom largely managed to conceal from the world outside East Germany and
which it will repay future generations of scholars to investigate.

The Lukács interpretation

The East German interpretations of Goethe's *Faust* owe much more to
Lukács's work than the post-1956 East German *Faust* literature openly
states. The problems with Lukács's approach, which tends to remain too re-
mote from the actual text and is thus too sparing in its reference to detail,
partly justify the accusation that his method is too abstract and even too close
to the method of Geistesgeschichte which he claimed to have left behind.
But it would be fruitful to look very closely at his presentation and analysis of
Faust: first, with a view to highlighting the substance of his interpretation
and second, with a view to ascertaining what the East German Marxists
themselves added or took away.

What impresses the reader of Lukács's *Faust* essays is both his unified
grasp of the work and the way he imbeds it into the historical background,
this latter including: the political history of Germany, where strong emphasis
is laid on the emergence of a middle class combating the feudal status quo;
European history — including the French Revolution, the Napoleonic re-
gime and the events leading up to 1830, with their effects on Germany — ;
cultural history from the Enlightenment onwards; the history of philosophy
reaching a climax with the publication of Hegel's *Phenomenology Of Mind* in
1807, just a year before *Faust Part One* appeared. Whatever about the inter-
pretation of some of these issues, it is undeniable that the Marxist tradition is
deeply concerned with them and by its very nature must be — since a serious
work of art is always seen by them as the product of an individual living not
in an historical vacuum but in all of the dimensions included above under the
term historical background.

With a view to comparing Lukács's interpretation with those of the East
German Marxists, it will be useful to pick out and present some of the main
aspects which interest him.

Historical dimension

One of Lukács's prime theses is: "What is depicted is, indeed, the fate of one
man, but the true content of the poem is the destiny of all mankind."
(127/157) This statement is grounded in various ways, but most immedi-
ately here by reference to the Faust saga. Lukács quotes Gorki as saying that

such sagas are not fruits of fantasy but exaggerations which are necessary and in perfect accord with the laws of real facts. (129/159)

A saga like that of Faust reflects for Lukács real historical tendencies (Lebenstendenzen), the essence of which has been seized on by the people and expressed in the form of a saga. In a saga like this, as also in the history of Götz von Berlichingen, Goethe was able to focus both on his own personal concerns and the deepest concerns of the epoch. Thus Goethe's work on *Faust* is seen as a reshaping of folklore material in such a way that, avoiding a clear break with the tradition, the writer achieves an organic continuation of the folk tradition and thereby grows with the new development, at the same time remodelling the character (Faust) without risking its destruction.

For Lukács, an important aspect of the Faust saga (and also of the Götz story) is its link with the Reformation, the German Renaissance, the battle between the small princes and the nobility, and the Peasants' War. (130/160f.) According to Lukács, this turning back to the past (around 1500) had nothing to do with an equivalent tendency found in the Romantics when they turned back to the Middle Ages. It was Europe *emerging* from the Middle Ages. It was the origin of the slowly developing middle class. This is an attempt on Goethe's part to make contact with his cultural roots, his inheritance. The Faust figure becomes a symbol for Goethe not just of his own personal problems with the shackles imposed on him as an individual in eighteenth century Germany; Faust also represents the much more general striving for freedom on a national basis in Germany since the Reformation. Of Götz Lukács writes:

> Götz's robber chivalry is for young Goethe only a symbol, an expression of the untamed, uninhibited need for freedom of the new man, of the ideological avant-garde of bourgeois society in Germany which was taking stock of itself. (133/163)

Then of Faust:

> The idea of the "self-reliant man" is even broader and deeper in *Faust*. The legend itself requires Goethe to pose the problem in all its universality. To this extent, the later recollection of Goethe, that the representation of both the great and the little world, of both the public and the individual life, was intended from the beginning, is surely correct. (133/164)

The microcosm of Faust's individual world and the macrocosm of the wider social and political world are both intrinsically related features of the work.

In tracing the development of the work from the *Urfaust* stage to the *Fragment* of 1790 and to the completion of *Part One* in 1808, Lukács is not preoccupied primarily with a philological task but is instead tracing the growth in Goethe's Weltanschauung in a series of highly significant steps. *Urfaust* deals with the relationship of conflict between a man and woman which has a tragic outcome. But in Lukács's interpretation of Goethe, the tragic is not the final principle. In the *Fragment*, where the scene "Forest and Cavern" (Wald und Höhle) appears for the first time, we find evidence of the new conception of nature developed by Goethe in his early Weimar years and deepened by his experience in Italy. But, according to Lukács, Goethe is not yet ready to apply — poetically and philosophically — his newly developing Weltanschauung to all aspects of nature and human experience. He will first have to cope with the political upheaval in Europe resulting from the French Revolution and the Napoleonic era. Where the *Fragment* does not end as in *Urfaust* with the death of Gretchen, but breaks off before the conclusion of the Gretchen episode, *Part One* ends with the death but also with the salvation of Gretchen. Furthermore, because the whole episode is now viewed within the framework established by the "Prolog in Heaven," the tragedy of Gretchen is no longer so central but is reduced to a decisive tragic step in the course of Faust's life, on the way to the full development of the human race. (141/174) In this way, *Faust*, no longer in danger of interpretation as depicting the fate of an individual, is established as a poem about the world (Weltgedicht). Lukács relates the development of Faust to the accompanying developments in German philosophy. It is

> the period during which German philosophy begins its transition from the subjective idealism of Kant and Fichte to the objective idealism of Schelling and Hegel: the period of the formation of the idealist dialectic. (140/172)

With regard to the eventual continuation and conclusion of *Faust*, the hopes of the students of Fichte and Schelling are expressed in the following words:

> If this tragedy is someday completed, it will represent the spirit of the whole of world history; it will be a true image of the life of mankind embracing past, present, and future. Humanity will be idealized in Faust; he will be the representative of humanity.[9]

What remains for *Part Two* is the treatment of "the greater world." In Act One and Act Four of *Part Two* Goethe will refer back to the feudal society he had already dealt with in *Götz von Berlichingen*. But he will be clearer and will go further than in *Götz*. He will give a more comprehensive picture of the decay of feudalism and of the rottenness of court life; he will show the main factor which finally destroys the old system: namely, the development of productive forces through capitalism. (142/175)

According to Lukács, Goethe accepts the Enlightenment ideal of progress. While he was opposed to the violence and turbulence of the French Revolution and was always in favor of social evolution, he was still convinced

---

[9] 140/173 (Lukács does not give the source of his quotation).

that progress was inevitable. Goethe shows this progress in *Faust* as the result of a series of individual tragedies:

> The tragedies occurring in the microcosm of the individual are the disclosure of the ceaseless progress in the macrocosm of the species: this is the philosophical factor common to both *Faust* and the *Phenomenology of Mind*. (147/181)

Faust's (Goethe's) vision of progress puts him in touch with reality in a way which, in the Earth Spirit scene, was only dreamed of. This progress takes place through involvement with praxis. Unfortunately, from Faust's and Goethe's point of view, the praxis now available is that determined by the development of industry with its capitalist implications. (157/193)

From a Marxist point of view, it is interesting that *Faust* finds himself in a contradictory situation for which there is no apparent, immediately available socio-political solution. If *Faust* seems, in the great final monolog towards the end of *Part Two*, to find a solution — with humanity looking forward to a rosy future of freedom achieved by its labor — this hopeful view clashes with the harsh reality that what the lemurs are digging for the blind *Faust* is nothing constructive, like a dyke, but the grave for his burial. The real situation in which Goethe finishes his *Faust* is a world in which Goethe can see no solution. He does not flee from the present, nor does he capitulate with the kind of progress capitalism represents. The dilemma of human progress remains unsolved, which is the reason, according to Lukács, that Goethe resorts to the theme of celestial Christian transcendence at the very end. (158/193) He believes in an indestructible core in the human being, in humanity; he believes in the salvation of this core both in and, above all, in spite of the concrete capitalist form of development which was the only one available to him around 1830.

Good and evil

One special characteristic of Lukács's *Faust* interpretation is to be found in his section on "Faust und Mephistopheles," where the central duel between the two characters is given a particular interpretation. The play does not represent a struggle for the possession of Faust's soul between the two traditionally understood principles of good and evil. Rather, both principles are part of Faust himself. Thus, Mephisto is partly identified with Faust. Yet at the same time Mephisto is related to a social dimension which is part of the external reality which Faust himself must confront. Mephisto seems to stand, within Faust, for that aspect of Faust which involves him in the only kind of social reality which gives him the possibility of development. His own personal development and his participation in human progress is only possible in the concrete, historical world, which at the time was, unfortunately, that of fast developing European capitalism. Lukács takes pains to show that Mephisto is not related to any transcendent realm but stands for the devilish, satanic elements in the social world. A reflex of this denial of transcendence is moral relativism. Faust is committed to personal self-development and to participation in human progress, and in this context:

> only the exact function in the given concrete stage of development determines whether a feeling, a thought, or an action is human or diabolical. Sometimes it is not even possible to come to a decision about this on the basis of an isolated moment, but only on the basis of the direction of the process it reveals and which will become visible only later. (160/197)

What seems good in Faust — his striving for fulfilment and his commitment to progress — seems possible only in social circumstances which involve him in evil: his turning to magic, to Mephisto and to what in Act Four and Act Five of *Part Two* Mephisto represents: the ruthless, exploitative and brutal forces of capitalism.

Thus Lukács finds in Goethe a dialectic which he sees as the foundation for Goethe's unshakable belief in the future of mankind. But, according to Lukács, the moral relativism implied does not lead to nihilism but, as with Hegel, is seen as a stage in human development which is then "aufgehoben" — overtaken and assimilated into a further stage:

> Goethe incorporates moral and social relativism poetically as an element in the total dialectic in the same way Hegel does philosophically. (161/197)

We will be looking at the role of the final scene as the poetic means for achieving this reconciliation which is not really possible in Goethe's concrete world. The dialectic which could not be resolved in Goethe's contemporary world gives rise, also in contexts other than *Faust*, to the creation of a utopia which is not an escape from reality but an anticipation of a social and political climate in which a resolution — in the Hegelian sense of "Aufhebung" — is really possible.

Nature

In the context of East German Marxist reception of Goethe, the meaning attached to nature is of the utmost importance. In the "Faust und Mephistopheles" chapter, Lukács's ideas on this subject are clearly laid out and should serve as an enlightening comparison with those presented in the GDL.

In the medieval world, just as everything connected with sensuality, the natural existence of man (Sinnlichkeit, das naturhafte Dasein des Menschen) is looked on as sinful (163/200), so too nature itself is seen as the sphere ruled by the devil. Only by following the ascetic dictates of the transcendent Christian God is it possible to escape being controlled by the devil's influence. For Enlightenment thinkers, however — and Goethe amongst them — man's own human nature, with all its passions, is seen in a purely positive light, and external nature is seen equally positively as a focus for man's search for knowledge and as a sphere of his intense activity. Goethe himself allows no compromise in these regards:

> On the one hand, from his early youth, Goethe rejected the Kantian postulate of the unknowableness of nature, the unknowableness of the thing-in-itself . . . But, perhaps even more passionately, he rejects the Kantian conception of the "radical evil" in man's empirical and physical nature.
>
> (164/201)

On this basis, Lukács's interpretation of the Earth Spirit is particularly significant. What the Earth Spirit says about himself represents the very core of Goethe's philosophy of nature — in Lukács's words: the ceaseless transformation and self-renewal of nature. If this is the case, why does the Earth Spirit reject Faust? Because Faust's ambition to know nature is based on the desire for a mystical identification of man and nature which Goethe, at this stage of his life (and along with him Faust), is soon to realize is impossible. Lukács points to the "Forest and Cavern" stage of Faust's development, where he no longer yearns for immediate identification with nature (loss of self in nature) but has reached the philosophical natural state. (164/201) This stage represents an advance on the previous one, but it is still not final. The beginning of *Part Two* brings the consideration of the healing powers of nature seen as a force which is both independent of man and indifferent to his moral status as good or evil. Then, when confronted with the rising sun, Faust, though forced to turn his back on its brilliance, is not turned away from knowledge and enjoyment of it: "we have life in its colorful reflection" (Am farbigen Abglanz haben wir das Leben). This particular scene represents a step forward, in that it provides the basis for a new conception of beauty — and, in *Part Two* itself, for the introduction of the Helena tragedy.

By contrast to the pantheistic conception of nature attributed to Goethe by East German scholars, we find in Lukács's essay the conviction that a central feature of Goethe's conception of nature is that it is independent of man and his moral (and other) concerns. Thus, the healing scene is not to be interpreted in any idyllic sense. Instead, Lukács stresses that at the end of the play there is an intense and many-faceted conflict between man and nature. Mephisto even envisages the entire destruction of Faust's life's work by the antagonistic forces of nature. We are naturally reminded of the role played by nature in ballads like "Der Erlkönig," "Der Fischer," "Der Zauberlehrling," and of the function of water as a threat and even as a destructive agent in *Die Wahlverwandtschaften* (Elective Affinities). According to Lukács, it is important to see that in man's dealings with nature he sometimes releases forces which have a life of their own and which he does not understand and certainly cannot control. Similarly, on a social level, progress and development take place as a result of man's passions but then leave him behind, not only becoming independent of his control, but making him dependent on the processes he himself initiated.

Here Lukács sums up his understanding of Goethe's ethic:

> The mastery of passion, its ennoblement, its orientation toward the really great goals of the human species — this is Goethe's ethic! (166/203)

Goethe is by no means amoral:

> His morality seeks a way which would allow *every* passion to express itself and develop in the interest of the species. By the mastery of the passions, he does not mean their rigorously ascetic suppression, as Kant does; he has in mind rather — like the great men of the Renaissance, and also Fourier — a state of humanity and human relations in which the interaction of men, the test of passion in human activity, would lead men to a real consciousness of themselves; that is, to a complete development of all their potentialities, to a harmonious equilibrium of the unfolding passions — in such a way that the inner harmony of man would be the motive force of his accord with his fellow man. (166/204)

Gretchen

It is worth focusing attention on Lukács's interpretation of the Gretchen tragedy. The story of the seduced lower middle-class girl serves to contrast the decayed moral values of the nobility with the healthy upright moral sense of the new middle class. It illustrates at the same time the powerlessness even of the most strident Storm and Stress voices against the established position of the feudal society. But, according to Lukács, Goethe does not stop short at this contradiction but takes pains to show that even within middle-class society itself there is a radical contradiction. The new society, while espousing the cause of full development of the individual, has within itself the very seeds which militate against this development: the need to build a career within this society — to establish a livelihood — is inimical to the spontaneous living-out of love and to early commitment of young people in love. Though Lukács develops this theme by reference to several of Goethe's early works, suffice it here to highlight his application of it to the relationship between Faust and Gretchen

> All the great tendencies of evolution are concentrated in the person of Faust. When, turning to life, he approaches Gretchen, the sad burden weighs on him of the scarcely surmounted tragedy of immediate knowl-

edge and his pact with the devil. And, at the height of his ecstasy with Gretchen, enraptured by the charm of her person and her nearness, there is at work in him the invincible aspiration: to go further, higher! Faust knows, even if he does not wish to admit it to himself, that he cannot long stay in the "little world" of Gretchen . . . With him, it is actually a question of a restless urge to perfection. (182/223f.)

One main focus of the irreconcilable differences between the two lovers is found in their conversation about religion. Subjectively — in their intense experience of love — they become inwardly very close. But, according to Lukács, we find a dialectic between the openness and upright honesty of Gretchen on the one hand and the deceit and self-deceit of Faust on the other. Lukács claims that this dialectic is inevitable, given the contradictions intrinsic to middle-class society at the time. In Gretchen, this openness and honesty can manifest itself as sheer naiveté when she says "You have no Christianity"; but she links this statement with references to Mephistopheles, whom she experiences as a major disturbance in her relationship to Faust. As Lukács points out, the impossibility of Gretchen's ever understanding Faust has nothing to do with the difference in intellectual level between the lovers, but with Faust's now unavoidable entanglement with Mephisto — which he has just previously admitted in "Forest and Cavern," but which he cannot admit to her. And it is precisely Faust's involvement with Mephisto that makes Gretchen refuse to be saved by Faust:

> she will not be rescued by a Faust to whom Mephistopheles is indispensable. This is why the voice from above can proclaim: "She is saved!"
>
> (185/227)

Perhaps paradoxically, at this point the full depth of Lukács's interpretation of the Margarete figure and of her significance for Faust are to be revealed: at the point where Lukács must explain Goethe's use of the Christian theme of salvation — in a Christian heaven!

In this context, the obvious point which Lukács needs to stress is that Goethe is in no way to be understood as a believer in transcendence. The final section of *Part Two* has to be understood as Goethe's expression of his knowledge that human perfection— whether for a Faust or for a Gretchen — is, in the historical and social conditions of Goethe's experience, quite impossible. Yet Goethe had the unshakable conviction that humanity would develop in the future, though in a way which he, of course, was in no position concretely to envisage (for the Marxists: through the emergence of the proletariat as the next phase in the history of human development). This conviction or belief could not yet be represented in anything directly founded in concrete human history, and so, to avoid the danger of lapsing into a feeble vagueness, Goethe resorted to the arbitrary choice of the

Catholic heaven as a final scenario. The conversation in which Goethe said as much to Eckermann is often referred to by the Marxists, and we shall have occasion to look at it more closely.

Within the formal structure of the so-called Catholic heaven, Goethe makes his own construct, where it is possible to envisage the eternal process of the perfection of the human race; (186/228f.) and if Lukács admits that the Catholic notion of divine grace is present in the text he counteracts this with the statement that the final lines: Eternal Womanhood leads us above (Das Ewig-Weibliche/Zieht uns hinan) are to be understood in terms of a pantheistic dialectic which is totally immanent (diesseits). Interesting as this idea is, the immediate connection of the passage with pantheism is obscure. Be that as it may, the important point is made:

> For Faust, then, heaven is the culmination of his development projected into the hereafter, a development of which the crowning highpoint is his reunion with Gretchen. All the rest is only milieu, mediation, decoration. Gretchen is the spirit of perfection in Faust's striving, just as Klärchen was the spirit of freedom for Egmont as he went to his death. (187/230)

The status of Gretchen, revealed in this way, is now clearly not just that of a middle-class girl who was destroyed in her innocence and left to pay the price. She has grown beyond this and has significance way beyond it. If her intellectual niveau was in one sense less than Faust's, her request "allow me to teach him" (Vergönne mir, ihn zu belehren!) has a most serious meaning and is seen to be of central, paramount importance to the whole of the drama. Here Lukács virtually summarizes his interpretation of Goethe's theory of human development towards perfection.

Lukács refers to "an extremely important variation and development, in Goethe's old age, of his conception of human perfection." (187/230) He speaks of a two-fold tendency, each element striving for the upper hand: first, the tendency to achieve the fullest possible development of the individual's capabilities to the point of complete mastery; second, the tendency to achieve an inner human harmony in the development of these capabilities; thus the development of the individual's gifts to the highest possible degree should not produce such highly specialized monsters as the capitalist system almost inevitably produces, but the growth of the individual capabilities should be accompanied by the harmonious growth of the whole person. In the real situation in which he lived, Goethe knew that this synthesis was not possible to achieve. But he did not lose from sight that the aim was not in itself impossible. It was not meant for an elite. Lukács quotes him as saying: "the least man can be complete if he moves within the limits of his capabilities and aptitudes." (188/231) Lukács highlights, perhaps too briefly to make his case entirely convincing, that Goethe finds this form of harmony more often in "plebeian" ranks than in higher strata of society. He is more convincing — because his case is more obvious — when he says this type of inner harmony is more often found in women than in men: he mentions Iphigenie, Philine, Klärchen, Ottilie, Natalie and Dorothea. Inclusions and exclusions could be debated, but the comparison seems valid in the case of the women whose human development is more limited in extent but is more intensively harmonious than is the case with the prominent men. (If this formula is valid, it applies especially to the Susanna figure of *Wilhelm Meister's Apprenticeship*, whom Lukács repudiates!) For the future, Goethe dreams

> that at later stages of mankind's development the highest intellectual attainments, the inner and outer unfolding of individual talents would, without foregoing any of these gains, reach the inner completeness, the moral and aesthetic harmony of such women. (189/232)

The relevance of these ideas to Lukács's interpretation of Gretchen is striking. Gretchen's personal qualities developed in the "kleine Welt" carry over into the "große Welt" in a continuous development which, far from becoming more ethereal, involves a mutual learning and teaching with Faust:

> Hence, the Catholic heaven at the conclusion is the human harmony and perfection, which grew out of the "great world" and the perpetual development of the personality founded on mutual assistance and instruction; a progress that has no need of Mephistophelian forces. All this, Faust must learn in heaven from Gretchen. (189/233)

In conclusion, it is worth noting Lukács's interpretation of the final words about "Eternal Womanhood":

> It is his last avowal of the possibility of a perfection of man on earth, a perfection of man as a physical and spiritual personality, a perfection founded on his mastery of the external world and the elevation of his own nature to spirituality, to culture and harmony, without a denial of its natural character. (190/234)

The *GDL* interpretation: secularization

The reception of Goethe's version of the Faust material poses quite specific problems for the Marxist interpreters, mainly because of its concern — at least on the surface — with religion. It is clear to everyone that Goethe (and, to a far lesser extent, his society) has moved a long way in the direction of secularization. A glance back at poems by Gryphius would make the difference abundantly clear. The only possible vexed question is: *how far* has Goethe's thinking become secularized? His *Faust* still has at least the trappings of religion: the framework beginning with a "Prolog in Heaven" and ending in what Lukács constantly refers to as the Catholic heaven; the struggle of Faust with the devil; Margarete's close involvement with the Catholic Church.

The question of Goethe's own Weltanschauung needs careful consideration. It is not sufficient any more to refer to Goethe simply as a pagan or as an atheist, as if this were a well established fact. It requires much more discipline to try to define in what Goethe's relationship to the divine consists rather than blindly to affirm that he had none. Significantly, the Marxist tradition, beginning with Lukács, undertakes this task. This tradition does have unity in this respect in so far as it always emphasizes that Goethe is no believer in transcendence. This says more than that he is fully committed to living out every possible aspect of what this *earthly* existence offers. Such a claim is theoretically compatible with some of the more liberal forms of modern Christianity, which would not demand a radical choice between commitment to *this* life and some kind of belief in immortality — a form of *after*-life. The additional Marxist element implied in this statement is that Goethe lives exclusively a life of immanence (as a "diesseitiger Mensch"), and it is precisely this element which requires the Marxist interpreters to offer explanations of how to understand the religious elements referred to. This they do in different ways.

Comparing the approach of Lukács with that of the *GDL* writers, we find that Lukács leans heavily on an Hegelian approach, stressing a dialectic which sees Mephisto as representing that part of man which has to cope with human passions, especially as these manifest themselves in corrupt society. Lukács shows the contradictions as necessary in the given historical context and as pointing to a future stage in the development of society, where the conflicts will be resolved. Thus the individual tragedies — like the destruction of Gretchen, the destruction of Philemon and Baucis — are seen as necessary in the course of social development. But, particularly in the case of Gretchen, this tragedy has a positive function in the education of the individual Faust; and Gretchen, as representative of Eternal Womanhood, has a function in the development and perfection of the human race. Indeed, Lukács's twinning of the fates of the individual and of the species enables him to look beyond Faust's individual death to a future which is not Faust's immortality but the future growth and progress of the human species. Not Faust but the human race survives Faust's individual death.

Spinoza

The *GDL* writers, though they mention the importance of Hegel for Goethe, emphasize Spinoza and pantheism. Lukács himself, in listing the various early influences on Goethe which led him to a dialectical view of the world, names Spinoza. Having mentioned in this context Giordano Bruno, Hamann and Rousseau, Lukács writes:

> There is the influence of Spinoza which also works in the direction of the dialectic. All these currents of thought profoundly influence the Weltanschauung of young Goethe. (135/166)

But Lukács takes much greater pains to stress the link of Goethe with Hegel:

> Goethe's *Faust* and Hegel's *Phenomenology of Mind* belong together as the greatest artistic and intellectual achievements of the classical period in Germany. (143/176)

Three of the most important aspects of Lukács's *Faust* interpretation depend on this link:

> Here three related conceptions of history intersect and interpenetrate. First, there is the historical progress of the individual from simple perception of the world to a perfect philosophical cognizance of it. Second, there is the historical progress of mankind from its most primitive beginnings to the cultural level of Hegel's time, to the great French Revolution and its conquest by Napoleon and the modern bourgeois society which emerged from this earthquake. And, finally, this whole historical development is conceived as the work of man himself: man creates himself through his labor.
>
> (144/177)

In this third point, Lukács underlines his (Hegelian based) view of secularization: man achieves his own development; he is not led on by any transcendent force, nor is his reward to be found in the individual's life after death.

The *GDL* writers naturally continue the idea of the dialectic in Goethe's Weltanschauung, but they base it very firmly in Spinoza's pantheism. This applies especially, but not exclusively, to Part One. To a non-Marxist reader, the *GDL* interpretation of the "Prolog in Heaven" brings some surprises. As we shall see, a pantheist view tries to situate the Lord, the arch-angels, Mephisto, and Faust within a unified system.

The treatment of the "Prolog in Heaven" is significant for a variety of reasons. The relatively detailed discussion of the Book of Job as a biblical source, without deserving the label of positivist, represents an advance on the more purely theoretical work of Lukács. Yet there is an obvious unease, or even a cavalier attitude, in dealing with the religious tradition. In general, it may be acceptable to say that, in the Book of Job, God and Job appear as eternal opponents. (*GDL* 7 207) But this opposition cannot simply be interpreted as a Christian dualism in which there is an equal status ("Ebenbürtigkeit") between God and Satan. Satan has usually, if not always, been interpreted — within the Christian tradition which is here under discussion — as an angel created by God and allowed to use his freedom even to turn against God. God, in the same Christian tradition, is understood to have the absolute power either to annihilate Satan or to leave him in existence as a subordinate. Thus, when the *GDL* highlights the fact that between the Lord and Mephisto there is no equality of status because Mephisto is subordinated to the greater scheme of things in the world, this does not of itself establish the difference between the traditionally Christian view and the one Goethe is presenting in the "Prolog." Nor does it immediately follow that Goethe, by his re-interpretation of the Job story, is attacking the theocentric world view found in religion and replacing it by an anthropocentric view of the world based on an understanding of man as devoid of all religion. It would take much effort to substantiate the thesis that Goethe, in his treatment of the poetic model (Book of Job), "had hollowed out and driven out its religious content." (207) There can be no doubt that a substantial degree of secularization has taken place, but defining this degree is an important task — which is not fulfilled by a simple denial of religiosity in Goethe's world view.

Given that Spinozist pantheism is an established tool in East German Marxist Goethe reception, the details of its application here are quite fascinating: the Lord appears in the traditional image of the Lord of Heaven, but his whole meaning and function is not that of a transcendent, personal God; but, as a poetic figure, he represents the immanent laws of the universe. (207) This means that he does not stand over against the universe as different from it and superior to it (as creator vis-à-vis the creature in terms of traditional theology), but rather he is a representation of it, symbolizes it as a totality and process with all the inherent contradictoriness (in ihrer widerspruchsvollen Ganzheit und Prozeßhaftigkeit). Furthermore, he is not the almighty, predetermining, judging and punishing Lord over human beings — not the traditional God over human creation — but allows them space for his own (!) free and independent development ("sondern gibt diesen Raum für seine (sic!) eigenständige, freie Entwicklung"). (208) The reader's first suspicion about the word "seine" is that, as a result of an oversight, it has crept in in place of "ihre," which latter would mean that 'the human beings' ("die Menschen") are left room for their independent, free development. But in the context of pantheism the word "seine" could stand, and thus the text would mean that the development which takes place in human beings is also the Lord's development in so far as he represents the totality and process just mentioned. But the words "free and independent development" seem to relate more to the world of the *natura naturata* — where there is at least an appearance of freedom — than to the more hiddenly necessitated aspect of the *natura naturans*.

The song of the arch-angels praises the natural universe with its governing system of laws and its dynamism. Here is no static harmony but a picture which expresses immanence and infinity, the inner conflicts and contradictions of the universe, as well as the laws which bind it into a unified system.

From this consideration of the macrocosm, focus shifts to the earth as an integral part of the natural universe, thus sharing in the contradictions intrinsic to it — symbolized by the changes between night and day and by the opposition of the various elements: earth, water, air, fire. In an even tighter focus, man comes to center stage with the arrival of Mephisto, who introduces the case of the human being, whereupon the Lord chooses to discuss the example of Faust. Mephisto is interpreted by the *GDL* as being limited in his activity to the earthly sphere. For this reason he is not on the same footing as the Lord, who thus has no need to take up his bet about Faust. By contrast to the "Christian" devil, Mephisto has no transcendent sphere of influence but is entirely integrated into the earthly sphere. He is related to the sphere of the Earth Spirit, the spirit in tune with the world and all its activity. (208)

When it comes to understanding Mephisto's own account of his identity, the text itself yields up some interesting bases for the pantheistic interpretation. The darkness of which Mephisto claims to be a part was a chaos where there was no distinction of anything from anything, where all was darkness and night — which was to become the mother of all being.

That is the image of a monstrous, immanent self creation intrinsic to nature's development. It is the poetic version of the dialectical principles of pantheism, *natura naturans* and *natura naturata*, nature as a creating and as a created principle in one. (208)

As part of the darkness — which gives birth to light — Mephisto is a negative, destructive principle corresponding to the Earth Spirit as the positive principle of creation, development and movement in the earthly sphere. Mephisto stands for all those nature elements in human experience which threaten to destroy man or to impede his development. Even though he has partial success, the results are never quite to his liking. He is "Part of the Power which would/Do evil constantly, and constantly does good" ("Er ist ein Teil von jener Kraft, die stets das Böse will und stets das Gute schafft").[10] In dealing with Faust, he operates as the same negative principle also in the social sphere and in the sphere of human history. In these more strictly human spheres, he acts in opposition to man. He is, in addition, a nihilist and a cause of chaos. Wherever there is inhuman, destructive and anarchic activity taking place, Mephisto has a role to play. But here, too, his negativity is never totally independent but is tied inescapably to the positive principle of development, so that in the end society and history — as well as the individual — benefit from his ill-intentioned activities.

Within the pantheist system they present, the *GDL* writers attempt to define the relationship between the Lord and Faust. The Lord, as representative of universal laws and development in nature (207f.), has a position and

---

[10] David Luke. *Faust Part One.* 42; HA lines 1335f.

function superior to that of Faust, who is seen as subject to this necessitating force as it were from outside himself. In this sense he is a servant (Knecht). But the necessitating force is not seen as absolute, for at least in some respects it leaves Faust the freedom to go his own way, to serve in his own confused (verworren) way. From a philosophical point of view, there can be no pretense that this relationship between necessity and freedom is easily intelligible — if it is intelligible at all. But the Marxists are not the first philosophers to be confronted with such insoluble antinomies.

Individual and species

But in this context, how is Faust himself to be understood? For the *GDL* Marxists he is, on the one hand, very clearly presented as an individual with the concrete problems one might expect in a scholar of his time; and, on the other hand, he represents humanity; (211) but this does not imply anything more than that he is like thousands in his generation. He is not the manifestation or the fore-grounding of a deeper reality the way the Lord is the representative of universal law and development. By contrast, Faust is just a case in point, one example amongst many possible examples. In this limited sense he is typical of other human beings. In this important respect the *GDL* Marxists differ from Lukács, for whom Faust is both individual and species (Gattung), so that, for example, what is tragic for him (his destruction of Gretchen and, later, of Philemon and Baucis) is not tragic for the species, because personal tragedies are seen as unavoidable steps in the course of its development. As we have seen above, Lukács ties the play in with the development of German philosophy, from the subjective idealism of Kant and Fichte to the objective idealism of Schelling and Hegel (140/172f.), so that already in 1790 students of Fichte and Schelling were hailing *Faust* as an idealization of humanity, depicting the life of mankind, encompassing its past, present and future. (140/173) This development of the species is seen by Lukács in relation to the development of the "World Mind" in Hegel's contemporaneously written *Phenomenology of Mind.*

While there is no explicit rejection of Lukács's view at this point, it is clear that the *GDL* Marxists have moved a long way forward. Lukács, in his study of Goethe, always stressed the inner harmony which many of his figures strove for and even achieved. Lukács (and Goethe) saw this harmony as capable of development to include harmony with the world at large — with nature and society — although both realized that, before this could happen on a broad scale, many sweeping and fundamental changes would have to take place in European political and social structures. Whereas Lukács is preoccupied with the theme of full and harmonious development of the individual in the context of society — and traces this theme back to the renaissance — the *GDL* interpretation passes it over. Despite Lukács's conscious rejection, in his *Theory of the Novel*, of his own earlier involvement with Geistesgeschichte, he is still accused, as we have seen above, of working with abstractions and looking for an inner core in man which resembles an essence. He sees the development of this core as intrinsically part of a developing "World Mind" à la Hegel. From what we have seen in the context of *Faust*, these accusations seem to be substantiated, and it is understandable that in the more modern, post-war context, Marxist literary theory would reject the emphasis on such a unified subject seen as inwardly secure and ultimately able to resist all the undermining social pressures which threaten to unbalance it. In fact, in interpreting the text where Faust speaks about expanding his individual self to become the self of humanity — a text which Lukács takes at its face value — the *GDL* takes a radically different view. Here Faust is seen as overbearingly confident, giving Mephisto a chance of causing Faust's downfall:

> Here Faust feels exalted. He overestimates himself and identifies himself with humanity. This is not the idea expressed in the Prolog, where there was no question of identification. This latter idea is a product of an exaggerated sense of his own importance. (216)

Optimism?

Lukács's optimism is not completely shared by the *GDL* Marxists. The Lord's confidence that Faust will not be brought down by Mephisto is interpreted by Lukács as representing Goethe's own view and is endorsed by Lukács himself. There is nothing wrong with Faust that could not be explained by the complex of circumstances in which he finds himself. The *GDL* Marxists see it differently. Similarly, the interpretation of the small world and the larger world marks a difference. For Lukács, the former is the microcosm, the personal world which Faust shares with Gretchen; and the latter is the macrocosm: the larger world of society and politics and of the future (i.e. all the spheres which provide for the development of the individual personality and for the development of the species). For the *GDL*, the main basis for distinguishing between the two worlds is that, while both are spheres of social life and are historically co-existent with one another, the small world refers to

> the sphere of the exploited and the oppressed, the unprivileged and those cut off from the process of making political and social decisions. It refers to the "lower" class — those who have not yet become aware of their social potential and have not yet become involved in the movement of history.
>
> (217f.)

By contrast, the "große Welt" is the sphere of those

> who rule and exercise power, who look on their privileged and dominant status as natural and eternal. From this blinkered position they exercise their controlling function. (218)

This latter distinction of the *GDL* authors reflects a more concretely politicized view than that of Lukács, and it could be argued that to this extent Lukács is more closely in touch with the play itself, whereas the *GDL* authors too rigidly suit the requirements of a more recent Marxist reception theory regarding the classics. They are certainly less interested than Lukács in promoting the organic conception of human harmony (based on an idealist "inner core" theory).

Gretchen

A further indication of a relatively dampened enthusiasm by comparison with Lukács can be seen in the interpretation of the role played by Margarete, not just in *Part One*, but in the play as a whole. The *GDL* sees Margarete as a working-class girl who is the victim of social circumstances. She suffers a double suppression: firstly, as a member of the lower classes and, secondly, as a woman. Thus, through her plight, the problem of the liberation of humanity, which is here claimed to be the central theme of the play, is brought sharply into focus. (219) In this interpretation, Margarete is taken seriously as an independent partner who retains her autonomy over against Faust. The integrity of her love for Faust is never in doubt, and she shows herself able to shoulder the whole burden of its responsibility. This love, seen as part of "that powerful force of love, understood pantheistically, which exerts its influence throughout the universe" (219) survives the ravages of her social and historical situation, even though she loses her life through them. She thus gives Faust the example of integrated humanity (integren Menschentums) (219) and, by virtue of this example, at the end of *Part Two*, her life has a function in the resolution of the Faust conflict, which, given the general tenor of her life, would perhaps have seemed improbable.

This *GDL* analysis of the importance and function of Margarete occurs in the section dealing with *Part One*. After the significance attached to Gretchen and Eternal Womanhood, the reader would expect an expansion and development of the analysis where it would be most appropriate — at the end of *Part Two*. But, in fact, here the comments about Margarete are extremely brief. She is mentioned twice: first, in a phrase registering that she is amongst the penitent women; and second, in the statement:

Gretchen symbolizes in this final scene the true and pure love which is as much a part of the true human being as is active striving. It is intrinsic to the concept of progressive and developing humanity. (734)

This account of Gretchen is, by comparison with Lukács's interpretation, extremely dry and limited. Lukács does not reduce the meaning of Margarete to true and pure love. He is here less abstract! As we have seen, he sees Margarete as having the function of the woman, who, on the basis of her particular qualities and experience of life, is in a position to teach the man; and he stresses that Eternal Womanhood is Goethe's last avowal of the possibility of human perfection *on earth*. (190/234) This is a perfection which, for the man, depends on his relationship to the woman and on the close link with nature (Naturhaftigkeit) which he retains (with her). Thus Lukács highlights the very human aspects of the Faust and Gretchen story, and, in doing this, he remains closer to Goethe's text than does the *GDL*, which does not even mention Eternal Womanhood in this final section.

Gnade (divine grace) and secularization

At this point we can return to the theme of secularization. Common to both interpretations is the quoting of Goethe's words to Eckermann about the need to produce a conclusion which will prevent the work dissolving into vagueness. How is the play to conclude? Not simply with the death of Faust, who in his blindness misinterprets the sounds of digging around him. The play is not meant to end with Faust's delusion.

Referring to the conclusion of both *Part One* and *Part Two*, Lukács says that human perfection (eine menschliche Vollendung), whether for a type like Faust or for a type like Gretchen, was thought by Goethe to be impossible in the contemporary social situation. Yet this knowledge was combined with an unshakable faith in human development in the future; and Lukács claims that, because Goethe's horizon remained that of the middle-class society, he had no means of producing even a utopian picture of what this future would be like. "This explains," says Lukács, "his (arbitrary) choice of the Catholic heaven as a concluding image." (185/228) At this point he quotes part of Goethe's conversation with Eckermann on June 6, 1831. Because parts of the relevant section of the conversation are usually omitted in the Marxist discussion, we need to quote the important passage in full.

Eckermann writes:[11]

We spoke then about the conclusion, and Goethe drew my attention to the lines:

[11] *Gespräche mit Goethe* June 6, 1831.

This noble spirit saved alive
Has foiled the Devil's will!
He who strives and lives to strive
Can earn redemption still
And now that love itself looks down
To favour him with grace,
The blessed host with songs may crown
His welcome to this place.

These verses, said Goethe, "contain the key to Faust's salvation. In Faust himself there is an ever higher and purer activity right up to the end, and from above there is eternal love coming to his aid. This is quite in keeping with our religious ideas, according to which we become blessed not purely through our own efforts but, in addition, through divine grace.

Moreover, you will agree that the conclusion, where the saved soul is taken upwards, was difficult to do and that I could easily have got lost in vagueness in dealing with such supernatural (übersinnlichen) things which we can hardly sense (ahnen) at all. To counteract this I had to give my poetic intentions a limiting form and firmness by using the clearly defined figures and ideas of the Christian Church." (*Gespräche* June 6, 1831)

The question of what exactly Goethe envisages after the death of Faust is difficult for any reader, but it proves, I think, particularly difficult for a Marxist to interpret. Who or what survives this death? Does Goethe make it clear that the individual Faust survives it in some form which is real but hard to imagine, i.e. does Goethe make some claim for a real form of immortality for the individual (as opposed to a metaphorical form of immortality through his achievements as they influence later generations)? Any theory of individual immortality is incompatible with Marxism; and the Marxists write as if it is incompatible with Goethe's thinking. Hence the form of survival they find in Goethe's conclusion to *Faust* is that of the species. At this juncture there is no significant difference between the views of Lukács and those of the later Marxists. The individual dies, but the human race continues on to new generations and to a new future.

The short-comings of the fundamental Marxist interpretation in this context can be observed through a close scrutiny of Goethe's statements. The commentary on the verses quoted from *Faust* falls into two parts. In the first paragraph, Goethe explains the meaning contained in the lines which he considers to hold the key to Faust's salvation. In the second paragraph, which begins with "Moreover" (Übrigens), indicating that this is not the main point he is making about the final verses (Schlußverse), Goethe explains the artistic difficulties he experienced in dealing with the phase where the redeemed soul goes upward. His intention is precisely to show that the soul *does* go upward. The problem is how to show it. Any belief in real immortality puts immense strain on the imagination, even in a modern Christian context, where the details of the Catholic heaven are no longer simply accepted at face value. Even for a Christian believer in immortality, the conception of what it must be like is vague, and the traditional details are seen only as an attempt at visualization. For artistic reasons, Goethe needed to avoid vagueness and used a variation on the Catholic heaven to express his meaning.

To return to the question of the first paragraph, (which the Marxists usually do not quote): this has to be seen as an elucidation of the verses Eckermann quotes. These verses are spoken by an angel "carrying the immortal part of Faust" (Faustens Unsterbliches tragend).[12] As a condition of Faust's salvation it is envisaged that love has played its part from above. In the Marxist context what can this love from above possibly mean? Lukács admits that in the vivid Catholic milieu there is a suggestion of something like grace (aus der katholisierend malerischen Umgebung klingt etwas wie Gnade mit). To counter this impression that grace has a role to play, he claims — not very convincingly — that these verses end in a completely earthly way (vollkommen irdisch) with the words: "Eternal Womanhood leads us above." This solution is literally far-fetched. These final two lines he quotes occur 170 lines — or five pages — later! and it is not at all clear that they help to counter the impression that grace is at work.

In his first paragraph Goethe gives his own interpretation of the verses spoken by the angel. He refers, on the one hand, to Faust's own activity: "an ever loftier and purer activity right up to the end" and on the other to the "eternal love coming to his aid from on high." This reference to the activity from above is far stronger than what for Lukács is a mere "suggestion" (Mitklingen). Then the next part of Goethe's commentary makes Lukács's position clearly untenable. Goethe explicitly excludes the notion that man can become blessed purely through his own power ("bloß durch eigene Kraft selig werden"); he needs equally the supplement of divine grace (hinzukommende göttliche Gnade). This notion of double activity involving one's own resources and divine grace corresponds, according to Goethe, to "our own religious ideas" (unserer religiösen Vorstellung) — which are not sought out purely for the sake of artistic convenience but are relevant to his own convictions.

It should be clear that the Marxist tradition has wrestled with the *Faust* text in such a way as to plumb some of its many depths. No single interpretation can do everything, and if some short-comings of the materialist position have emerged, this is not to deny that the Marxist tradition, inherited

---

[12] HA before line 11934.

and developed in East Germany, has served to highlight the relevance of Goethe and his *Faust* to important aspects of modern intellectual life in Europe.

New discussions:
Faust and *Urfaust*

It is a puzzling fact that, in the extensive *GDL* passages dealing with the *Faust* material, there is no discussion of Goethe's *Urfaust*.[13] As we saw above, there was, in the 1970s, a shift to a more critical view of the Faust figure, reflecting a new cultural policy. In fact, the *GDL*'s Faust interpretations themselves, being far less rigid than the earlier official views, contributed to new conditions where ultimately the 1984 *Urfaust* production by the Berliner Ensemble was feasible. While this was not a reversion to Brecht's *Urfaust*, it represented a break with the official policy typical of the 1950s and 1960s. Goethe and his Faust were no longer on a pedestal but were more usefully assimilated as an essential part of the Marxist inheritance.

In the late 1980s, well before there could be any expectation of the events of 1989, the *Weimarer Beiträge* were publishing a series of essays centered on the interpretation of Goethe's *Faust*. This discussion revived the old controversy. Günter Hartung spoke of the renewal of the "old debate about whether Goethe's Faust is to be seen as a figure of warning or a shining example."[14] More precisely, he recalls a debate with his colleague, Hans-Günther Thalheim in which, in contrast to Thalheim, he had put forward the view that

> the Faust figure was presented by the author as problematic and that to interpret Faust unconditionally as a model is a straight contradiction of the author's intention. (Hartung: 285)

In his new essay, Hartung aimed at examining the structure of Faust's character as intended by Goethe. He wanted to

> grasp the poetic idea, the main thrust in so far as this could be done from a study of the plans, sketches, paralipomena, and any other personal testi-

---

[13] This is curious, since the conception of literary history expressed in the *GDL* is certainly broad enough to include the discussion of "fragments." But by the late 1970s, when volumes 6 and 7 of the *GDL* appeared, Gerhard Scholz's particular method of analyzing the basic elements (such as the *Urfaust* scenes) and the way they were transformed when incorporated into a finished work (such as *Faust Part One*) was no longer in vogue, though it was central to his own important *Faust* book.

[14] "'Wilhelm Meisters Lehrjahre' und das Faustische." In: *Weimarer Beiträge* 36 (1990): 284

mony given by Goethe. Reference to the finished text should be a final consideration and should only be used as a check. (285)

Jens-F Dwars takes issue with this method:

> The question of the author's intention is not necessarily able to throw light
> on the "'idea" of the work and thus on its poetic density . . . Shouldn't the
> search for a not necessarily deliberate structure of Faust's character go hand
> in hand with a definition of the not necessarily deliberate structure of the
> text — with its own particular aesthetic laws? By going back to the historical structures and the experience the author has of them this could be
> achieved.[15]

Here Dwars is high-lighting a largely neglected approach to interpreting the Faust figure. He refers to the Marxist global interpretation of both Lukács and Scholz, which had shown Goethe's view of his era as the element which provided the unity of the text. They had interpreted the text as a drama of the human race or a drama of human liberation. Dwars criticizes these methods for not showing how the aesthetic transformation of Goethe's experience can be revealed in the literary structure of the text. Instead of this, these authors focus on a human core

> which breathed life into the human inheritance as a defense against Fascism
> and as a means of fostering a budding socialist society with all its heroic illusions. Emphasis on this core resulted in an ideological narrowness in the
> attempt to provide a text analysis related to social history. (Dwars: 1731)

Dwars's reference to the two authors exemplifies the main social and political preoccupations of the early East German intellectuals, in the context of which the scholarly writing is to be understood: the promotion of anti-Fascism and the construction of a budding socialist society. The core (Kern) smacks of a a pre-Marxist conception of the nature of man, and the new socialist developments are seen in too unrealistic a light (Illusionen). In contrast both to Hartung's interpretation and to the general trend of Marxist criticism, Dwars stresses the need to focus on the literary structure of the work. Thus he sets himself the task of sketching out the master and servant relationship as one of the motifs which give expression to the character of the age. He does not want to limit himself to separate analyses of certain themes like religion, art, nature, politics, or economics, but he wants to study the shape they take as aesthetic manifestations of a particular historical subjectivity.

---

[15] Jens-F. Dwars. "Dichtung im Epochenumbruch. Goethes Historisierung des 'Faustischen' im Spannungsfeld von Herrschaft und Knechtschaft." In: *Weimarer Beiträge* 36 (1990): 1731.

Dwars's starting point is the "Prolog in Heaven." He sees as a particularly relevant element of structure analysis the function of the Lord:

> As a quasi authorial narrator he has an overview of the whole of the work and points to a level of meaning which is opened up to an alert audience though it is beyond the grasp of the figures in the play. (1733)

Here he is introducing an element of interpretation which features too little in Marxist criticism. Although Manfred Naumann made important theoretical contributions to a Marxist study of "Autor-Leser-Adressat" (author, reader, addressee), his ideas seem to have been insufficiently used in the business of interpreting actual texts.

Dwars's idea of the quasi authorial narrator can be developed much further. We can ask whether the author does, in fact, reveal to us his opinion about the Faust figure, and if so, what this opinion is. Above all, it can be shown that the newer views suggested by Hartung and Dwars can be applied back further than the 1808 *Faust Part One*. It can be shown that, even without the authorial figure of the Lord, Goethe reveals, within the text, an authorial critical attitude towards the Faust figure.

In approaching this problem regarding the *Urfaust* text we can find a clear analogy with the *Werther* text, which dates from roughly the same period — both being products of Goethe's Storm and Stress phase. If, in *Werther*, the author (within the text) was not sufficiently taken into account, perhaps a similar problem prevails in the *Urfaust* text — with similar consequences. If, as Peter Müller showed (*Zeitkritik*: 18–28) the reception of the *Werther* text by Lessing, Nicolai, and Goeze on the one hand, and Wieland and Lenz on the other, was quite different because of the *a priori* points of view, it would seem that the text itself would have played too insignificant a role — with the result that the contributions of these writers tells us more about them and their own views of life than about Goethe's text itself.

For his revision of the *Werther* text for the 1787 version, Goethe was able to comment on his text by certain new insertions. His intentions could be revealed in two ways. Firstly, a comparison of the two texts would indicate Goethe's dissatisfaction with certain impressions made by the earlier text and a desire on his part to change them. Secondly, the actual insertions themselves and their particular function within the text provide another way of indicating the author's intentions (those of the author-within-the-text).

Similarly, by the addition of the "Prolog in Heaven" to *Faust Part One* Goethe was able to achieve a certain obvious distance to his Faust figure, a vantage point from which he could be critical. The Lord and Mephisto express two different opinions about Faust. The bet they enter into highlights the difference in their views. Thus the reader is prepared for the first appearance of Faust and is ready to interpret him from two different perspectives.

The question about the outcome of the bet is already implanted in the reader's mind: will the Lord's or will Mephisto's view be supported by the text? What Faust himself says will not be simply accepted at face value on the basis of a Faust and Goethe identification. Faust himself will speak and act considering himself a free agent, while in fact he will be led from above and at the same time be exposed to manipulation by his dependence on Mephisto's magic.

But what of the Faust figure in *Urfaust*, where there is no "Prolog" to help establish these "superior" points of view? The question arises whether and by what means the author's voice can be found within the play. Of course, there is no narrator in the Brechtian sense, but it is possible for the author to introduce alienation effects into the text which distance the reader from the central Faust figure.

It could appear at first sight that, without the presence of some form of independent narrator, the task of finding the voice of the author in the play would be more difficult than in an epistolary novel like *Werther*, though the task of relativizing the central figure in a play would be easier than that of relativizing the protagonist in the novel. Faust's self-interpretation is more easily relativized because, aside from his monologs, other voices and points of view are heard and considered which are independent of him and his own self-understanding. When in the *Werther* novel other voices like those of Lotte, Albert, the Amtmann, and Wilhelm are heard, this happens largely to the extent that Werther himself permits it. Their opinions affect the reader only indirectly. Their status in the novel depends on what Werther tells the reader about them. Any weight they may have is the weight which Werther himself attributes to them. If we take the extreme case of the people at court, we find that in their contempt for him they represent a particular interpretation of him as a person. But their opinion is not able to relativize the reader's opinion of Werther, because Werther is able to discredit them by what he reports in his letters. Naturally, once we become convinced of the extreme onesidedness of Werther's ideas, we might start to surmise that his critics at the court have a valid point to make — but this remains to a large extent surmise. Much the same applies to the weight attributed to Lotte and the other characters mentioned.

With *Urfaust* it is different. Even the mighty monolog in the "Night" scene, in which Faust gives free expression to his views on the world and his place in it, turns out to be not simply a monolog. Given that the Earth Spirit, who is seen to be in every respect superior to Faust and totally independent of him, knows about the wishes, hopes, and longings expressed by Faust in the "Monolog" and who appears in response to what Faust says there, the "Monolog" is really to be seen as a dialogue. Despite the fact that the Earth Spirit appears in response to Faust's conjurings, he is in no way Faust's servant or creation. He belongs to a higher (or lower) sphere in which, it is clear, a man like Faust cannot survive or function. In this first encounter with the independently "other," Faust realizes that his self-interpretation has no absolute validity but is relativized by the opinion of a figure who has a higher status and is totally independent of him.

What opinions of Faust are relativized? When he thinks of himself as a God-like figure, this presumption is removed by the Earth Spirit's ironical reference to him as Faust the superman who, when confronted with the spirit he summons up, is filled with "pitiable fear." The extent of his disillusionment is underscored when, on the disappearance of the Earth Spirit, the gap is filled by Wagner, the "dry-as-dust toady" (trockener Schwärmer). Disappointed in his ambitions to raise himself up to a higher world populated by spirits, he now has to cope with the world of his "famulus" (or academic servant), which he experiences as shallow. Thus Faust's self-understanding is relativized not merely for the reader but, in this case, also for himself. There will be other instances where the reader will be led to see Faust's behaviour as unacceptable even where Faust himself does not. The scenes of the "Gretchen Tragedy" are, of course, revealing.

The "Gretchen Tragedy"

Here Faust is seen at first in a quite negative light. His behaviour is accompanied in the text by a three-fold "commentary" by the author, which drives a wedge between what Faust thinks of himself and what the reader thinks of him. The first of these "commentaries" is the brutal nature of the language which the author puts in his mouth. After the refined, if exaggerated, expressions with which he greets Margarete, the uncouth language he uses in persuading Mephisto to procure her for him alienates the reader and functions as a kind of unconscious self-commentary on the part of Faust. It is the language of a rough, insensitive, immature young man who, when attracted by a young woman, sees her as something to be had, something he can easily get — in a word, as an object to be possessed for a time. Thus, the gift he asks Mephisto to procure for Margarete is not seen as a joy in store for the girl, but quite simply as a handy means to seduce her. Significantly, it makes no difference whether Mephisto or Faust himself seeks out the present.

In this context, the Marxist commentaries are never severe enough in their judgment of Faust. The "hero" is often seen too positively as a representative of a progressive class (thus Lukács, Scholz, Werner[16]), with the result that the irresponsible attitudes of Faust are either ignored or condoned;

---

[16] Hans-Georg Werner. "Probleme einer sozialistischen *Faust 1*–Aufführung." In: *Weimarer Beiträge* 4 (1971) 127–160.

even where, as with Gert Liebich[17] and Heinz Hamm,[18] Faust's behaviour is seen in a negative light, their judgment of Faust turns out to be very mild. In this way the seriousness of Goethe's "commentary" is not fully appreciated. This phenomenon is partly to be explained by the Marxist tendency to shift the focus rapidly from the individual to the social conditions which produce the individual.

The second commentary on Faust's behaviour is given in Mephisto's remarks and jests, in words like "Come, this is Randy Andy talk" (Sprichst ey wie der Hans Lüderlich); and: "Well, now you're almost talking French" (Ihr sprecht schon fast wie ein Franzos). Then the low, libertine language of Mephisto, expressing the level on which he expects Faust to operate:

> . . . after long preparation
> And complicated titillation,
> To make her willing and soft to the touch;
> In Italian tales you'll have read as much[19]

is capped by Faust, whose reply: "I've appetite enough without all that" shows that he is operating at an even lower level.

A third commentary is to be found in the presentation of Gretchen's genuine loveliness and innocence, qualities which Faust at first does not appreciate. "She's over fourteen," he says, brutally implying that any girl of that age is ready for seduction. When he first accosts her in the street he behaves à la Don Juan. In the "Evening" scene, when, with Mephisto's help he gains access to her bedroom, his attitude soon changes. In the "Welcome, sweet twilight" monolog (Willkommen süsser Dämmerschein) the reader hears tones of the contemplative Faust from the "Night" scene: "Oh sad full moon, my friend" (O sähst du voller Mondenschein) etc. But the reader-audience naturally perceives the unsavory character of Faust's behaviour before Faust himself becomes fully conscious of it. Thus the otherwise fine-sounding, lyrical words:

> How this whole place breathes deep content
> And order and tranquillity!
> What riches in this poverty,
> What happiness in this imprisonment!   (2691–4)

---

[17] Gert Liebich. *Faust und Mephisto im "Urfaust."* Diss. Leipzig, 1975. Cf. Especially 156–158.

[18] Heinz Hamm. *Goethes "Faust." Werkgeschichte und Textanalyse.* Berlin: Volk und Wissen, Volkseigener Verlag, 1988, 57–58.

[19] Lines of *Faust* are quoted from HA volume 3. The line numbering in David Luke's translation is identical.

which are followed by Faust's awakening to the indecency of his situation, are revealed as cloaking a suspect attitude. This fine language is akin to the high-sounding language of seduction which, through its religious overtones, will confuse Margarete. As he draws back the curtains at her bed-side with the words

> Here the child lay, her tender heart
> Full of warm life, here the pure love
> Of God's creative forces wove
> His likeness by their sacred art! (2713–6)

his language reveals the mixture of eroticism and religion which the innocent girl cannot resist. Faust himself suddenly becomes aware of the dishonesty of what he is doing. He realizes at this point that he has no right to be here. His better instinct tells him to leave forever. Of course, his resolve is too weak to survive Mephisto's goadings, and when he leaves the room and then Margarete enters, the unsavory feeling experienced by the reader is contrasted with the impact made by the total innocence and goodness of the girl. The "King of Thule" song, which reveals her capacity for loyalty and complete dedication, provides the stark contrast with what the reader will learn — and already suspects — of Faust's behaviour. This contrast functions as a continual commentary on the Faust figure.

Of special importance is the author's constant interest in drawing the reader-audience's attention to the dangers lurking in Faust's language. The abstractions which are a natural part of it: "simple innocence," "humble lowliness," "value," etc. are lost on Margarete. (3102) She can't live in his world. All she can do is interrupt his flow of language and take her turn at speaking. Yet behind her language, for all its simplicity, there is a direct awareness of which Faust is not yet capable. It is clear she thinks he will abandon her. She says forthrightly that she will have time enough to think of him — i.e. when he is gone! Here Faust learns from her. He takes her point and manages to listen without interruption. But how little he learns is seen from the continued contrast: her account of the simple family life she leads, with its mixture of basic happiness and drudgery, and the simple game with the flower show her world as separated by a chasm from that implied in Faust's language. His reply to the result of her simple game (he loves me, loves me not) is over-powering:

> Yes, my love! (Kind) The flower speaks,
> And let it be your oracle! He loves you:
> Do you know what that means? He loves you! (3184–86)

and

Don't be afraid! Oh, let my eyes,
My hands on your hands tell you what
No words can say:
To give oneself entirely and to feel
Ecstasy that must last for ever!
For ever! — For its end would be despair.
No, never-ending! Never ending!   (3188–94)

Naturally, we are reminded of Mephisto's taunts that Faust will dazzle her
with talk of eternal love and fidelity — which, of course, he does, with disas-
trous consequences. This combination of "commentaries" — the contrast
with Margarete's world and the prophecy of Mephisto — should leave the
reader in no doubt as to the author's critical judgment of Faust. The author
has a judgment, and he makes his judgment clear.

It is worth concluding this chapter with a somewhat surprising perspec-
tive which opens up within the East German Marxist ranks.

Günter Mieth

The fact of secularization in Goethe's thinking and writing is not simply a
skepticism with regard to tradition; instead, Goethe had found in Spinoza a
more modern view which seemed to explain life more fully and with greater
validity. One has to disagree with the early East German Marxist tendency to
use Spinoza to show how, under his influence, Goethe was fundamentally
materialist in his thinking. To be accused of atheism was, of course, the fate
of Spinoza in his time. Goethe was himself under suspicion of atheism when,
in the mid-1780s, his commitment to Spinozist ideas hit the headlines. But
these judgments about Spinoza and Goethe are all extreme. Goethe himself
referred to Spinoza as the most Christian of men, an opinion on his part
which invites some clear distinctions: Goethe was convinced that, in some
central aspects, the organized Churches were corrupt and therefore un-
Christian, and that certain central dogmas (about sinful human nature and
the need for redemption) were simply false, but that one could reject all of
these and still be inwardly Christian. Without wishing to develop this line of
thought any further here, let us simply record that, in his focus on Spinoza,
Goethe thought he saw in him and his work more real Christianity than was
to be found anywhere in the Churches.

In Spinoza, two main facets attracted Goethe. The first one is highlighted
best, to my mind, and perhaps ironically, by a scholar writing in the East
German Marxist tradition. Günter Mieth's essay on the final scene of *Faust*.

Part Two[20] shows the Spinozist elements in Goethe's writing and, paradoxically, draws attention to the specifically Christian aspect of Spinoza's mind which greatly appealed to Goethe. Mieth's analysis of the final *Faust* scene is centered on the close relationship between love and vision, and it is precisely in this respect that Mieth underlines the intimate affinities between Spinoza and Goethe.

The second facet of Spinoza's work which attracted Goethe was that it posited the existence of *one* single substance, implying the absolute identity of God and nature, the *natura naturans* and the *natura naturata* — the producer of nature and the nature produced being merely two aspects of the same thing. This conception was radically different from the creator-creature relationship of the Christian tradition, which insisted on the absolute independence the Creator enjoyed and the absolute dependence of the creature on the Creator. The East German Marxist tradition of Goethe scholarship had relied heavily, in interpreting Goethe, on Spinoza's formula *deus sive natura* (God *or* nature). This identification of God and nature enabled the scholars in the Marxist tradition to cope smoothly with the many passages in which Goethe's respect and enthusiasm for the Divine was evident. It proved possible — and for a Marxist-Leninist it was certainly desirable — to substitute the word nature for the word God and thereby be operating on much more familiar ground. But though the God and Nature identification is extremely important for an understanding of Goethe's work, Günter Mieth pointed out, in his quite daring article published in 1986, that it is only *one* important aspect of the relationship between Spinoza and Goethe. In our present context, by far the more important aspect, according to Mieth, is the link between love and vision.

In a letter of 1786 to his friend Friedrich Heinrich Jacobi, Goethe, defending Spinoza, writes:

> If you say one can only *believe* in God, then I must tell you that I lay great store by *vision* and when Spinoza speaks of the scientia intuitiva and says: "hoc cognoscendi genus procedit ab adaequata idea essentiae formalis quorundam Dei attributorum" (this mode of knowledge proceeds from the adequate idea of the formal essence of certain attributes of God), these few words give me courage to devote my whole life to the contemplation of concrete things."[21]

Günter Mieth points out that, in Spinoza's philosophy, intuitive vision and intellectual, spiritual ("geistige") love form a direct unity. Vision and love are, in this system of knowledge and ethics, inseparable from one another.

---

[20] Günter Mieth. "Szene 'Bergschluchten' in Goethes *Faust*" — spinozistisch verstanden." In: *Impulse* 9 (1986). Berlin: 175–186.

[21] Quoted by Mieth 176f. from the Weimarer Ausgabe 4 214.

The main thrust of Mieth's article is then to show that the final scene of *Faust* is essentially structured by the way in which vision and love are correlated. (Mieth: 177)

Mieth differentiates between three central voices in the scene. The first is the "pater ecstaticus," who, "floating on high and below," expresses in his words an inner state of unrest which alternates between pain and pleasure and keeps him bound to the sphere of subjective sense experience, a level of knowledge which in Spinoza's system is the lowest: the *imaginatio*. The next voice is that of the "pater profundus," who sees (schaut) the landscape with its woods and boulders. He is aware of natural reality and understands it as the work of *love*. His knowledge — the next higher step on the ladder — corresponds to the adequate knowledge of the *notiones communes* in Spinoza's system. But, while he grasps nature *sub specie aeternitatis* (under the aspect of eternity), his response on the level of feeling is inadequate. Only the "pater seraphicus" reaches the highest level of Spinoza's *scientia intuitiva*. Occupying a middle region, he has eyes attuned to the world and the earth. He mediates between the earth and the world first by making real insight into the earth possible and then by drawing attention to the presence of God in it.

With Spinoza, Goethe thinks in terms of an identity between nature and God, so that God and nature are one and the same substance. For Goethe, nature is not a source of images which can be used to help grasp something of a far higher order, the natural being used as an avenue for approaching the supernatural. The unity of substance for Goethe — adapting Spinoza — does away with the distinctions between the natural and the supernatural altogether.

After the debacle in which, by the end of *Part One*, Faust has destroyed Margarete's existence and has himself reached the brink of despair, we find him at the beginning of *Part Two* collapsed on a grassy bank where he is then gradually revived by nature's spirits. When he reaches the threshold of full consciousness, he hears the approach of dawn as the brilliant sun comes up over the mountains. As he turns to confront its brilliant light, he is, like Dante in the latter stages of the *Paradiso*, blinded. He turns away with a searing pain in his eyes. He is forced to fix his gaze on the earth, and he concludes: "So let the sun remain in my back."[22] But his attention is caught more and more by a massive waterfall which throws its spray high into the air producing a rainbow with what he calls changing permanence (Wechseldauer). Its outline is at one moment brilliantly clear and at the next moment it has disappeared, only to reappear again seconds later. This changing but constant rainbow he interprets as the mirror of human endeavor. If we think

[22] HA volume 3, line 4715.

about this, he says, we will understand that we possess the light, not in its purest form but refracted as in the brilliant colors of the rainbow. Given Goethe's identification of God and nature à la Spinoza, this perception that there is another dimension to life raises questions. There is not the clear and explicit belief in an after-life as understood by the orthodox Christian and as expressed by Dante in the *Paradiso*. Yet, by the same token, the more rigid of the Marxists are simply wrong, I think, when they treat Goethe as an atheist. Goethe shifted his gaze from transcendence to immanence in such a way that the intensity of his focus on nature, on this world, amounted to profound religiosity. His preoccupation with science was not a contradiction of this but rather a ratification. When, from within the Marxist ranks, Günter Mieth emphasizes the importance of *love* and *vision* in the closing pages of *Faust* — and implicitly in the closing stages of Goethe's life — , he is at least indirectly pointing to Goethe's religious experience. Love of what, vision of what? For the orthodox mediaeval Christian (e.g. Dante) the answer was clear: love of God, vision of God. For Goethe, the modern man for whom Spinoza's religious thinking wrought as radical a change as that brought about by Immanuel Kant for generations of other modern thinkers, the answer is less clear. Love of what, vision of what? We can't simply say: love of God, vision of God. Nor can we simply return to the subjective inner glow of the Storm and Stress: "feeling is everything" (Gefühl ist alles). This idea cannot fit a man who, for decades, had been passionately committed, as Goethe was, to scientific studies. So perhaps we can do no better than suggest that, whereas the orthodox Christian enjoyed security and clarity of vision in his adherence to a relatively fixed theological position, Goethe based his security on retaining a fiercely intense focus on aspects of nature which he considered inseparable from a divine presence. It was, according to Spinoza, not possible to separate God from nature, and Goethe had no desire to do so.

11: *Elective Affinities (Die Wahlverwandtschaften)*

Whereas the earlier novels lent themselves readily to a sociological inter-
pretation — in the one instance because of Werther's obvious conflict
with society and in the other instance because Wilhelm Meister was clearly
being led out of his subjective world and taught to take his place in soci-
ety — *Elective Affinities* posed more serious problems for the Marxist inter-
preters. As we have suggested in the case of *Wilhelm Meisters Apprenticeship*,
the playing down of the role of Susanna's pietism in the novel presented
grave difficulties. But in the context of the whole novel it must be admitted
that the social aspect is of paramount importance.

With regard to *Elective Affinities*, it is also clear that the social dimension
plays an important role. The author's treatment of the marriage between
Charlotte and Eduard, of the relationship between the Major and Charlotte,
and of that between Eduard and Ottilie, inevitably engages the reader in the
problems of the society whose conventions give rise to the interpersonal
problems dealt with in the novel.

In this chapter, however, it will be useful to attempt an evaluation of the
aptness of the Marxist interpretation of this particular novel. It is worth ex-
amining in detail how Goethe portrays Ottilie, who undoubtedly plays a
central role. It is no doubt clear that the social issues are vital. But it should
become equally clear that the level of secularization represented by the
Marxist stand-point is not appropriate for an appreciation of at least one issue
profoundly involving Ottilie: namely, the religious dimension of her experi-
ence. It will be necessary to deal with this issue in detail, so as to high-light a
central area in Goethe's writing and in his experience (behind the writing)
which on principle is not accessible to a purely materialist Marxist interpreta-
tion.

Social theme

The reader of the section in the *GDL* which deals with *Elective Affinities* is
struck by the focus on the social dimension. The four main characters are
criticized because their activity is geared towards the total satisfaction of their
need for contemplation and enjoyment. (7 636) The exaggerated subjectiv-
ity of the main characters who are totally out of touch with the problems of
their period is seen to reflect the real social state of the landed nobility. After

the spiritual adultery, only the Captain becomes aware that he is not fulfilling his full potential and that he is merely whiling away his time in leisurely activities. (636)

Later, in the treatment of the novella within the novel, the youth's heroic action is seen first and foremost as a contribution to the common good. In this internal plot, the lovers have a social orientation which distinguishes them radically from the main characters in the novel. The utopia of this novella is made to shine like a beacon into the novel. The novella, in which nature and culture, the individual and society are in harmony — despite their contradictoriness — shows up what is lacking in the broader context of the novel itself. In this way, the novel is seen by the authors of the *GDL* as "sozialkritisch." (637)

The social characteristics of the young hero of the novella carry over into the novel through the agency of the Captain, who is seen to be the only figure in the novel who clearly develops and seeks to engage in a socially useful activity. (638) Ottilie, as a member of the middle-class, is seen to have a hidden affinity with the Captain in her (seemingly fruitless) search for a meaningful social activity. What separates or links the four main characters is the degree of their orientation towards the community. The least important in this respect are Charlotte and Eduard, as representatives of the landed nobility. (638)

As a counter-poise to this strong emphasis on the socially critical aspect of the novel, we need to highlight the important and — in the Marxist interpretations — largely neglected topic of the religious dimension to Ottilie's experience.

Ottilie's religious orientation

The social orientation of the novel is relativized by consideration of the fact that its main proponent, the Captain, departs towards the end of the first part of the novel and thereafter exerts no significant direct influence on the other characters. A development takes place within Ottilie which is not primarily social and which had already begun to manifest itself in the boarding school — before she came under the Captain's influence. It is important to look at this other theme: the holy, the inner life, which is contrasted with the social dimension though not divorced from it.

When we read in the *GDL* (638) in relation to the final chapter of the novel, that the traditional Christian motifs are made by Goethe to serve the presentation of the wholly secularized content — activity geared towards the common good — we need to question this claim. How obvious is it that we are dealing with a wholly secularized content? Is it not far more obvious that the religious motifs, which we shall see are inextricably woven into the novel, are in fact reliable indicators of the main preoccupation of the novel?

The Marxist collective finds the final chapter problematic. Having tried to situate Ottilie within the ranks of the active (productive) middle class, they now have to face the problem that the success they attribute to her is coupled with her physical death, her victory with defeat, so that the novel ends in a contradiction. According to the collective, this does not amount to a conflict situation within Ottilie herself. The contradiction is an artistic one attributed to Goethe himself and stemming from the fact that he used the same figures and motifs to portray both socially critical and utopian aspects of the novel. Even more candidly: the contradictions involved in the conclusion of the novel indicate limitations in Goethe's ability to give artistic shape to his novel (Grenzen des Goetheschen Gestaltungsvermögens). (639)

Given the extreme nature of such judgments, it is imperative here to submit the text of the concluding chapter to close scrutiny to determine whether the problem is solved by recourse to Goethe's weakness as an artist or whether the chapter (and therefore much of the novel itself) should be interpreted quite differently: whether the reader needs to attribute to the whole religious sphere a role at least as significant as that of the social aspect; and whether Ottilie's experience, because belonging to the substance of the novel, is presented in its own right and not merely, as the Marxists would have it, as purely subordinate to the process of conjuring up a Goethean utopia.

H. Trevelyan's article on "Ottilie and Sperata" goes straight to the heart of the matter.[1] He claims that Sperata, the mother of Mignon, is in nearly every respect an earlier version of Ottilie. This extraordinary statement is quite crass and dismissive of Ottilie by comparison with the Marxist interpretation; yet both approaches empty out the specifically religious (not necessarily Christian) value and meaning with which I think Goethe imbues his final chapter.

A careful reading of *Wilhelm Meister's Apprenticeship* makes it obvious that Goethe, despite his compassionate portrayal of Sperata, sees her in a negative light. She is the victim of religious superstition which Goethe associates with the Catholic Church of the period and which is seen as endemic. Sperata, along with the Harpist and Mignon, forms part of a constellation of characters who are doomed to destruction, because, unlike Natalie and Wilhelm, they are not in harmony with nature. Sperata is classified with the sick

---

[1] Though not directly referred to by the *GDL*, this brief article has close affinity with the materialist orientation of the Marxist interpreters wherever revealed religion is under discussion. Thus it functions here as a contrast to what I am convinced is a more justifiable interpretation of Goethe's text.

and Natalie with the healthy. Both characters are separated by a gaping chasm.

Trevelyan highlights the common elements in the stories of Sperata and Ottilie: in both cases a man and a woman are drawn together into a passionate relationship under circumstances which make the fulfilment of their love be seen as a breach of morality. In the beginning both women give in to their passion but later realize the sinfulness of their action. They repent and freely renounce their love. In both cases the end is brought about by the loss of the child, whereby in both cases the drowning in the lake is a feature. Towards the end both women feel more and more elevated above earthly existence. They no longer feel the need to eat and drink, and death overtakes them gently. After death miraculous healing powers are attributed to both of them.

Operating with the familiar polar opposites — law and passion, necessity and freedom, polarity and intensification (Steigerung), conflict and reconciliation — Trevelyan maintains that because of her passionate attachment to her child (though it is the fruit of a forbidden, incestuous relationship with her brother) Sperata can, in death, be led on to a higher existence. Similarly, Ottilie, in whom the polar opposites are eventually reconciled, enjoys at this moment a resulting higher form of existence beyond that of normal human life.

The very basic structuralism of this interpretation, which does not distinguish between Sperata's higher existence and that of Ottilie, results in an unacceptable over-simplification. For an understanding of either novel it is important to distinguish the differences between the two figures.

If it is true that the superstitious preoccupation with animals' bones and the illusory conviction that her child had come to life again— Goethe's irony is evident, since we know that the child, Mignon, in fact had not died! — are characteristic of the disturbed mind of Sperata, what of the final chapter of *Elective Affinities*? What of the superstition and illusion here? To what extent is Goethe's irony, here too, at work? To uncover Goethe's meaning in both of these contexts, we need to examine the narrative perspectives.

The Sperata story

This story, being told only in retrospect and occurring in the second last chapter of the novel, makes Sperata seem like a memory captured in an old photograph album. The reader does not really know her, although, in order to make Mignon's origins and character understandable, Goethe produces this part of the jig-saw puzzle at the last moment. Within the whole structure of the novel the story of the Marquis and his brother, sister, and niece (the

Harpist, Sperata and Mignon) is totally subordinated to the main story concerning Wilhelm and the effect Natalie and her surroundings have on Wilhelm. The story of Sperata is inserted in the novel in the context of the death and burial ceremonies of Mignon. The funeral ritual does not take place in a church or chapel, but in the classical surroundings under the surveillance of the rationalistic Abbé, the enemy of all that could be considered "Romantic" — a term which can justifiably be applied to the constellation of characters comprising Sperata, the Harpist, and Mignon. It does not need to be said explicitly in the novel that the Abbé would abhor virtually everything associated with Sperata and with Mignon's origins: the strictness and foolish vanity of Sperata's father; the lie about Sperata's origin — which, with catastrophic results, served to obscure the brother and sister relationship; the total emotional instability of her brother; the defenseless position of Sperata, who is left to the mercy of the powerful and authoritarian clergy. These are all manifestations of a society against which the Abbé and the other members of the Tower Society are determined to protect their charges. Ironically, Goethe puts his criticism of the whole Sperata story in the mouth of the Harpist himself: when nature abhors something it makes its message clear. The creature which is not meant to be, cannot develop (werden); the creature which lives falsely is destroyed early. Barrenness, a wretched existence, early dissolution are the curses which characterize nature's severity. It is precisely this severity which typifies the "healthy" attitude towards life promoted by the Abbé (and Goethe).

Highlighting some elements of the Sperata story which run counter to this Goethean idea of nature and health will provide a sound basis for pointing up the difference between Sperata and Ottilie:

1. Sperata is a young woman who can neither read nor write, whereas Ottilie is described not only as one who has received a good education but as one who even seemed suitable to the Assistant to become an educator herself.

2. Ottilie falls in love with a married man, Sperata with a monk, so that each of the relationships implies a challenge to a comparable bond (marriage and religious vows); but in the case of Sperata there is, in addition, the "unnatural," incestuous dimension which does not obtain for Ottilie.

3. The physical union actually takes place between Sperata and the monk, her brother — she consents to breaking the religious vows of her partner. Ottilie, in her relationship with Eduard, holds back and waits for Charlotte to decide first about her relationship with Eduard.

4. Perhaps the most important difference between Sperata and Ottilie is their contrasting involvement with religion. As we will see in detail, Goethe shows Ottilie's religion as something completely internal: there

is no place in her life for involvement in the hierarchical Church with its external practices, its priests, community, and laws. By contrast, the religiosity to which Sperata is inclined by nature is entirely bound up with these things. Her lover was totally at the mercy of the Order and of the bishop. The family's confessor was in a position to manipulate the young mother: in terrifying imagery Goethe highlights this power which induced her, as a poor sinner, willingly to offer her neck to the executioner's axe and to beg to be separated from her brother. In Ottilie's life there is not the slightest trace of this clerical domination so abhorrent to Goethe. Ottilie's own passionate attachment to Eduard is able to disorient her, but outside forces cannot touch her. The zealous Mittler, a former pastor, can do damage to relationships but he is incapable of exercising any moral influence on Ottilie, who remains autonomous. Even where she decides to wait for Charlotte's decision about divorcing Eduard this is unrelated to the Church, it is an expression of loyalty to one who has always treated her lovingly as if she were her own daughter.

5. Sperata is a prisoner not only to the Church but to the superstitious society whose folklore induces her to think that, if she finds the bones of her drowned child and takes them to Rome, the Pope will restore the child to life and sanctify the relationship between the parents. The obvious simple-mindedness, ignorance, illusion, even insanity of Sperata hardly invite comparison with the mentality of Ottilie.

Yet there is the problem of the final chapter of Elective Affinities. There is a question of miracles being worked and the people believing in them and being influenced by them. But these "occur" after Ottilie's death. Thus they do not imply superstition on Ottilie's part. To find out Goethe's meaning in his relating of Ottilie's death, we need to examine the narrative perspective of the final chapter. What is presented by the narrator as fact and what is not?

Elective Affinities, final chapter.

The narrator reports how Nanny (Ottilie's young maid), despite all efforts to deter her, manages, from the vantage-point of a high room, to observe the approach of the funeral cortege bearing the corpse of Ottilie. The reader is first given the narrator's objective view-point in the simple statement: "The procession wound its way through the village on the path strewn with leaves." The next sentence shows the reader what Nanny saw. Here is a change in the perspective:

Nanny saw her mistress clearly beneath her. She had a clearer, more complete and lovelier view of her than all those in the procession.[2]

While it is clear that with this view the narrator is referring to one distinct from his own, it is also clear that he gives it a certain authority (a better view than that of those in the procession).

And now we learn what, according to Nanny's own conviction, came to pass: "Ottilie seemed, supernaturally, as if carried on clouds or waves, to make a sign to her maid." Then the focus shifts to what the narrator purely objectively reports: "And Nanny, confused, swaying, staggering crashed down." This objective report by the narrator also contains the mention of Nanny's "confusion," so that later her credibility as a witness is partly called into question. But her fall is presented as an objective fact. So too is the following report:

> The crowd was scattered in all directions with a fearful scream. In the ensuing tumult, the pall-bearers were forced to put down their burden. The young maid lay on the ground close by; every bone in her body *seemed* to have been broken. She was picked up and by chance or by some stroke of fate (Fügung) she was made to lean over the corpse; she herself *seemed* with the last ounce of life in her to try and reach her beloved mistress. Her trembling limbs had hardly touched Ottilie's garment and her limp fingers had hardly made contact with Ottilie's folded hands when the maid sprang up, raised her arms and eyes first towards heaven (the New Testament phrase "gen Himmel"), then fell on her knees before the coffin and with devotion and ecstasy looked up at her mistress. (486)

There is nothing in this report but the viewpoint of the narrator. The word "seemed" is twice used in this report (I have italicized these usages in the text). In the first instance, did the word "seem" refer to the narrator or to the bystanders? We have no need to choose: in the circumstances of Nanny's fall, everyone who saw her crash to the ground must have had the same impression. The objectivity of the impression is vouched for where the narrator makes his own observation about her trembling limbs and limp fingers.

In the second instance, the word "seemed" indicates that every external observer, whether the narrator himself or the witnesses accompanying the cortege, is able to interpret her actions as based on an inner process — her will or intention — but, because it is internal, it is not able to be directly verified. In the whole report, the distinction between interpretation (or surmise) and fact is made clear.

The narration goes a step further: Nanny says to the people:

> You saw what happened — how she raised herself up and, with her hands folded, blessed me; how she looked at me in such a friendly way. You all

[2] HA volume 6 486.

heard, you are witnesses of how she said to me: "You are forgiven." I am
no longer a murderer amongst you (she felt guilty for having secretly eaten
Ottilie's food instead of reporting her mistress's attempts to starve herself).
She has forgiven me, God has forgiven me and no one can have anything
against me. (486)

Here we need to note three things: first, Nanny herself speaks about Ottilie's
actions and words of forgiveness; second, it is by no means clear that the
people also saw and heard these things; third, Nanny's horizon is the specifi-
cally Christian (Catholic) one: for her, Ottilie is a saint who works miracles
and speaks of the forgiveness of sins. Since Goethe himself is writing from a
far more secularized point of view, we will need later to discuss what his in-
tention is in employing this Catholic imagery.

Between the arrival of the cortege at the church and the description of
the people's reaction to Nanny's account of Ottilie's death, the narrator re-
ports the architect's reaction. In this context Nanny's witness is given further
weight. In an effort to console him in his overwhelming sorrow she

spoke to him with so much truth and force, with so much good-will and
certainty, that, astounded by the eloquence of her speech, he was able to
collect himself. (488)

Because of the clear distinction between the narrator's and Nanny's view-
points, the reader is naturally inclined to be skeptical about the status of
Nanny's view: was it purely her own possibly unstable subjectivity interpret-
ing events? Yet the reader is surprised to find that anything Nanny would say
would have such a profound effect on the architect as to steady him in his
sorrow and to make him feel that the beautiful Ottilie (his "schöne Fre-
undin") now lived and functioned (wirkte) in a higher sphere.

The narrator further confirms this positive impression about Nanny when
he introduces the evidence of the surgeon. In this passage it is as if Goethe is
deliberately anticipating the reader's skepticism about Nanny with a view to
refuting it. The surgeon, portrayed as a soberly professional man, is not
treated with irony in the novel but as an objective observer. Of him we read:

The surgeon was anticipating bizarre reactions from Nanny: he thought she
would speak of nocturnal tête-à-têtes with Ottilie and of other such phe-
nomena; instead, she was natural, quiet and fully self-possessed. Her mem-
ory of all past events and circumstances was extremely accurate and nothing
in what she said went beyond the ordinary bounds of truth and reality ex-
cept for the events in the funeral procession, which she repeated often and
with joy: how Ottilie raised herself up, blessed her, forgave her and thereby
gave her lasting peace. (488)

Nanny's totally steady behaviour, while she still insisted on her version of
events, overcame the skepticism of the surgeon, and prevents the reader from

dismissing her as a simple-minded religious crank. This still leaves unanswered what point Goethe is making.

If we see the architect and the surgeon, both positive in their view of Nanny, as one group, we find this group divided by a deep chasm from a further group — represented by the ordinary people. These latter wanted to see Ottilie and

> each one wanted to hear the unbelievable story from Nanny's own lips, some so that they could mock, most to show their skepticism and a few to accept the story in faith. (488)

The faith mentioned here is that of the people who *need* to believe something. The irony and skepticism of the narrator, who links faith with the need of faith, is aimed at this latter group, which resembles the people we have met around Sperata in the *Apprenticeship*. There is no irony concerning the objective facts reported by the narrator: that Nanny fell from a height, was unaccountably healed by contact with Ottilie's garment and her folded hands. It is not acceptable simply to follow the opinion of Goethe's friend Reinhard, according to whom the force that seems to go out from Ottilie is only a natural phenomenon which we do not yet know how to explain.[3]

Michael Niedermeyer, the Marxist scholar, adopts Reinhard's view in his dissertation,[4] although with some modifications. In any case, it is significant that for both Reinhard and Niedermeyer Goethe is writing of an event which he portrays as real and as needing an explanation (whether "scientific" or otherwise). For the narrator the healing took place.

Other testimony

If it is true that in the final chapter Ottilie plays a central role, this possibility has been highlighted from early on in the novel. The Assistant and (especially in the second book) the Architect are two characters to whom Goethe gives an insight into Ottilie's inner being. Neither of them sees in Ottilie a modest, quiet, untalented beautiful girl. Instead, they see her as a person with great inner depths which are gradually revealed, to the point where the narrator presents her as a holy woman who works miracles. The witnesses of the Assistant and particularly of the Architect (since his presence beside Ottilie's coffin achieves the organic continuity of the last chapter with the body of the novel as whole) make highly implausible the view that the novel breaks down artistically with the author resorting to a utopian leap. We need to show that

---

[3] Letter of K. F. Von Reinhard to Goethe, February 16, 1810, quoted in HA 6 670.

[4] Diss. Berlin. 1983: 79.

Goethe was not artificially extricating himself from an otherwise insoluble problem by moving from the individual plane to that of the whole human species (the "Gattung") as Geerdts[5] and Lukács[6] would have it, but that this holiness of Ottilie emerges early in the novel and becomes ever more obvious, so that the manifestation of her holiness by the miracle-working in the final chapter should not shock the reader. Of course, it would be nonsense to attribute to Goethe a belief in miracle-working. He is not to be considered in any formal sense a Christian, let alone a Catholic! On the other hand it is unsatisfactory — because the text does not endorse it — to reduce all that is holy about Ottilie to her unconscious (and uncontested) harmony with nature. A careful examination of the text should help to determine in what Ottilie's holiness consists.

The Assistant

The witness of this man occurs as early as the third chapter of the novel. Commenting on the judgments made by the school principal about Ottilie he refers to his charge as a fruit which has not yet opened but which is genuine, with a real kernel to it and which, sooner or later, will open out and develop to a full life. Of her type of intelligence he says that she does not understand anything which is isolated from the context from which it arises, but if the right links are made she can understand the most difficult things. Furthermore, she learns, not as one who is to be educated but as one who wants to educate; not as a pupil but as a future teacher.

The qualities referred to here point to an inner growth and development taking place in Ottilie. The image of the gradually opening and ripening fruit contains the motif of inwardness ("Innerlichkeit") which we see developed and deepened in the novel.

A further image introduced in the letter to Charlotte in Chapter Five reinforces this theme. Having said that he knew of no instance where Ottilie had demanded or earnestly asked for anything for herself, the Assistant says that there were, if rarely, occasions when she tried to resist demands made on her. She did this with a gesture which, for anyone who understood its significance, could not be opposed. She pressed the palms of her hands together, raised them aloft and brought them to rest folded against her breast, bowing forward slightly and fixing whoever was making the demand with a gaze which would make him desist from everything he demanded or wished of

---

[5] Cf. Hans-Jürgen Geerdts. *Goethes Roman "Die Wahlverwandtschaften."* Weimar: Arion, 1966: 185.

[6] *Goethe and His Age* passim.

her; and so the Assistant asked Charlotte, should she ever witness this ges-
ture, to think of him and to spare Ottilie.

With this gesture Ottilie expresses her autonomy, the inner (if not outer)
independence and ultimate privacy of the individual. If Edward reads out this
letter with a smile and a shake of the head, towards the end of the novel he
will not mistake the meaning of the gesture. Even for the passionate Edward,
Ottilie is unreachable when she makes this gesture in refusal of the request in
his letter that she commit herself to him. The refusal is absolute, final. The
joined palms raised on high and then brought to rest on her bosom express
the link between a higher authority and her inner self. With her "Nein" she
seems to withdraw herself from Edward (and from the outer world) and to
have no further life than the life of the inner self. She has closed herself off in
order to shield herself from everything which might threaten to take her by
storm. We are dealing here with the irreducible inner pole of Ottilie's experi-
ence which cannot be mistaken for or confused with the *social*. This inner
realm is where Ottilie's religious experience is centered and presented as a \
value independent of any social values.

As for the status of the Assistant in the novel, we need to note the fol-
lowing: first, after Charlotte read the Assistant's note we are told:

> Charlotte rejoiced when she read this note. The content was very much in
> line with the notions she herself had about Ottilie. (HA 6 265)

If she smiles at seeing the Assistant so favorably disposed towards Ottilie (an
attitude which the examiner also notices at a later stage), she sees these lean-
ings in a positive light in a world where indifference and aversion are so
much at home. Second, what the Assistant wrote about Ottilie's gesture was
correct and was understood and respected by Edward.

The Architect

With regard to the Architect's status in the novel, it is worth noticing that it
was precisely the Captain who introduced him into the circle as his trainee.
This occurred at a time when he himself had to leave the circle of friends and
wanted to make sure that work on the project on Edward's and Charlotte's
property should continue to flourish. He saw in the Architect one who
would advance the work and ensure its success and permanence. Through
the introduction of the Architect the Captain was secretly pleased that his
departure would not impinge. And in a certain sense this is what happened.
At the beginning of Part Two, Goethe seems to present the Architect as a
replacement for the Captain (and for Edward!):

After the departure of the Captain and Edward the Architect grew in importance. He proved to be exact, competent and active. His positive influence was radiated in every direction. (360)

His first action was to deal briefly with Charlotte's problems concerning the cemetery. Here he had some good suggestions to make. His next task was focused on the church. At this point the church is not to be seen merely as part of the landscape. Instead, it is of central importance for our present discussion. This is where the Architect will spend his time; here he will, together with Ottilie, practice his art until he too departs; here he will be found at Ottilie's side after her death and will learn from Nanny the details surrounding her death and the funeral procession. It is obvious that the church motif deserves close scrutiny.

The graveyard theme in the first chapter of Part Two brings to the foreground the theme of death and of the relationships which may be possible between the living and the dead. This is, in a broad sense, a religious theme. That discussions on this topic do little to enlighten the reader is to be expected. Ottilie herself writes dryly in a section of her diary with which Chapter Two closes that, while we might think of life after death as a second life — in which we are commemorated in stone or in writing — , this second life also comes to an end sooner or later. In the next extract from her diary she will return to the same theme.

In the meantime, the Architect has been asked by Charlotte to focus his attention on the church. This church is not to be seen as something at all foreign to these people, apart perhaps from the fact that it conjures up thoughts of an earlier epoch. It had a certain architectural quality and value. One could see that the builder of a nearby monastery had brought his insight and dedication to bear on his work on this smaller building. The theme of Catholic Christianity is treated positively here in a way which should predispose the reader to view the similar theme in the final chapter in an equivalently positive light:

> The building made a solemn and pleasant impression on the observer although the new interior adapted to the Protestant service had taken somewhat from the atmosphere of peace and majesty. (366)

There is a resonance here of what a little later Goethe will write in *Dichtung und Wahrheit* (Poetry and Truth) where he describes the Catholic sacramental system, showing that, although he is far from being a Christian in any strict sense, he is still capable of appreciating certain aspects of the Christian faith and liturgy. But how do we account for Goethe's introducing the theme of Catholic Christianity at this point?

When he discovers a small chapel within the church, the Architect is astounded and delighted. The decoration and finishing are even more pleasing and detailed. The chapel contains, in its sculptures and paintings, remains of "that older (i.e. Catholic) religious cult" which had known how to mark the various feasts by the use of various images and objects and to celebrate each in its own particular way. It is precisely this Catholic chapel to which the Architect devotes his attention. In this chapel Ottilie will be given an increasingly central role to play.

The accompanying theme of the past is developed where the Architect keeps his promise and shows the women samples of his collected treasures: these were mostly of German origin, things which preoccupied the imagination of earlier times; and since (through his work) the church itself grew, as it were, closer and closer to the past, one had to ask whether one really lived in the newer age. Perhaps it was only in a dream that one lived with quite new manners, habits, customs and convictions.

Particularly significant in this context is the religious dimension: the Architect produces a collection of mainly human figures. The faces and gestures are characterized by a spirit of recollection; ready acknowledgment of something above us deserving of our reverence; quiet surrender in love and hope. The old man, the young boy, the cheerful youth, the serious man, the transfigured saint, the hovering angel — all seem blissful in innocent pleasure and pious expectation. The most ordinary event has a tinge of heaven, and any liturgical action seems in tune with the nature of each person.

Are these ideas utopian — in line with the Marxist tendency to interpret religious themes in Goethe's works? It seems not. Goethe seems to anticipate the possibility that these lines could be interpreted in terms of hankering for a better world in the past: "Most people look to such a region in search of a golden age which had disappeared, or a lost paradise." (368) But in direct and explicit contrast to such people, Ottilie is seen to find in these images relevance to the present rather than the past, so that rather than "living" in some utopia she feels moved by the images because they have relevance to her own inner life, her religious experience.

When in the third chapter the Architect begins work on the dome, he does not create completely new figures but bases them on figures like those mentioned above. It is significant that Ottilie's talents, here developed, are now put to use by the Architect, as he has her help him with the artistic work. With paint and brush she was able to follow his instructions with considerable success. Furthermore, when the Architect began to paint the faces, they all began to resemble Ottilie. Goethe's endeavor to link Ottilie with the holy figures reaches its climax where, from the last face painted on the ceiling of the dome it was as if Ottilie herself were looking down from heaven.

When the dome was finished and the walls, as the earthly sphere, were to be painted brown, Ottilie again took on an important role: under her influence it was agreed to depict flowers and hanging fruit whose function it was, as it were, to join up heaven and earth. Here Ottilie was in her element. (372)

Her function in this context indicates that she is not understood as belonging exclusively *either* to the heavenly sphere *or* to the earthly, social sphere — but that she combines *both* heaven and earth.

The Architect asked all the women to stay away from the church for a week during the final stages of the restorations. When the time was up, Ottilie was the first to arrive at the church. The church door was open. She went in, walked to the chapel door, which though heavy with bronze fittings, opened easily at her touch — a sign of her easy access to the religious sphere.

Death

At this point we are to see Ottilie deeply preoccupied with the theme of death. This theme, treated profoundly by Goethe, moves us into areas which can have no direct relevance to a specifically Marxist and atheist standpoint.

When Ottilie sits down on one of the ancient choir stalls in the chapel, she is taken back centuries to earlier artistic periods. (373) Immediately, as she looks up above and around her, it is as if she existed and yet did not exist, as if she was aware of herself and yet not aware of herself, as if everything would disappear from her, and as if she might disappear from herself. (374) This was like a premonition of death. The state of reverie was disturbed for her when she realized that the sun had gone down: she "awoke" and hurried from this tomb-like place to the security of the residence.

The next excerpt from her diary pursues this theme. She writes about ancient beliefs which obviously impress her: people in this tradition think of their ancestors as sitting around silently on thrones in big caves. When they are joined (in death) by a new-comer, if they find him worthy they stand up from their thrones and bow towards him as a sign of welcome. From her "throne" (the choir stall) Ottilie thinks: why can't you stay sitting here for a long, long time — silently and deep in recollection — until your friends finally join you and you can stand up and, with a friendly bow, indicate to them their place. (375) It is clear that Ottilie sees herself as if already dead, having gone ahead and waiting for the death of her friends. She thinks of this new state as a kind of twilight, symbolized by the effect which the stained glass has on the sun-light which penetrates it. This twilight situation mediates between, and is distant from, both the day (the sphere of the living) and complete darkness (the state of absolute non-existence). Ottilie concludes that an eternal lamp should be provided so that even the night would not remain wholly dark. The eternal light in the darkness has important connotations: here death is not absolute, as it must be in the atheist system of thought; something positive, signified by the term light, not only exists but will always continue to exist. The extent to which Ottilie's (and Goethe's) conception of death is foreign to any atheist tradition is indicated by the obvious link with the Catholic tradition: the lamp burning constantly in a Catholic church signifying the presence of Christ=God in the tabernacle. The effect of this image is to underline the transcendence aspect (the "Jenseitigkeit") of Ottilie's religious experience.

Sight and light

For Ottilie this light is far from a vague, flickering hope for an after-life. On the contrary: Goethe's treatment of the theme of sight and light is powerful and impressive. The next idea which Ottilie introduces is striking: "Try as we might, we can't help thinking of ourselves as always *seeing*." Ottilie says:

> I think a person dreams only so as not to stop seeing. It could well be that the inner light will some day shine out of us so that we would need no other light. (375)

Considered in isolation, this notion might appear fanciful, but Goethe roots it firmly in the biblical tradition and hence further underlines the transcendence character of Ottilie's experience: in the last book of the New Testament we read that at the end of the world the heavenly city, the new Jerusalem, will not need the light of the sun and the moon. Light will have another source: the glory of God.[7] This text is already anticipated in the Old Testament in Isaiah 60:19. What Ottilie's idea and the biblical texts have in common is the notion that there is a state in which light comes not from the *natural* source (sun, moon etc) but from *another* source: in the Bible the source is expressly the glory of God, for Ottilie the source is within the human person — implying some form of personal immortality. Although "God's glory" is not simply identical with the inner personal self from which Ottilie envisages light ultimately emanating, it is not immediately obvious that Goethe has in mind two radically different sources of light — one interior and the other exterior to the person. Goethe was so well acquainted with the Christian tradition, both Protestant and Catholic, that he would certainly know that faith is the inner vision of the believer and that God is the believer's inner light.

Goethe further develops the connection between Ottilie and the inner light where he has the Architect deeply involve her in his preparations for the celebration of Christmas. In his representation of the Mother of God in the crib (a Catholic tradition), he chooses Ottilie as the Mother. Goethe uses this means to highlight Ottilie's inner qualities. He does this through his reliable

[7] Cf. Apocalypse 21, 23; 22, 5.

witness, the Architect, and through reference to Ottilie's diary, where she writes:

> The whole space suggested *night* rather than *twilight*, and yet no detail of the surroundings was obscure. The artist had managed, through the clever use of lighting, to communicate the superb idea that the child was the source of all light. (403)

Here is an example of a human person from whom light emanates in such a way that natural sources of light are not needed. In this scene Goethe portrays Ottilie not simply as able to play the part of Mary but also as able to *identify* with the role.

Her relationship to the Architect, who clearly loves her, is specified in such a way that yet again her involvement with a transcendence dimension is underlined. It appears that her relationship with Edward leaves no room in her for more than a sisterly friendship with anyone else. In this context we read:

> Her heart was completely filled with her love for Edward, and only the godhead, which penetrates everything, could possess this heart simultaneously with Edward. (390)

On the level of personal human relations she had an exclusive bond with Edward; yet Goethe makes it clear that on another level (reaching beyond the purely human sphere) there is a complementary relationship: of Ottilie to God. In the context of Catholic thought this is not problematic: God as Creator is present to all His creatures at all times, not just in the act of creating them but also in the process of preserving them — a process without which they would fall back into the absolute nothingness from which he created them.

In his portrayal of Ottilie, Goethe leans so heavily on the Catholic-Christian imagery that he offers us a serious alternative to the Spinozist interpretation of reality. Goethe's treatment of God and the divine, as shown in the case of Ottilie, is not simply reducible to terms of Spinozist pantheism as the East German Marxist tradition would have it. Even if the Assistant's Protestant objections to the Catholic imagery and ritual are voiced, this is not in favor of a more immanentist conception of the divine; on the contrary, the Protestant tradition voiced by the Assistant represents an even more severe view about God's distance (implying transcendence) from the human sphere.

In conclusion: the intrinsic link set up by Goethe between Ottilie and the Western religious tradition of biblical and Catholic Christianity seems to have *no negative function*. Instead, it leaves the reader with the impression that the inner (as opposed to the social) aspect of Ottilie's life deserves to be considered as an important aspect of her personal experience. Despite Goethe's "progress" in the direction of secularization in his way of thinking and living, he seems, in his portrayal of Ottilie, to want to hold onto the idea of an inner core, or center, which he sees neither as a basis for confessing Christianity nor as an organ for experiencing a pantheistic openness to the cosmos, but as a focus of a deep personal religious experience — which, however, is not accompanied by any need to identify the precise object to which this religious orientation is directed. The *agnostic* element which characterizes this experience cannot be denied, yet it does not negate the *religious* aspect of the experience. If we want to determine the degree of secularization Goethe has reached at this point in his life, passages of the text such as we have studied here need to be considered; and conversely, it is not possible to do justice to the text of Goethe's novel if the consideration of the process of secularization in his life and work is undertaken without due differentiation.

12: Resonance in the West

While it is clear that the Berlin Wall resulted in more than physical isolation of the GDR from the western world, it is not easy to measure the extent of cultural isolation which resulted. Naturally, in the earliest years of the GDR the task of achieving political stability and recognition for the new State influenced developments on various aspects of the cultural front. The need to dissociate the State from Germany's National Socialist past, seen as the logical out-crop of capitalism, went hand in hand with attempts to identify what was the authentic tradition on which the new Marxist state could be built. The humanism of Classical Weimar was quickly to become the cornerstone of the new culture. Goethe, Schiller, Herder and the later Wieland were viewed in a new light. Goethe in particular, and especially his "Faust" figure, underwent new scrutiny.

The GDR policy of laying claim, particularly to Goethe and Schiller, as their inheritance was viewed in the West — as was to be expected — as a political and cultural ploy which could not go unchecked. The result was an atmosphere of polemical discussion and often bitter controversy. Much of the early East German writing on Goethe was clearly doctrinaire,[1] dictated by party-political cultural policy. Goethe, and even his "Faust," had to be held up as heroic, progressive members of a middle class responsible for the advance of democracy and humanism around 1800. Until the death of Stalin in 1953, there was no question of challenging the party line on this. In such a climate it was simple for the West to dismiss the Marxist claims as having nothing but political significance. Only well after the erection of the Berlin Wall, when, in the late 1960s and early 1970s, the GDR gradually became inwardly more stabilized, was it feasible for more fruitful contact between the GDR and the West. Around this time it was possible to have open inner-Marxist discussions in the GDR. There was important controversy about Peter Müller's "Werther" book when it first appeared in 1969. This attracted attention of left-wing Germanists across the Wall, but it also sparked off hefty discussion amongst GDR scholars as well. *Die Klassik-Legende*, the "Second Wisconsin Workshop," edited by Reinhold Grimm and Jost Hermand and published in 1971, sparked off a controversy within the GDR about the relevance of the Classical Weimar tradition. The central position occupied by

---

[1] An extreme example of this would be the book by Herbert Lindner, *Das Problem des Spinozismus im Schaffen Goethes und Herders.* Weimar: Arion-Verlag, 1960.

Goethe and Schiller was up for discussion. It was now possible to treat even the "Faust" figure with much more differentiation.

Looking back, as we are attempting to do in this work, on a tradition of Goethe interpretation which has now run its course, scholars can treat the work of the GDR Germanists less polemically — since, in one sense, the fight is over. The process of assessing the true achievement of these scholars is, in the case of Goethe studies, only beginning.

Two important accounts of this tradition, one by Karl Robert Mandelkow and the other by Rüdiger Scholz, need to be mentioned here.

In the second volume of his *Goethe in Deutschland*, in the section where he deals with the reception of Goethe after World War Two, Mandelkow gives an excellent account of the different factors influencing both West and East German reception and includes in his study the achievements of Germanists abroad — on the North American Continent, in Australia, and in Great Britain.

With regard to East Germany, Mandelkow highlights both the importance of the "Materialien"[2] and the attention which these interviews give to the role played by Gerhard Scholz. In general, Mandelkow's book offers a detailed and enlightening overview of the history of the various approaches to interpreting Goethe, showing how they are related to — or even grow out of — their particular historical and political situation. It is not our task here to summarize or to discuss this important survey (reaching far beyond East Germany). However, it is worth noting that in chapter three, where Mandelkow sets out to study the main tendencies to be found in interpretations of Goethe in West Germany, Switzerland and the GDR in the 1950s and 1960s, he states that, whereas scholars in the first two countries continued to deal with much the same problems and to use much the same methods as before 1945, the situation in East Germany was radically different — for the reasons we have explained above in the introductory chapters to Part One. Yet even Mandelkow's contribution, while informative and virtually offering, among other things, a compendium of subjects which might be examined in detail, does not engage in an actual study of the GDR contributions. The nature of his book is to categorize more than to give evaluations based on detailed analyses. Thus there is the gap to be filled. The preceding chapters of this book represent an attempt to begin the task of description, appreciation, and evaluation.

Of Rüdiger Scholz's two important books on Goethe's *Faust* the first is an "Einführender Forschungsbericht": *Goethes "Faust" in der wissenschaftlichen Interpretation von Schelling und Hegel bis heute*. In this report he shows how most of the interpretations of *Faust* he discusses are in the final analysis

---

[2]   See above, Part One, Chapter three.

unscientific because, whether unwittingly or not, they all have recourse to some kind of absolute which they cannot account for by rational analysis. Scholz's second book, *Die Beschädigte Seele des Großen Mannes*, rationalizes the various "absolutes" by explaining both Goethe and Faust in terms of their direct relationship to concrete history (the "bürgerliche Gesellschaft").

A brief glance at Scholz's analysis in his Forschungsbericht will show how he characterizes the approaches of most *Faust* interpretations in the West and how the "materialist" interpretations — amongst which he includes Lukács, Bloch and the GDR authors — could be expected to differ from these.

He begins with a consideration of Schelling's and Hegel's response to Goethe's *Faust. Ein Fragment* (1790), since this is the work on which their main comments are based. He quotes Schelling:

> In so far as it is possible to judge Goethe's *Faust* from the fragment of it that is available, this poem is nothing other than the innermost, purest essence of our epoch: material and form created out of that which included within itself the whole era and out of that with which the whole era was — and still is — pregnant. For this reason it has to be called a truly mythological poem.[3]

He explains that, according to Schelling, the poem participates in the absolute, even through the finite characteristics which make it part of the modern world of decay. "Goethes *Faust*," glosses Scholz,

> is not the great poem of the World Mind, but the mythology of the historical subject Goethe. In the fragmented modern world, only isolated individuals are in a position "to know and to portray the tendency to the absolute." Schelling sees the "Genie" as the individual human subject able to open up access to the absolute; it is "so to speak, a piece of the absoluteness of God." (7)

Subjectivity is here understood dialectically: negatively, as an impure representation of the absolute, and at the same time, positively, as participation in the absolute. Also, in so far as the poem has a national character, dialectically it is seen positively by Schelling as participation in the truth of the absolute and negatively as a limitation of the same. As a work of art, the poem, for Schelling, has the task "of canceling out the contradictions of the present historical situation by reconciling them in the absolute." (8)

Perhaps the main point to stress here is that for Schelling the aim of art is to achieve truth as an eternal, absolute value, as *being*, about which no further questioning is possible. (8)

Scholz's analysis of Hegel's position yields similar results:

---

[3] Rüdiger Scholz. *Goethes "Faust" in der wissenschaftlichen Interpretation von Schelling und Hegel bis heute*. Rheinfelden: Schäuble, 1985: 6.

The Phenomenology of Mind (1807), published after Fragment (1790) and
just before *Part 1* (1808) is so close in its sequence of themes to those
arising in *Faust* that the *Phenomenology* has been seriously considered as
providing an interpretation of *Faust*. (10)

According to Scholz's view, where Goethe presents Faust as the skeptic
with regard to all the established sciences, as aspiring to direct possession of
nature, as looking to found his identity in activity and striving, as having two
souls and as seeking access to the world through sense experience in his con-
crete existence, Hegel includes all of these themes in his system according to
which the Mind develops itself, moving from the certainty experienced by
the senses to the stage where the Mind knows itself *as* Mind — in its abso-
lute knowledge.

Hegel underlines the important distinction between the World Mind and
the absolute individual:

> Hegel defines the Mind as the absolute, real being (Wesen) which is com-
> plete in itself (sich selbst tragend) (*Phänomenologie*, 314), "the particular
> individual is the incomplete Mind." (Scholz: 11)

As the development of the World Mind takes place, the rift between indi-
viduality and generality occurs in various stages. At the end of this dialectical
division of the Mind into its different facets occurs the new unity between
"being and self, individual and species, and subjectivity and objectivity" (Sein
und Ich, Individuum und Gattung, Fürsich und Ansich). While this unity
only reaches its fullest form in scientific knowledge (Wissenschaft), where the
Absolute Mind is fully identical with itself, a high level of progress towards
this unity is reflected in art. More specifically: *Faust* shows, on the one hand,
the division within the Mind and, on the other hand, significant progress to-
wards achieving the final unity and identity. (12)

It is within this idealistic context, whether of the Schelling or Hegel vari-
ety, that, where the idealist tradition is adhered to, many of the central con-
cepts are frequently interpreted: truth, fate, necessity, the good, guilt, virtue,
duty, justice. These concepts, understood as manifestations of the World
Mind's development while still divided within itself on the way to achieving
its full identity, are part of an absolute system which cannot be challenged by
any historical considerations. While unfolding in history, these concepts, as
constructions of the World Mind, are paradoxically at the same time "ahis-
torical."

When Scholz then proceeds to examine the so-called "bürgerliche" *Faust*
interpretations, he finds that they fundamentally rely on some kind of abso-
lute being which puts them beyond the grasp of rational investigation. Thus
the relationship between literature and society, in so far as it is considered at
all, is, in the course of the nineteenth and twentieth century, progressively

dehistoricized to the point where in Fascism it is becomes no more than a supra-historical national myth and, after the war, is reduced to Christian, existential or other unhistorical conceptions of "being" and "mind." (94) Thus Scholz summarizes the failure of the new middle class society to capitalize on the use of its own empirical, rational scientific methods and on its opportunity to historicize the world into which it was born. Summing up the positive achievements of this basically rationalist middle-class tradition of *Faust* interpretation in the West, Scholz refers to the establishment of an authentic *Faust* text, to the thorough work of the the Goethe biographers, to the study of Weltanschauung both in the drama and in Goethe's own life, and to the comprehensive research devoted to the history of motifs and the history of ideas. But this tradition falls far short of its own possibilities:

> Instead of scientific research you have biblical exegesis; Goethe and Faust are figures with whom people identified, arousing emotional and irrational interest, with the result that the requisite scientific detachment is destroyed.
>
> (94)

A result of accepting the idealist limit imposed on what can be investigated is that Goethe's own interpretation of the world and of the function of creative literature is absolutized. Concepts like the divine, fate, genius, work of art, the tragic, (das Göttliche, Schicksal, Genie, Kunstwerk, Tragik) etc. are not subjected to scientific scrutiny.

It is not our task here to examine Scholz's second book, in which, using methods drawn from psychology and psychoanalysis, he attempts just such a scrutiny, historicizing both Goethe and his *Faust* and, without trying to destroy their significance, aims at putting them more scientifically into their true social and historical context. Scholz's analysis presented in brief outline in the last few pages shows what serious problems he has with the *Faust* interpretations in the West and identifies the root problem as a completely insufficient handling of the social and historical perspective. (In this outline we have not referred to Scholz's discussion of Gervinus, Vischer and Ziegler, because, although they make gestures in this direction, their progress is not significant. (18–24)

In his treatment of the so-called materialist interpretations, where history could be expected to provide the counter-balance to the ahistorical or supra-historical absolute elements which the materialists would reject, Scholz expresses disappointment at what he finds. The materialist tradition (i.e. the interpretations based on Karl Marx's theory of history) aims, in its interpretations of *Faust,*

> to work out — without recourse to metaphysics, without the use of absolutes which are supra-historical, and without irrational identifications — the way drama and author are bound up with history and society. (97)

His critical judgment is as follows:

> This attempt is only successful in embryo. It has not led, on the whole, to an explanation of elements of content and form in drama on the basis of the process of social development. (97)

When Scholz turns to the GDR *Faust* interpretations, his first sentence highlights the dominant influence of Georg Lukács's *Faust-Studien*. (98) Scholz finds that the weakness of Lukács's *Faust* theses lies in their generality. While linking the play with various aspects of capitalism, Lukács ignores the various historical phases of its development. Goethe's own exposure to aspects of capitalism is not discussed, let alone where these aspects appear in his play. Nor are the absolutizing elements banned from Lukács's work: Goethe is for Lukács the great "Genie" and the great humanist, and as such he is relevant to a socialism which is trying to produce its own brand of humanism. But, according to Scholz, humanism is for Lukács a supra-temporal concept, by using which

> he abandons the field of interpretation based on historical materialism and is caught in the slip-stream of bourgeois ideology. Concepts such as *the tragic* and *fate* are not given a foundation but are simply retained and have the same function as in bourgeois ideology . . . This ideology of (Lukács) contains — in the concepts of humanism, the great individual, and realism — three central ideas of authentically bourgeois ideology. (100)

Referring to the writings of Alexander Abusch in the Goethe centenary year of 1949, Scholz sees that the glorification of Goethe is here modified by the recognition that there were contradictions in Goethe's life and work which needed explanation. In particular, Scholz quotes two statements by Abusch: "Goethe was no middle-class revolutionary, not even in his youth"; and, with reference to Goethe's rejection of the French Revolution: "no matter how much social reality saddened his consciousness, Goethe was conquered by the German *Misere*." (104)

In general, Abusch agreed with Lukács about Goethe as a genius and a humanist but stressed more strongly that Goethe was not an example of pure humanity but rather the most perfect example of his class — the progressive middle-class.

Despite the modifications introduced into the GDR interpretation of Goethe, Scholz claims that Abusch's work is still limited by his adherence to party policy. The official theory that literature has to mirror the social circumstances is hard to reconcile with the notion that, in his thinking, Goethe projects beyond capitalism to an order of things which, in his own experience, does not exist even im embryo. A criticism levelled at most of the GDR Goethe interpreters is the gratuitousness of the claim that, when Goethe identifies the limits of the capitalist system and thus transcends its horizon, what beckons on the other side is socialism. It would have to be shown that Goethe does not envisage a different alternative such as a feudalistic reactionary world or a middle-class utopia — perhaps a modified form of capitalism.

Referring to the development of the GDR tradition, Scholz claims that, until about 1974, which sees the publication of work by Höhle and Hamm leading to the publication of volume seven of the *GDL*, the ideas of Lukács are continually repeated but in a more rigid form and becoming more and more an expression of state ideology. (107) When towards the end of the Stalinist era Hanns Eisler's *Johann Faustus* dismantled the image of Faust as hero and humanist, his work was (as we have seen above) utterly rejected. Drawing on the work of Hans Schwerte[4] and André Dabezies,[5] Scholz stresses that the official *Faust* interpretation highlights nationalist and titanist traits which had already served the cause of the Third Reich. Scholz finds the continuation of this heroic interpretation even in Gerhard Scholz, Edith Braemer and Walter Dietze (all leading figures in GDR Goethe studies in their time), who around 1966 white-wash Faust and lay the blame for the destruction of the "Wanderer" and of Philemon and Baucis on the victims themselves.

With the arrival of the *GDL* volume seven in 1978, Rüdiger Scholz identifies attempts to modify the official Faust interpretation — by turning back the clocks nearly thirty years: to 1949! An earlier version of Höhle's and Hamm's section on *Faust Part Two* had already appeared in *Weimarer Beiträge* in 1974. A significant advance was achieved around 1978 in Hamm's own book *Faust* book,[6] where he maintains that Goethe, as a thinker, was a middle-class man (not a socialist).

In general, Scholz finds the GDR achievement disappointing. Even Hamm seemed to operate only within Goethe's own view of the world. (114) The Marxist interpreters' attempts to deal with the concrete historical situation of Goethe's period are for Scholz not as effective even as those of Lukács. While Scholz lists the achievements of the tradition — centered especially around the activities of the *Nationale Forschungs-und Gedenkstätten der klassischen deutschen Literatur* — he finds a certain stagnation and a tendency to conserve the treasures of the past.

To sum up Scholz's position: against the GDR interpretation it must on the whole be said that it does not consistently pursue the historical and dialectical path of Marxist interpretation which it had set out to follow. There is no route which leads from Lukács's argument — teasing out the general

---

[4] *Faust und das Faustische.* Stuttgart: Klett, 1962.

[5] *Visages de Faust au XXe siècle.* Paris: Sorbonne, 1967.

[6] Heinz Hamm. *Goethes* "Faust." *Werkgeschichte und Textanalyse.* Berlin: Volk und Wissen, 1978.

manifestations of capitalism in his attempt to discover the dialectic between literature and historical reality — to literary practice; no route which leads to the investigation of the real connections between idea, content, and form on the one hand and history on the other. There was no scientific inquiry to supersede the work of Lukács. (115)

When Scholz identifies the cause of the problem, he is clearly setting the stage for his own response (in his *Die Beschädigte Seele des großen Mannes*.) The cause is the canonization of the Faust image which is seen to be unshakable. Behind Faust Goethe had to be the "Genie," the great humanist, the progressive "Bürger" with socialism in his sights. Naturally, the application of psychoanalytic categories to the interpretation both of the drama and of its author would unsettle the official picture of Goethe and of his play.

Rüdiger Scholz's survey of East German interpretations of *Faust* in particular would leave the reader with the suspicion that Marxist interpretations of Goethe in general were dictated, on the one hand, by an overwhelming debt to Lukács and, on the other hand, by SED party policy. With regard to *Faust* it is obvious that Scholz was concerned to show that virtually all major interpretations — whether in the West or in the GDR — were a prisoner either to idealist thinking stemming from Schelling and Hegel or to Goethe's own view of life and art. In particular, he accused the Marxists, as we have seen, of an insufficient understanding of how German classical literature relates to the historical and social conditions from which it originates. Despite all seeming awareness of the problem, the Marxists, he feels, did not deliver. Thus he sets out in his own book to provide both the necessary information and to indicate the relevant links in Goethe's *Faust*. While it is valid, in the context of his thesis, to focus on the links with idealism and on a consequent diminution of contact with history, Scholz leaves the reader with the false impression that Marxist Goethe interpretation lacks differentiation and personal insight.

The same negative impression is conveyed by Walter Hinderer in his contribution to *Die Klassik-Legende*,[7] a book which provoked vigorous discussion in the GDR. Hinderer's essay, entitled "Die Regressive Universalideologie" contains the following statement:

> If one surveys the various conceptions of "Klassik" from Franz Mehring to the *Weimarer Beiträge* and compares the concepts and notions of "Nationalliteratur", there emerges — if one leaves aside the handful of original contributions — a rather sad "Unisono" seen in the specially designed phraseology, which in every age has been the language of the ideologies. What provokes criticism is not the stereotyped repetition of the same results which are based on the scattered statements by Marx and Engels, on the

[7] *Die Klassik-Legende. Second Wisconsin Workshop.* Edited by Reinhold Grimm and Jost Hermand. Frankfurt am Main: Athenäum Verlag, 1971.

views expressed by Lenin, and on the aesthetic writings of Lukács; nor even the over-eager suggestions in favor of a still more thorough investigation of German Classicism. What provokes criticism is the mere fact that here — what Hans Albert says is true of all "secular, political religions" — we see the rule of blind prejudice (here "Parteilichkeit"), obedience based on faith and an irreversible engagement.[8]

The response to this dismissive, anti-Marxist passage and to the *Klassik-Legende* in general was found in the "Klassik-Debatte," published in *Sinn und Form*.[9] This response appeared in the perhaps more important context of the book by Werner Mittenzwei on *Brechts Verhältnis zur Tradition*,[10] in which the author attempts to give a differentiated account of Brecht's reception of Goethe and Schiller. In 1973, an essay by Mittenzwei, based on his book and entitled "Brecht und die Probleme der deutschen Klassik," was printed in *Sinn und Form*[11] and provided the opening of the debate. This essay was followed by Helmut Holtzhauer's "Von Sieben, die auszogen, die Klassik zu erlegen" — a direct response to *Klassik-Legende*. A third essay was by Hans-Heinrich Reuter (in direct response to Mittenzwei's opening essay): "Die deutsche Klassik und das Problem Brecht — Zwanzig Sätze der Entgegnung auf Werner Mittenzwei." A fourth, very important essay, was the incisive but conciliatory contribution of Hans-Dietrich Dahnke on "Sozialismus und deutsche Klassik." Other essays followed, by Lothar Ehrlich: "Bertolt Brecht und die deutsche Klassik " and Wilhelm Girnus: "Die Glätte des Stroms und seine Tiefe — Betrachtungen über unser Verhältnis zur literarischen Vergangenheit."

Perhaps the most significant feature of Mittenzwei's contribution is that he demolishes the impression that the GDR Goethe reception was largely limited to the repetition and slight development of the insights of Lukács in the 1930s. Mittenzwei, an authority on Brecht, voices the ideas and ideals of an entirely different stream within the Marxist tradition. Already in an early version of his essay "Die Brecht-Lukács Debatte"[12] he underlines the history of the basic conflict between the two great Marxist writers, and it becomes evident that two clearly divergent points of view remained in conflict with one another from the time of the expressionist debates of the 1930s, through the early years of the the the GDR (until Brecht's death in 1956), and, after

---

[8]   *Klassik-Legende.* 144

[9]   Cf. Helmut Holtzhauer. "Von sieben, die auszogen, die Klassik zu erlegen." In: *Sinn und Form* 25 (1973) no. 1, 169–188.

[10]   Berlin: Akademie Verlag, 1973.

[11]   Mittenzwei's essay and the others listed here were collected by Mittenzwei and published in: *Wer war Brecht?* West Berlin: DEB, 1977.

[12]   Printed in an early version in: *Sinn und Form* 19 (1967) no. 1, 235–269.

Brecht's death, into the late 1970s. It is true that the Lukács tradition played a more obvious role in the GDR interpretation of Goethe, because, even though Lukács fell from favor with GDR officialdom after the Hungarian uprising in 1956, his central ideas and methods suited the demands of GDR cultural policy. The "great" Goethe and the "great" *Faust* were needed as a cornerstone of the Marxist cultural policy. Brecht (and his disciples and advocates) enjoyed a less comfortable relationship to the establishment. As the outstanding dramatic writer of his generation Brecht was another "flagship" of GDR culture and was suitably accommodated with his Berliner Ensemble in the theater at the Schiffbauerdamm. But his opposition to the classical Goethe (and Schiller) became notorious, as evidenced by his involvement in the *Urfaust* productions of 1952 and 1953. Though at this time it was not possible to flout the official view in public, and Brechtian opposition to Goethe (and Schiller) remained outside the academic main-stream, it was still a force to be reckoned with, all the more so when in the 1970s the new German literature taking shape showed both hostility to Goethe and a much greater openness to Romanticism than was usual amongst the academics themselves. In the mid-seventies the tight focus on Goethe and German Classicism in GDR literary history was openly challenged. Thus from here on there is even less basis for speaking of a monolithic, undifferentiated approach to the discipline: Hinderer's "blind obedience" motif is by this stage out of date, even if it is true that such a narrow-minded attitude characterized many scholars in the early decades and some scholars right up to 1989.

Works Consulted

Primary Texts

Eckermann, Johann Peter. *Gespräche mit Goethe.* Leipzig: Hesse and Becker, 1913.

Goethe, Johann Wolfgang von. *Faust. Part One.* Translated by David Luke. Oxford and New York: Oxford UP, 1987.

—— *Werke*, Hamburger Ausgabe. Edited by Erich Trunz. Volumes 1–7, 12. Munich: Beck, 1981.

——, *Die Leiden des jungen Werthers.* Erste und Zweite Fassung. Edited by Erna Merker. Berlin: Akademie-Verlag, 1954.

Hegel, Georg Wilhelm Friedrich. *Phänomenologie des Geistes.* Frankfurt am Main: Suhrkamp, 1977.

Secondary Literature

Abusch, Alexander. "Faust — Held oder Renegat in der deutschen Nationalliteratur." In: *Sinn und Form* 5 (1953):179–197.

Beharriell, Frederic. "The Hidden Meaning of Goethe's 'Bekenntnisse einer schönen Seele.'" In: *Festschrift für H. Henel.* Edited by J. L. Sammons. Munich: Fink, 1971: 37–62

Böttcher, Kurt. Editor. *Erläuterungen zur deutschen Literatur.* Berlin: Volk und Wissen, Volkseigener Verlag, 1956–1970.

Böttcher, Kurt and Geerdts, Hans-Jürgen (Editors). *Kurze Geschichte der deutschen Literatur.* Berlin: Volk und Wissen, Volkseigener Verlag, 1981.

Boyle, Nicholas. *Goethe. The Poet and the Age*, Oxford: Clarendon Press, 1991.

Braemer, Edith. *Goethes Prometheus und die Grundpositionen des Sturm und Drang.* Berlin and Weimar: Aufbau-Verlag, 1959. 1968 (3).

Braemer, Edith and Wertheim, Ursula. *Studien zur deutschen Klassik.* Berlin: Rütten und Loening, 1960.

Bunge, Hans. *Die Debatte um Hanns Eislers "Johann Faustus."* Berlin: Basis, 1991.

Childs, David. *The GDR. Moscow's German Ally*, Allen and Unwin, London, 1983.

Dabezies, André. *Visages de Faust au XXe siècle. Littérature, idéologie et mythe.* Paris: Sorbonne, 1967.

Dahnke, Hans-Dietrich. "Zeitverständnis und Literaturtheorie. Goethes Stellung zu den theoretischen Bemühungen Schillers und Friedrich Schlegels um eine Poesie der Moderne." In: *Goethe-Jahrbuch 95* (1978), 65–84.

———. "Im Schnittpunkt von Menschheitsutopie und Realitätserfahrung: *Iphigenie auf Tauris*." In: *Impulse* 6 (1983), 9–36.

———. "Humanität und Geschichtsperspektive. Zu den Goethe-Ehrungen 1932, 1949, 1982." In: *Weimarer Beiträge* 28 (1982) no. 10, 66–89.

Dietze, Walter. *Kleine Welt, große Welt. Aufsätze über Goethe.* Berlin: Aufbau-Verlag, 1982.

———. *Poesie der Humanität. Anspruch und Leistung im lyrischen Werk Johann Wolfgang Goethes.* Berlin: Aufbau-Verlag, 1985.

———. "Der 'Walpurgisnachtstraum' in Goethes *Faust*." In: *PMLA* 84 (1969), 476–491.

Dwars, Jens-F. "Dichtung im Epochenumbruch. Goethes Historisierung des 'Faustischen' im Spannungsfeld von Herrschaft und Knechtschaft." In: *Weimarer Beiträge* 36 (1990), 1729–1753.

Eisler, Hanns. *Johann Faustus.* Edited by Hans Bunge. Berlin: Henschel, 1983.

Eissler, Kurt. *Goethe. A Psychoanalytic Study, 1775–1786.* Detroit: Wayne State UP, 1963.

Farrelly, Daniel. *Goethe and Inner Harmony.* Shannon: Irish UP, 1973.

———. *"Schöne Seele" Studies. Essays on Goethe.* Dublin: Blackwater Press, 1978.

Gaier, Ulrich. *Goethes Faust-Dichtungen. Ein Kommentar,* Band 1, *Urfaust.* Stuttgart: Reclam, 1990.

Gallas, Helga. *Marxistische Literaturtheorie. Kontroversen im Bund proletarisch-revolutionärer Schriftsteller.* Neuwied and Berlin: Luchterhand, 1971.

Geerdts, Hans-Jürgen. *Goethes Roman "Die Wahlverwandtschaften." Eine Analyse seiner künstlerischen Struktur, seiner historischen Bezogenheiten und seines Ideengehalts.* Weimar: Arion, 1966.

Geschichte der deutschen Literatur von den Anfängen bis zur Gegenwart, volumes 6 and 7. Berlin: Volk und Wissen, Volkseigener Verlag, 1978–1979.

Grimm, Reinhold and Hermand, Jost. *Die Klassik-Legende. Second Wisconsin Workshop.* Frankfurt am Main: Athenäum Verlag, 1971.

Hahn, Karl-Heinz. "Zeitgeschichte in Goethes Roman *Wilhelm Meisters Lehrjahre*." In: *Deutsche Klassik und Revolution,* ed. Paolo Chiarini (et alii). Rome: Edizioni dell' Ateneo, 1978: 169–194.

Hamm, Heinz. *Goethes "Faust." Werkgeschichte und Textanalyse,* 5th impression. Berlin: Volk und Wissen, Volkseigener Verlag, 1988.

———. *Der Theoretiker Goethe. Grundpositionen seiner Weltanschauung, Philosophie und Kunsttheorie.* Berlin: Akademie-Verlag, 1975.

Härtl, Heinz (Editor). *Die Wahlverwandtschaften. Eine Dokumentation der Wirkung von Goethes Roman 1808–1832.* Berlin: Akademie-Verlag, 1983.

Hartung, Günter. "*Wilhelm Meisters Lehrjahre* und das Faustische." In: *Weimarer Beiträge* 36 (1990), 284–312.

Hartmann, Horst. *Faustgestalt, Faustsage, Faustdichtung.* Berlin: Volk und Wissen, Volkseigener Verlag, 1979.

Heukenkamp, Rudolf, "Problematische Künstler. Bemerkungen zu *Faust, Dichtung und Wahrheit* und *Torquato Tasso.*" In: *Weimarer Beiträge* 28 (1982) no.10, 124–141.

Höhle, Thomas and Hamm, Heinz. "*Faust. Der Tragödie Zweiter Teil.*" In: *Weimarer Beiträge* 20 (1974) no. 6, 49–89.

Holtzhauer, H. and Zeller, B. *Studien zur Goethezeit. Festschrift für L. Blumenthal.* Weimar: Böhlau, 1968.

Hörz, Herbert (Editor). *Philosophie und Naturwissenschaften. Wörterbuch zu den philosophischen Fragen der Naturwissenschaften.* Berlin: Dietz Verlag, 1983.

Kaufmann, Hans. *Versuch über das Erbe.* Leipzig: Reclam, 1980.

Klingenberg, Anneliese. "Das Verhältnis von Individuum und Gesellschaft in seiner Entwicklung von den Lehr- zu den Wanderjahren." In: *Weimarer Beiträge* 28 (1982) no. 10, 142–145.

———. *Goethes Roman "Wilhelm Meisters Wanderjahre." Quellen und Komposition.* Berlin: Aufbau-Verlag, 1972.

Korff, H. A. *Geist der Goethezeit. Versuch einer ideellen Entwicklung der klassisch-romantischen Literaturgeschichte,* Part 1, *Sturm und Drang,* Part 2, *Klassik.* Leipzig: J. J. Weber, 1923, 1930.

Kortum, Hans, and Weisbach, Reinhard. "Unser Verhältnis zum literarischen Erbe. Bemerkungen zu Peter Müllers *Zeitkritik und Utopie in Goethes 'Werther.'*" In: *Weimarer Beiträge* 16 (1970) no. 5, 214–219.

Krauss, Werner. *Gesammelte Aufsätze zur Literatur- und Sprachwissenschaft,* Frankfurt am Main: Klostermann, 1949.

———. *Grundprobleme der Literaturwissenschaft. Zur Interpretation literarischer Werke,* Hamburg: Reinbek, 1968.

———. *Studien und Aufsätze.* Berlin: Rütten und Loening, 1959.

Kühl, Hans-Ulrich. "Kunstproblematik und 'klassische' Romanform bei Goethe. Von der *Theatralischen Sendung* zu den *Lehrjahren.*" In: *Kunstperiode. Studien zur deutschen Literatur des ausgehenden 18.Jahrhunderts.* Von einem Autorenkollektiv. Berlin: Akademie-Verlag,1982, 144–176, 237–242.

———. "Das Poetische in *Wilhelm Meisters Lehrjahre.*" In: *Goethejahrbuch* 101 (1984), 129–138.

Lange, Victor. *Das klassische Zeitalter der deutschen Literatur, 1740–1815.* Munich: Winkler, 1983.

Leistner, Bernd. *Sixtus Beckmesser. Essays zur deutschen Literatur.* Berlin and Weimar: Aufbau-Verlag, 1989.

———. *Unruhe um einen Klassiker. Zum Goethe-Bezug in der neueren DDR-Literatur.* Halle-Leipzig: Mitteldeutscher Verlag, 1978.

Liebich, Gert. *Faust und Mephisto im "Urfaust."* Diss. Leipzig, 1975.

Lindner, Herbert. *Das Problem des Spinozismus im Schaffen Goethes und Herders.* Weimar: Arion, 1960.

Link, Hannelore. *Rezeptionsforschung: eine Einführung in Methoden und Probleme.* Stuttgart: Kohlhammer, 1976.

Lukács, Georg. *Goethe and his Age.* Translated by Robert Anchor. London: Merlin Press, 1968.

———. *Goethe und seine Zeit.* Bern: A. Francke, 1947.

———. *Theorie des Romans,* Neuwied and Berlin: Luchterhand, 1971.

———. *Writer and Critic and Other Essays.* Edited and translated by A.Kahn. London: Merlin Press, 1970.

Luke, David (Translator). *Faust Part One.* Oxford: Oxford UP, 1987.

———. *Faust Part Two.* Oxford: Oxford UP, 1994.

Mahl, Bernd. *Brechts und Monks "Urfaust"-Inszenierung mit dem Berliner Ensemble 1952–52. Studien zur Goethe-Zeit und Goethe Wirkung,* Band 1. Stuttgart: Belser-Verlag, 1986.

Mandelkow, Karl Robert. *Goethe in Deutschland. Rezeptionsgeschichte eines Klassikers.* Vol 2, 1918–1982. Munich: Verlag Beck, 1989.

Mattenklott, Gert, and Scherpe, Klaus (Editors). *Westberliner Projekt: Grundkurs 18. Jahrhundert.* Kronenburg: Taunus, 1974.

Mayer, Hans (Editor). *Goethe im XX Jahrhundert. Spiegelungen und Deutungen.* Frankfurt am Main: Insel, 1987.

———. "Der eliminierte Mythos in Goethes *Iphigenie.*" In: Hans Mayer, *Das unglückliche Bewußtsein,* Frankfurt am Main: Suhrkamp, 1986, 246–254.

———. "Werthers *Leiden.*" In: Hans Mayer: *Das unglückliche Bewußtsein,* Frankfurt am Main, 1986, 137–146.

Mieth, Günter, "Die Szene 'Bergschluchten' in Goethes *Faust* — spinozistisch verstanden." In: *Impulse 9,* Berlin: Aufbau-Verlag, 1986, 175–186.

———. *Vom Beginn der großen Französischen Revolution bis zum Ende des alten deutschen Reiches 1789–1806.* Berlin: Rütten and Loening, 1982.

Mittenzwei, Werner. "Die Brecht-Lukács Debatte." In: *Sinn und Form* 19 (1967), 235–269.

——. *Brechts Verhältnis zur Tradition.* Berlin: Akademie-Verlag, 1973.

—— (Editor). *Positionen. Beiträge zur marxistischen Literaturtheorie in der DDR.* Leipzig: Reclam, 1969.

——. *Der Realismus Streit um Brecht.* Berlin and Weimar: Aufbau-Verlag, 1978.

—— (Editor). *Wer War Brecht. Wandlung und Entwicklung der Ansichten über Brecht.* Berlin: DEB, 1977.

Müller, Joachim. *Der Augenblick ist Ewigkeit. Goethestudien.* Leipzig: Kochler und Amelang, 1960.

—— *Neue Goethe-Studien.* Halle: Niemeyer, 1969.

—— *Prolog und Epilog zu Goethes Faustdichtung.* Berlin: Akademie-Verlag, 1964.

——. "Phasen der Bildungsidee im *Wilhelm Meister.*" In: *Goethe* 24 (1962), 58–80.

Müller, Peter. "Goethes 'Prometheus.' Sinn- und Urbild bürgerlichen Emanzipationsanspruchs." In: *Weimarer Beiträge* 22 (1976) no. 3, 52–82.

——. *Zeitkritik und Utopie in Goethes Werther.* Berlin: Rütten und Loening, 1969; 1983 (2).

Naumann, Manfred. *Gesellschaft Literatur Lesen. Literaturrezeption in theoretischer Sicht.* Berlin and Weimar: Aufbau-Verlag, 1976.

——. *Blickpunkt Leser. Literaturtheoretische Aufsätze.* Leipzig: Reclam, 1984.

Niedermeyer, Michael. *Das Ende der Idylle. Zum Charakter der Weltbeziehung in Goethes Roman "Die Wahlverwandtschaften."* Diss. Berlin, 1983.

Peacock, Ronald. *Goethe's Major Plays.* Manchester: Manchester UP, 1959.

Reincke, Olaf. "Goethes Roman *Wilhelm Meisters Lehrjahre* — ein zentrales Kunstwerk der Klassischen Literaturperiode in Deutschland." In: *Goethe-Jahrbuch* 94, Weimar, 1977, 137–187.

Reuter, Hans-Heinrich. "Der gekreuzigte Prometheus: Goethes Roman *Die Leiden des jungen Werthers.*" In: *Goethe-Jahrbuch* 89 (1972), 86–115.

Rilla, Paul. "Wilhelm Meisters theatralische Sendung." In: *Essays.* Berlin: Henschel, 1955, 125–132.

Schlenker, Wolfram, *Das "Kulturelle Erbe" in der DDR. Gesellschaftliche Entwicklung und Kulturpolitik 1945–1965.* Stuttgart: Metzler, 1977.

Schmeer, Hans. *Der Begriff der schönen Seele besonders bei Wieland und in der deutschen Literatur des 18. Jahrhunderts.* Series: *Germanistische Studien* 44. Liechtenstein: Nendeln, Klaus Reprint, 1967.

Schmitt, Hans-Jürgen. *Die Expressionismusdebatte. Materialien zu einer marxistischen Realismuskonzeption.* Frankfurt am Main: Suhrkamp, 1973.

Schmitt, Peter. *Faust und die "Deutsche Misere." Studien zu Brechts dialektischer Theaterkonzeption.* Erlangen: Palm und Enke, 1980.

Scholz, Gerhard. *Faust-Gespräche.* Leipzig: Reclam, 1983.

Scholz, Rüdiger. *Goethes "Faust" in der wissenschaftlichen Interpretation von Schelling und Hegel bis heute.* Rheinfelden: Schäuble, 1985.

——. *Die beschädigte Seele des großen Mannes. Goethes "Faust" und die bürgerliche Gesellschaft.* Rheinfelden: Schäuble, 1982.

Stellmacher, Wolfgang. "Drama und Theater beim klassischen Goethe." In: *Weimarer Beiträge* 29 (1983) no. 7, 1232–46.

Streller, Siegfried. "Der gegenwärtige Prometheus." In: *Goethe-Jahrbuch* 101 (1984), 24–41.

Teller, Jürgen. "Der Prometheus des Eins-und-Alles. Zum Spinoza-Verständnis des jungen Goethe." In: *Impulse* 8 (1985) 25–42.

——. "Gedanken zu Goethes *Wahlverwandtschaften.*" In: *Impulse* 4 (1982), 118–147.

Träger, Christine. *Novellistisches Erzählen bei Goethe,* Berlin: Aufbau-Verlag, 1984.

Träger, Klaus "Kritik der Stilkritik. Emil Staigers 'klassisches' Goethebild." In: *Weimarer Beiträge* 7 (1961), 212–254.

Trevelyan, Humphrey, "Ottilie und Sperata." In: *Goethe. NF des Jahrbuchs der Goethe-Gesellschaft,* 11 (1949) 78–80.

Viëtor, Karl. "Deutsche Literaturgeschichte als Geistesgeschichte." In: *PMLA* 60 (1945), 899–916.

Viëtor-Engländer, Deborah. *Faust in der DDR.* Bern: Peter Lang, 1987.

Werner, Hans-Georg. "Antinomien der Humanitätskonzeption in Goethes *Iphigenie.*" In: *Weimarer Beiträge* 14 (1968), 361–384.

——. *Text und Dichtung — Analyse und Interpretation.* Berlin and Weimar: Aufbau-Verlag, 1984.

——. "Peter Müller, *Zeitkritik und Utopie in Goethes 'Werther.'*" In: *Weimarer Beiträge* 1970, no.7, 193–199.

Wertheim, Ursula. *Goethe-Studien,* Berlin: Aufbau-Verlag, 1968.

——. "Klassisches in *Faust.Der Tragödie erster Teil.*" In: *Goethe-Jahrbuch* 95 (1978), 112–149.

Wruck, Peter. "Goethes 'Prometheus'-Gedicht — erneut gelesen." In: *Wissenschaftliche Zeitschrift,* Berlin, 35 (1986), 766–772.

Index

Abusch, Alexander, 6, 8, 89, 94–7, 152
Academy of Sciences of the GDR, 45
Academy of Social Sciences, 45
Akademie der Künste, 94
Akademie der Wissenschaften, 9, 14, 17
Aktion, Die, 6
Albert, Hans, 155
aristocracy, 72, 85

Bachmann, Ingeborg, 27
Baierl, Helmut, 98
Balzac, Honoré de, 6, 26, 56, 81, 90
Becher, Johannes, 6–8, 27
Beethoven, Ludwig van, 65
Beharriell, Frederick, 73f.
Bennewitz, Fritz, 90, 97
Berlin Wall, 147
Berliner Ensemble, 88, 91f., 94, 98, 119, 156
Beutler, Ernst, 95
Biedermeier, 9
Bitterfeld, 8f., 90
Bloch, Ernst, 6, 149
Bortfeldt, Hans Robert, 88, 89
Böttcher, Kurt, 10
Boyle, Nicholas, 50
Braemer, Edith, 23, 153
Brecht, Bertolt, 6, 9–11, 17, 20, 26f., 88, 89, 91, 97f., 122, 155
Büchner, Georg, 7, 25
Bunge, Hans, 91, 93f., 96

capitalism, 5f., 17, 27, 30, 35, 39, 55, 80f., 85, 94, 102f., 107, 147, 152, 154
Cervantes, 76, 81
Columbus, Christopher, 37, 90
communist party, 17
Copernicus, 90
cultural policy, 5–7, 13, 16, 45, 119, 147, 156
Czechoslovakia, 9, 97

Dabezies, André, 153
Dahnke, Hans-Dietrich, viii, 23, 45, 155
Dante, 128
Deus sive natura, 33, 51
deutsche Misere, 92f., 96, 152
Diderot, Denis, 6
Diersen, Inge, 12
Diesseits, 34, 107
Dietze, Walter, 153
Dilthey, Wilhelm, 28f.
Dresen, Adolf, 97
Dwars, Jens-F., 120–1

Earth Spirit, 36, 102, 104, 111f., 122f.
East Germany — *see* GDR
Eckermann, Johann Peter, 48, 107, 116, 118
Ehrlich, Lothar, 155
Eichendorff, Joseph, Freiherr von, 7f.
Eisler, Hanns, 6, 11, 88f., 97, 153

Eissler, Kurt, 50
Engels, Friedrich, 154
Enlightenment, 3, 17, 19, 25f., 52,
  95, 99, 101, 104
Enzensberger, Hans Magnus, 27
Erbe (*see also* "heritage,"
  "inheritance")
Eternal Womanhood, 93, 97, 107,
  109, 115f., 118,
Euripides, 65
executors, 10
Expressionism debate, 6

Farrelly, Daniel, 83
Fascism, 6, 15, 24, 120, 151
Faust Part Three, 9
feudalism, 33f., 59f., 63, 66, 72, 80,
  85, 94, 101, 105
Feuerfach, Ludwig, 55, 90
Fichte, JohannGottlieb, 101, 113
Fielding, Henry, 6
Fischer, Ernst, 92
Fontane, Theodor, 7
Forderung des Tages, 16, 22
formalism, 7
Forster, Georg, 8, 17
Fourier, François-Marie-Charles, 80,
  105
Frank, Leonard, 27
French Revolution, 45, 65, 80, 99,
  101, 110, 152
Frings, Theodor, 25
Fühmann, Franz, 18

Galileo, 90
GDR, 147
Geerdts, Hans-Jürgen, 10, 12, 17,
  18–20, 139

Geistesgeschichte, 3, 19, 27, 29–30,
  31, 35–39, 99, 114
Genie, das, 51, 149, 151f., 154
German Democratic Republic, 3, 98
Germanistik, 3, 13, 15, 16, 21, 23,
  26
German Jacobins, 9
Gervinus, Georg Gottfried, 151
Girnus, Wilhelm, 31, 155
Gnade, 116, 118
Goethe, Cornelia, 50
Goethe, Johann Wolfgang von,
  works by:
  Egmont, 64–5, 107
  Faust, 14, 22, 36–39, 43, 46, 50,
    52, 54, 88–192, 149–52
  Faust Part One, 5, 89, 110
  "Forest and Cavern," 101, 104,
    106
  "Prolog in Heaven," 33, 35, 90,
    101, 109f., 121
  Faust Part Two, 5, 8f., 11, 89, 93,
    101–4, 106, 115, 128, 153
  Faust. Fragment, 100f., 149
  Urfaust, 88, 91, 98–100, 119–
    126, 156
  Elective Affinities, 14, 18, 34,
    104, 130–146
  Götz von Berlichingen, 64, 100f.,
    128
  Iphigenie auf Tauris, 21, 64–71
  Poetry and Truth, 31, 141
  Tasso, 64–71
  Werther, 10, 14, 17, 48, 54–63,
    82, 98, 121f.
  Wilhelm Meister's Apprenticeship,
    14, 17, 34, 44, 46, 72–87,
    108, 119, 130, 132, 138
  *Wilhelm Meister's Vocation to the
    Theater*, 72

"An Schwager Kronos," 50, 52
"An Werther," 48
"Artist's Evening Song," 49
"Artist's Morning Song," 49
"Aussöhnung," 48
"Der Autor," 49
"Der Erlkönig," 104
"Der Fischer," 104
"Der Wandrer," 50
"Der Zauberlehrling," 104
"Ganymed," 50f.
"Hymnen," 50
"Mahometsgesang," 50f.
"Maifest," 47
"Prometheus," 50–2
"To Connoisseurs and Lovers,"
    49
"Wandrers Sturmlied," 50
Goetze, Johann Melchior, 62, 121
Gorki, Maxim, 99
Greifswald, 14, 23
Grimm, Reinhold, 10, 147
Grotewohl, Otto, 89
Gründgens, Gustav, 90
Gryphius, Andreas, 108
Gysi, Klaus, 97

Haase, Horst, 13, 16
Hacks, Peter, 97
Hager, Kurt, 10
Hähnel, Klaus-Dieter, 12
Halle, 45
Hamann, Johann Georg, 110
Hamm, Heinz, 31, 124, 153
Hartung, Günter, 119f.
Hegel, Georg Wilhelm Friedrich,
    35f., 38, 73–79, 99, 101, 103,
    109f., 113, 114, 148, 154

Hegel, Georg Wilhelm Friedrich,
    works by:
    Phenomenology of Mind, 74, 99,
        102, 110, 113, 150
Heine, Heinrich, 7f., 17
Heinz, Wolfgang, 97
Heise, Wolfgang, 15
Henel, Heinrich, 73
Herder, Johann Gottfried, 4, 31,
    47f., 147
heritage, 5, 7, 10, 18f., 21, 81
Hermand, Jost, 10, 147
Hermlin, Stephan, 27
Herwegh, Georg, 8
Heukenkamp, Ursula, 13
Heym, Stefan, 27
Hillich, Reinhard, 12
Hinderer, Walter, 154
Hitler, Adolf, 17
Hochschulreform, 15, 16, 21
Höhle, Thomas, 45, 153
Hölderlin, Friedrich, 8, 17
Holtzhauer, Helmut, 10, 155
Honecker, Erich, 10
Hörnigk, Therese, 12
Huchel, Peter, 27
Humboldt University, viii, 12, 14,
    15–17, 23, 45
Hungarian Uprising, 15f., 19, 156
Hutten, Ulrich von, 94

immanence, 31, 34, 54, 109, 111,
    129
inheritance, 5–7, 9f., 88, 100, 119f.,
    147

Jakobi, Friedrich, 32, 48, 127
Jena, 14, 23, 45

Jenseits, 34, 37
Job, 110f.
Joyce, James, 27

Kafka, Franz, 27, 97
Kahn, A., 80
Kant, Immanuel, 101, 104f., 113, 129
Kaufmann, Hans, 11–13, 20f., 23
Kaufmann, Ulrich, 13
Keller, Gottfried, 7
Klatt, Gudrun, 12
Kleist, Heinrich von, 7
Klein, Alfred, 12
Klettenberg, Susanna von, 32, 65, 68, 75
Klinger, Maximilian, 92
Korff, Hermann August, 14, 20, 25–30, 35–39, 52–54
Kortum, Hans, 57
KPD, 6
Krauss, Werner, 14, 24f.
Krenzlin, Leonore, 12
Kühl, Hans-Ulrich, 12
Kulturbund, 21
Kurella, Alfred, 8

Langhoff, Wolfgang, 88f.
Lavater, Johann Caspar, 32
Leipzig, 14, 24–26
Leistner, Bernd, 11
Lemke, Lisa, 12f.
Lenau, Nicolas, 8
Lenin, Vladimir I., 5, 6, 24, 155
Lenz, Jakob Michael Reinhold, 62f., 121
Lessing, Gotthold Ephraim, 16, 31, 62, 95, 121

Levetzow, Ulrike von, 48
Liebich, Gert, 124
Lindner, Herbert, 31, 147
Link, Hannelore, 61
Literary history, 3, 12–16, 19–21, 24f., 27–29, 35, 44f., 119, 156
Literaturwissenschaft — *see* Literary History
Lukács, 5–7, 9–11, 14–17, 20, 26f., 29f., 34, 44, 54–6, 59, 72, 76, 79, 82, 85, 89f., 95–6, 99–109, 113–8, 120–123, 139, 149, 152–5
Luke, David, 5, 9, 124
Luther, Martin, 95
Lutheran Church, 33

Mandelkow, Karl Robert, 43
Mann, Heinrich, 17, 27
Mann, Thomas, 27, 90
Markov, Walter, 24
Marlowe, Christopher, 95
Marx, Karl, 24, 151, 154
Marxism, 5, 10, 15, 17, 21, 31, 117
Materialien, 16, 27, 148
Mattenklott, Gert, 55
Mayer, Hans, 14, 16, 25–7, 29f.
Mehring, Franz, 95, 154
Melanchthon, Philipp, 68
Middle Ages, 94, 98, 100
middle class, 5–8, 19, 21f., 24, 26, 28f., 38, 49, 56f., 59, 80, 85, 89, 95, 98f., 105, 107, 116, 131, 151–3
Mieth, Günther, 31, 126–9
Mittenzwei, Werner, viii, 9, 11, 98, 155
modernity, 7
Monk, Egon, 91, 98

Moscow, 5–7

Müller, Heiner, 98

Müller, Peter, viii, 23, 54–63, 121, 147

Mundt, Theodor, 74

Napoleon, 99, 101, 110

National Socialism, 3f., 6, 14, 17, 88f., 147

Nationale Forschungs– und Gedenkstätten — *see* National Research Center

National Research Center, 8, 14, 153

natura naturans, 38, 111f.

natura naturata, 38, 111f.

nature, 33, 36–39, 43, 47, 49, 52, 54f., 58, 101, 104, 116, 120, 127f., 131f., 134, 139, 142, 150

Naumann, Manfred, 25, 121

Nicolai, Fritz, 62, 121

Niedermeyer, Michael, 138

Ottwalt, Ernst, 6

pantheism, 31, 35–39, 43, 47, 51, 54f., 58, 104, 107, 109–112, 145f.

Peacock, Ronald, 70

Peasants' Revolt, 91f., 96, 100

Pietism, 33

Plenzdorf, Ulrich, 10

Politbüro, 10

Popular Front — *see* Volksfront

Proletariat, 5, 10, 20

private property, 5

Raabe, Wilhelm, 7

Reformation, 34, 95, 100

Reimann, Paul, 19

Reinhard, Karl Friedrich von, 138

Renaissance, 34, 72, 90, 93, 95, 100, 105, 113

Restoration, 9

Riehter, Hans, 13

Reuter, Hans Heinrich, 58, 155

Romanticism, 19, 29, 32, 44, 45, 73–4, 78, 82, 100, 134, 156

Rostock, 14, 23

Rousseau, Jean-Jacques, 110

Rudolf, Johanna, 91–4

Sagert, Horst, 98

Sammons, Jeffrey L., 73

Schaginjan, Marietta, 96

Schelling, Friedrich Wilhelm Joseph von, 101, 113, 148–50, 154

Scherpe, Klaus, 55

Schiller, Friedrich, viii, 4, 8, 13, 16, 32, 45f., 65, 66, 74, 80, 88, 155–6

Schlegel, Friedrich, 72

Schmeer, Hans, 73f., 79

Schmitt, Hans-Jürgen, 17

Schmitt, Peter, 88f.

Scholz, Gerhard, 12, 16, 20–24, 26, 119f., 123, 148, 153

Scholz, Rüdiger, 148f., 153

schöne Seele, 34, 73–87, 108

Schönemann, Lili, 50

Schroth, Christoph, 98

Schulz, Gerhard, 43

Schwerin, 98

secularization, 34, 37f., 84, 108, 110–1, 116, 126, 130

SED, 7, 45

Seghers, Anna, 27

Shakespeare, 47

Shdanow, Andrei, 6

Siegrist, Christoph, 44

socialism, 3f., 7–10, 18, 20, 24, 27–30, 46, 80, 89, 97, 120, 153–5

Social Democrats, 17

Soviet Union, 3, 5, 7, 9, 15

SPD, 6

Spinoza, Benedictus de, 31–33, 43, 47–49, 54, 67, 109–112, 126–8, 145

Staiger, Emil, 3, 25

Stalin, Joseph, 6, 147, 153

Stein, Charlotte von, 68

Stellmacher, Wolfgang, viii, 23, 44–46

Stendhal, 81

Storm and Stress, 16, 20, 22, 32, 34, 36, 50, 52, 64, 65, 67f., 90, 92, 98, 105, 121, 129

Streller, Siegfried, 12, 26, 27, 28

Szymanowska, Marie, 48

Teller, Jürgen, 31

Thalheim, Hans-Günther, 12, 17–20, 22–24, 26–28, 119

Thirty Years War, 34

Tolstoi, 26, 90

Träger, Claus, 12, 17, 24f., 29

Trakl, Georg, 27

transcendence, 31, 34, 111, 129

Trevelyan, Humphrey, 132f.

Trunz, Erich, 51

Ulbricht, Walther, 5, 8, 10

utopia, 18, 72, 80, 103, 131, 153

Viëtor, Karl, 3

Viëtor-Englander, Deborah, 5, 88, 90, 98

Vischer, Friedrich Theodor, 151

Volksfront, 6f., 17

Vollstreckungstheorie, 8

Vormärz, 9, 20, 26

Weber, Peter, 23

Weerth Georg, 8

Weimar Classicism, 3–5, 7 ,9f., 16, 19, 34, 44, 46, 98, 147, 155–6

Weimar Republic, 14

Weisbach, Reinhard, 57

Werner, Hans-Georg, 13, 16, 18–20, 45, 57, 123

Wertheim, Ursula, 12 , 15, 17f., 21–23

Westberliner Projekt, 55

Wieland, Christoph Martin, 63, 73f., 121, 147

Wruck, Peter, viii

Ziegler, Konrat, 151